Historical Literacy

Historical
Literacy

THE CASE FOR HISTORY
IN AMERICAN EDUCATION

Edited by PAUL GAGNON

and

The Bradley Commission on History in Schools

Macmillan Publishing Company

New York

Collier Macmillan Publishers

London

Macmillan Publishing Company
866 Third Avenue, New York, NY 10022
Collier Macmillan Canada, Inc.

Library of Congress Cataloging-in-Publication Data

Historical Literacy: the case for history in American education /
   edited by Paul Gagnon and The Bradley Commission on History in
   Schools.
       p.   cm.
       Includes bibliographies, index.
       ISBN 0-02-542111-5
       1. History—Study and teaching (Elementary)—United States.
   2. History—Study and teaching (Secondary)—United States.
   3. History teachers—United States.   I. Gagnon, Paul A.
   II. Bradley Commission on History in Schools.
   LB1582.U6F87   1989   89-7978   CIP
   375'.9—dc20

Macmillan books are available at special discounts for bulk purchases for sales promotions, premiums, fund-raising, or educational use. For details, contact:

Special Sales Director
Macmillan Publishing Company
866 Third Avenue
New York, NY 10022

10 9 8 7 6 5 4 3 2 1

Designed by Jack Meserole

PRINTED IN THE UNITED STATES OF AMERICA

History, by apprizing them of the past, will
enable them to judge of the future.

THOMAS JEFFERSON,
Notes on Virginia, 1784

CONTENTS

vii

PREFACE

In the history of attempts at educational reform in America, the many committees and commissions at work have generally taken one of two approaches to the production of their reports and recommendations. On the one hand, some have been content to leave the tasks of conceptualizing and writing largely to their supporting staffs, with commission members themselves limited to quick reviews of drafts submitted by the staff, followed by ratification and signature. Others have chosen to be veritable working commissions, with all or most members directly engaged in generating the central ideas and arguments involved, in detailed discussion of these throughout their working sessions, and in giving final line-by-line approval of the entire document to be issued.

The Bradley Commission on History in Schools chose the latter method. Its many distinguished and experienced members carried on an open-ended conversation among equals to arrive at the final consensus expressed in their report, "Building a History Curriculum: Guidelines for Teaching History in Schools." Here reprinted in Chapter Two, its recommendations and supporting arguments represent a wholly collaborative effort, with each passage the product of the Commission's working meetings and subject to each member's approval.

In contrast to that initial report, what follows in this volume, the second publication to appear under the aegis of the Bradley Commission, has not been designed to achieve consistency or consensus. Our authors are, of course, all engaged in extending the arguments and spelling out the implications of "Building a History Curriculum," but they were enjoined to speak for themselves, to say what they wished in their own voices, to be as opinionated as they chose. Readers will find that they have done just that. From chapter to chapter, quite different tones and emphases emerge, as do different views of goals and methods for teaching history. This book, one could say, embodies the collective—but not agreed-upon—wisdom of the members of the Bradley Commission who contributed, and of several new colleagues.

As editor of this volume, I was privileged to work with some twenty authors, each with his or her own distinctive message to people who love history, who love to learn from it, and who love to teach it. But distinctive as these essays are, readers will find several common threads running through them. Of these, two stand out. One is the conviction that a sea change is needed in the social studies curriculum of most American schools if we are to have the possibility of teaching the amount and quality of history that is indispensable to the education of the individual and the citizen in a modern democratic society. The other is readiness to set forth the many obstacles and difficulties we face, over and above the constrictions of the present curriculum. There is an enormous lot to do before we can expect to reach our goals. The tasks ahead range from reminding ourselves and the public of the larger purposes of historical study all the way to devising imaginative classroom methods for conveying what is most worth knowing to our many diverse learners at all grade levels. We need to reconsider the kinds of history we teach, to reorder our ways of preparing teachers, and to alter drastically many of the conditions that teachers labor under in the schools. Our enterprise will require action on many fronts at once, and uncommon patience to keep at it for years to come.

Perhaps the most vital task ahead was expressed by the late Hazel Hertzberg, whose death brought great personal and professional sorrow to us, her colleagues on the Commission:

> There is nothing we can do that is more important than to develop within the historical profession a renewed and lasting commitment to the schools and a renewed *partnership* between teacher-

historians from the elementary school through graduate school . . . based on mutual respect, mutual knowledge, and mutual advantage.

As the chairman of the Bradley Commission, Kenneth T. Jackson, said in his letter of last November notifying us of Professor Hertzberg's death in Rome, the best gift we could give in her memory would be to dedicate our work toward making her dream for the profession a reality.

The readers, authors, and editor of this volume owe much to a number of people without whose devotion it would not have appeared in timely fashion or proper condition. Elaine Wrisley Reed and Joseph P. Ribar conquered the nearly endless logistical problems inherent in a multiauthored work and lent invaluable support to me. At Macmillan, our copyeditors, Jane Herman and David Frost, provided excellent assistance, and our editors, John Glusman and Robert Kimzey, offered unfailing encouragement and patience beyond normal expectations.

PAUL A. GAGNON

Cambridge, Massachusetts
March 1989

PART I

*A Time to Look
Forward*

CHAPTER 1

Why the Time Is Right to Reform the History Curriculum

by KENNETH T. JACKSON and

BARBARA B. JACKSON

Although men and women have been living and dying on this planet for many thousands of years, history itself is relatively young as an academic discipline and school subject. In 1880, as the late Hazel Hertzberg reminds us in Chapter 4, there was no department of history in any American school or college, and formal instruction about the human past usually emphasized recitation and memorization, not critical analysis of documents or the understanding of broad trends and questions.[1]

The 1880s, however, witnessed a revolution in the nation's schools as a more modern curriculum—which included history, modern languages, and science—slowly pushed out the classical core of Latin and Greek. The American Historical Association (AHA) was founded in 1884, and soon thereafter scores of college graduates crossed the Atlantic Ocean to continue their study in the prestigious seminars of German universities. Their objective was to become more critical and especially more scientific about the study of history.

In 1892, as part of a broad reexamination of the secondary school curriculum, the National Education Association (NEA) appointed nine subcommittees to consider the needs of the vast majority of American youngsters who would never go to college. The subcommittee on History, Civil Government, and Political Economy, chaired by Charles Kendall Adams, president of the University of Wisconsin, trumpeted the need, especially in a democracy, for a broad-based knowledge of the past. Adams's committee recommended that all students, regardless of their career choices, should take four years of history at the secondary level. Such a history-centered curriculum, it declared, was essential to an understanding of human affairs and to intelligent citizenship.

Between 1890 and 1920, history in the American secondary school curriculum had a larger role than it ever enjoyed before or since. Its decline after that date can largely be attributed to the 1916 report of the National Education Association Committee on the Social Studies, a remnant of the progressive movement that elevated civics, geography, sociology, and "problems of democracy" at the expense of ancient, medieval, early modern, and English history. Its recommendations, as Professor Hertzberg noted, ultimately led to the basic social studies curriculum found today in most American secondary schools.

The erosion of history in favor of a more utilitarian approach began almost immediately. Indeed, the decline was evident as early as 1918 with the publication of *The Cardinal Principles of Secondary Education*, generally considered one of the most important documents in the history of American education. Declaring that the mission of modern schooling was "social efficiency," *The Cardinal Principles* defined social studies as those disciplines with a "subject matter related directly to the organization and development of human society, and to man as a member of social groups." Thus, the ideal history course would be directly relevant to students' interests or personal and professional growth and development. Within this scheme, ancient or premodern studies seemed both irrelevant and superfluous.[2]

The movement by social studies educators to replace history with more contemporary-oriented courses continued through the interwar period and gained further strength after 1945. Indeed, many social studies educators, such as the late Edgar Wesley, wanted to eliminate history-centered instruction altogether. In a 1967 article entitled "Let's Abolish History Courses," Wesley argued that history met no "needs that pupils can appreciate." In his view, history should be changed from a course to a resource: "No teacher at any grade level, however, should teach a course in history as content. To do so is confusing, unnecessary, frustrating, futile, pointless, and as illogical as to teach a course in the World Almanac, the dictionary, or the Encyclopedia." According to Wesley's prescription, history should be "utilized and exploited—not studied, learned, or memorized."[3]

This supposedly utilitarian approach, ignited by the 1916 statement and fanned by such ardent supporters as Wesley, proved disastrous to the study of history. Courses in current events, modern issues, and student-focused units gradually supplanted history in the core curriculum. Some of the new courses deserved a place in the education of America's young, but the simple fact was that there was only so much time in the school day that could be devoted to social studies. With the introduction of more contemporary issues and concerns, there was little space left in the schedule for history. Even courses that did center on history were in many cases splintered into a multiplicity of diverse minicourses and study units with little or no consistent historical threads seaming them together into an articulated curriculum of scope and sequence.

Especially during the 1960s and 1970s, this trend resulted in the "balkanization" of the history curriculum. The classroom began to serve as a microcosm of democracy-in-action. Units of study were developed that emanated from student interests and concerns rather than from any coherent pattern of essential knowledge. Thus, many secondary schools offered myriad minicourses on a variety of topics over a six- or nine-week time frame with little attention to historical context. With the relationships between social, economic, and political factors not made apparent, certain historical events were emphasized far beyond their significance while others were either slighted or ignored. In many instances, this imbalance created a distorted historical perspective.[4]

In addition, federally financed curriculum development projects during the 1960s and 1970s contributed to the do-your-own-thing formlessness of social studies. The traditional core content and the direct instruction model of teaching history were discouraged in favor of the inquiry method that had been utilized primarily in the study of science. With this new methodology, history instuction revolved around the student rather than the subject, with teachers designing activities in which youngsters would have the opportunity to think and act like historians. Some of these case studies designed for hands-on experiences were highly motivational for the youngsters, but the limited scope of the study units did not provide for most students the solid foundation of historical knowledge necessary for informed inquiry.[5]

The weakening of history in the schools was exacerbated by the situation in the nation's colleges, where the new social history, emphasizing quantification, theory, and narrowly defined topics, turned much scholarly writing and teaching away from questions of broad general interest. This change of focus at the higher levels of education facilitated the disintegration of history studies even more than the political pressures on schools. Offering a smorgasbord of courses rather than a common core curriculum, history departments deemphasized broad survey courses that integrated the various topics. Thus college graduates, confronted with teaching survey courses in high school as novice teachers, had both a weak and fragmented knowledge base upon which to draw. They either taught the area of speciality they had studied, or they taught from a textbook.

As Diane Ravitch has noted, by 1973 the social studies

program was in a state of "curriculum anarchy." Not only had there been a splintering of history within each secondary school's curriculum, but also a discontinuity nationally as each American public school district exercised curricular independence.[6] A 1977 study by Richard E. Gross of Stanford University found that social studies programs at that time were characterized by increased fragmentation and dilution of curricula, by a growth of elective and minicourses, by the rapid spread of social science courses, and by a drop in required courses.

History's struggle to maintain a secure position in the secondary school curriculum was also recognized in a 1975 study by the Organization of American Historians (OAH). The report gave specific examples of the sapping and segmentation that had occurred in the discipline: In New Mexico, the trend was toward ethnocultural courses; in Hawaii, toward integrating history into a social science framework focused on problem solving, decision making, and social action; in Minnesota, teachers were encouraged to shift from historical study toward an emphasis on concepts that transcended any specific historical situation. One OAH representative from California predicted that history would continue to yield to such "relevant" topics as multicultural studies, ethnic studies, consumer affairs, and ecology. Reports from other states substantiated the claim.[7] Indeed, the prediction was fulfilled. The Bradley Commission on History in Schools found in 1988 that many high school students could satisfy their social studies requirements for graduation by taking such diverse, disconnected courses as current events, drug education, sex education, civics, values education, economics, and psychology and never take a history course at all.

By 1980 it was clear that history no longer held the prominence it had earlier in the century. Its place in the curriculum had been weakened not only by the newer social sciences but also by ineffective teaching of the subject. Both political and ideological trends outside the classroom had contributed to the decline, but the key issue of the continuing debate over history's rightful place in the curriculum was the value of history itself. Over the years, historians themselves had been unable to agree about the purpose of historical study; only a few gave serious thought to basic questions dealing with the relevance of their discipline. The profession failed to convince those outside it of the worth of historical study. As Edgar E. Robinson observed in 1947, "the purpose of the study of history, the scope . . . , the choice of subject matter, and most of all, the value of the discipline, are more and more at the center of the discussion given history by the laymen."[8]

Other historians also admitted the difficulty of defending history, confessing that many of its alleged virtues were difficult, if not impossible, to prove even to themselves. In 1949, Jennings Bryan Sanders surveyed the objectives of college and university departments of history and found that "to provide an understanding of the present" was the foremost reason given for historical study, with citizenship training trailing cultural training and development of perspective.[9] In 1958, G. D. Lillibridge wrote that "we have failed to suggest some meaning and purpose for the study of history which can make its value and practicality apparent to the student."[10] Although some, such as Crane Brinton in 1960, warned against historians overemphasizing the value of history in the "common-sense meaning of 'useful,' " the attempts in the last twenty-five years to make the study of history relevant have precipitated the subsequent revision of objectives, content, and methods in secondary and elementary schools throughout the nation.[11] The result, in general, has been both a substantial reduction in the amount of history offered and a subjugation of the discipline to contemporary issues and realities.[12]

THE TASK AHEAD

Why is it, then, that in 1989, after decades of decline and indecision, the time seems right for restoring history to the center of the American school curriculum? Why, especially in a postindustrial age, when high-technology communication systems threaten to revolutionize the way we live, should the study of the past command our attention and our resources? What does history have to say to the ghetto youngster who has to deal with poverty and racism? What does history have to contribute to the farm youth whose family must contend with foreclosures and declining government subsidies? What does history have to suggest to the young woman who wants to juggle family and career or to the young man who wonders why his regiment is stationed in West Germany with the Seventh Army? Is history relevant to contemporary reality, or is it a relic?

The Bradley Commission on History in Schools was created in 1987 to respond to these questions as well as to a perceived absence of sustained history instruction in our nation's school systems. Composed of distinguished authors and outstanding classroom teachers, it follows in a long tradition of commissions that have set similar goals. What is different now is that the political and psychological climate in the final decade of the twentieth century may be more receptive to curricular reform than at any time in the past eight decades.

Since 1957, when the Soviet Union rocketed Sputnik into orbit around the world and challenged the United States for technological supremacy, the American public has been barraged with a series of bad report cards on the nation's schools. The news has been unrelenting: Johnny can't read, Johnny can't write, Johnny can't add, and Johnny can't think. The most publicized assessment came in 1983, when the National Commission on Excellence in Education issued "A Nation at Risk," a thirty-five-page open letter to the American people that suggested that the very future of the republic was threatened by the "rising tide of mediocrity" in high school classrooms. Challenged by an emerging Asia and a resurgent Europe, the United States was exhorted to set higher standards of educational excellence for its secondary schools.

The Bradley Commission on History in Schools is one of many reassessments of the American educational enterprise that have thus far been produced in the 1980s. In particular, it builds upon the foundation put in place by many others, such as David Van Tassel of National History Day, Kermit Hall of the History Teaching Alliance, Arthur S. Link and Fay Metcalf of the National Commission on the Social Studies, Charlotte Crabtree of the UCLA/NEH Center for History in the Schools, James Howard and Thomas Mendenhall of the Council for Basic Education's Commission on the Teaching of History, and Matthew Downey and Paula Gillett of the Clio Project of the University of California at Berkeley. Both the Organization of American Historians and the American Historical Association have established special divisions and committees to focus on history in the classroom, and teachers themselves have begun to organize in a variety of ways.

The Bradley Commission on History in Schools, therefore, speaks not as a voice in the wilderness, but rather as part of a growing and broad-based national demand for improvement. Quite simply, it affirms what many of us intuitively know: that no matter what the time or place, human beings need a sense of self, a sense of how they got where they are in order to understand and evaluate where they are going next. History answers not only the what, the when, the where, and the who about the course of human experience on our planet but, more importantly, the why. It provides the basis for understanding such other disciplines as philosophy, the arts, religion, literature, law, and government. Through the study of the past, individuals are empowered to develop a more informed way of seeing, knowing, and coping with the larger human society in which they live. Precisely because the average university student faces the prospect of five or more career changes over a lifetime, young people need to be well grounded in disciplines that will help them in whatever they do and wherever they live.

Thus, the Bradley Commission is not simply another national commission primed only to point out the deficiencies of our nation's students, this time in the area of history. Our more global mission is to bring to public attention the unanimous opinion of a distinguished group of professional history educators—representing elementary, secondary, and higher education—that in an increasingly technocratic society, Johnny needs what history has to offer more than ever. The Bradley Commission declares that in a nation concerned about its children's future, there are specific steps that can be taken to assure that each student receives the best possible preparation in this vital discipline.

The first objective of the Bradley Commission was to evaluate the present state of the history curriculum in the United States. Remarkably, neither the federal government nor any other national body could provide such information. When the staff of the Commission completed its survey of requirements in the fifty states, the result was even more dismal than had been expected: History is typically a forgotten subject in the elementary schools, where an "expanding environments" approach assumes that preadolescents cannot understand historical concepts. And in the upper grades it fares only slightly better. A shocking 15 percent of the nation's youngsters do not study American history in high school, and a full half of them do not take any European or world history courses during those years. Four states do not mandate any American history in high school, and thirty-four states do not require any world history in order to graduate. Is it any wonder that some of our graduates do not even know which side Germany was on in World War II, or that almost half of them do not know that Stalin was the wartime leader of the Soviet Union?

While recognizing that individual initiative and local freedom are fundamental to the American system, the seventeen-member Commission, representing diverse instructional levels, regions, interests, and political perspectives, expressed a surprising unanimity of agreement about a basic foundation in history. They were fully cognizant of the importance of local involvement in the design and implementation of any particular plan of study and they were opposed to a "national curriculum." But they also believed it imperative that general guidelines be shaped by professionals in the classroom rather than by outside experts or those representing political interests in state assemblies. Thus, the decisions about what to teach in history were made by Commission members who not only shared a passion for the discipline but who also were well acquainted with the daily realities of the American school.

With the conviction that history is an integrative discipline, the panel, unsurprisingly, calls for the return of a more history-centered curriculum at both the elementary and secondary levels. Unlike the majority of earlier reform efforts that focused primarily on the high school, the Commission looked first at the elementary school and its importance in developmental learning. It proposes that instruction in the prevalent, egocentric, "expanding horizons" curriculum of the early grades, which revolves around the young student's family, neighborhood, and community, be expanded if not replaced by introducing history, as well as biography, literature, and geography, into the social studies framework. Historical enrichment in the early grades would be followed with substantial history courses in grades four, five, and six that would provide a developmental sequence.

At the secondary level, the Commission calls for requiring at least four years of history for all students sometime during their six years in grades seven to twelve. Requirements, we believe, can in fact liberate, and history itself can both entertain and civilize. The Commission is quite clear about what constitutes history. It is not computer education, psychology, driver education, or any of the "new courses" that have weathered quite well in the past decades under the social studies umbrella. It is American history, Western civilization, and world history. This is not to say that contemporary real-world issues cannot be integrated; indeed, the practice is encouraged. Students need to see the relevance of history to contemporary events and issues in order to understand their present lives and to envision future possibilities and alternatives. Stressing only the present, however, leads to a narrow focus, superficiality, and distortion. Studying the civil rights movement of the 1950s and 1960s, for example, makes little sense without an understanding of slavery, the Civil War, Reconstruction, peonage, and the Jim Crow laws.

It is one thing to plan history instruction; it is another thing to put it into effect, and the Commission is fully aware of this reality. For change in history instruction to occur, it must, like all other changes, occur not from the outside by external mandates but from within the schools themselves. This is not to say that policymakers do not have a profound effect on the course of public education. They do. But as anyone with experience in a public school can attest, while legislators and boards of education can dictate what they want, nothing happens until it happens in the classroom. As Michael Timpane, president of Teachers College at Columbia University, has astutely stated, principals and teachers must be at the center of the reform.

To ensure that the Commission's report would not be seen as another dust collector on a school's shelf, that it would be a valid and pragmatic document, we knew that equal participation on the panel of outstanding public school teachers was a necessary prerequisite. At our early meetings, they, in general, politely deferred to the views of the distinguished university scholars on the panel. But as they came to realize that they were not to be blamed for what was wrong with history education in the public schools, that they were asked to participate in order to share a wisdom gained from teaching history over the years and to present their visions for the discipline in the future, their voices grew louder. It was clear that a renewed partnership between teacher-historians from elementary school through graduate school was necessary, not just on this Commission but throughout the country, in order that history instruction not only be restored as the core curriculum but also, and more important, that it be restored effectively.

Blaming teachers is not the answer; they already have too

much with which they must cope. What teachers need is encouragement, support, and the power to shape their own work so that history will no longer be rated by students, as John Goodlad maintains in *A Place Called School*, as their least favorite and least interesting course. A major problem is that history is too often taught as a dull calendar of dates and events to be memorized, not as an exciting subject that can yield insights relevant to everyday life. As Thucydides wrote several dozen centuries ago, "History is philosophy learned from examples."[13] Thinking historically demands evidence and rational thought. It forces us to try to understand individuals and groups whose attitudes and aspirations are different from our own. It encourages us to reject stereotypes and to be alert for the individual person who lurks behind all generalizations.

Good teachers need adequate academic preparation. This means teacher-training courses that are intellectually challenging. It also means that persons should no longer be certified to teach social studies, as is now the case in some states, without taking a single college course in history. If properly prepared, teachers may feel more secure in their knowledge base and may use textbooks less as a course and more as a resource. The Commission realizes that teachers are hampered by inflexible scheduling, heavy clerical duties, and many other obstacles, but adequate training and collaboration with colleagues can bring them the excitement and confidence about their subject that is difficult for students in their classes to miss.

We do not mean to suggest that there are easy answers to any of the dilemmas facing either history or the American school. Nor is the fault for the current ahistorical bias in our culture easy to assign. But to recognize that the study of the past is important to all our citizens whatever their backgrounds or future plans, we need to enlist the aid of all the constituencies involved—teachers, students, parents, professors, textbook writers, school board members, and interested laymen. The time is right for commitment, and the Bradley Commission hopes to move people along that path.

NOTES

1. The Hertzberg essay in this volume is an abridged version of her longer work, Hazel Whitman Hertzberg, *Social Studies Reform, 1880–1980* (Boulder, Colo.: Social Science Education Consortium, Inc., 1981).

2. Diane Ravitch has written more extensively on this subject than any other person. See, for example, Ravitch, "The Precarious State of History," *American Educator*, Spring 1985, pp. 12–15; and Ravitch, "From History to Social Studies: Dilemmas and Problems," in Ravitch, *The Schools We Deserve* (New York: Basic Books, 1985).

3. Edgar Wesley, "Let's Abolish History Courses," *Phi Delta Kappan*, September 1967, passim.

4. Clair W. Keller, "Improving High School History Teaching," in *Against Mediocrity*, ed. Chester E. Finn, Jr. et al. (New York: Holmes and Meier, 1984), pp. 79–88.

5. Ibid.

6. Ravitch, "Precarious State," pp. 12–15.

7. Richard S. Kirkendall, "The Status of History in the Schools," *The Journal of American History* 62 (September 1975): 557–70.

8. Edgar Eugene Robinson, *Scholarship and Cataclysm: Teaching and Research in American History, 1939–1945* (Stanford, Calif.: Stanford University Press, 1947).

9. Jennings Bryan Sanders, "Objectives of College and University History Departments," *Higher Education* 5 (April 15, 1949): 189–90.

10. George D. Lillibridge, "History in the Public Schools," *Social Education* 22 (March 1958): 110–15.

11. Crane Brinton, *A History of Civilization: Prehistory to 1795*, 2nd ed. (Englewood Cliffs, N.J.: Prentice-Hall, 1960), p. 4.

12. For a recent overview, see Matthew T. Downey, "The Status of History in the Schools," in *History in the Schools*, ed. Matthew T. Downey (Washington, D.C.: National Council for the Social Studies, 1985), pp. 1–12.

13. John Goodlad, *A Place Called School: Prospects for the Future* (New York: McGraw-Hill, 1984), pp. 209–12.

CHAPTER 2

Building a History Curriculum: Guidelines for Teaching History in Schools

by THE BRADLEY COMMISSION ON HISTORY IN SCHOOLS

The Bradley Commission on History in Schools was created in 1987 in response to widespread concern over the inadequacy, both in quantity and in quality, of the history taught in American elementary and secondary classrooms. While other social science disciplines and many new fields, such as sex and health education, driver education, and computer education, have expanded their roles in the curriculum, the number of required courses in history has declined. Currently, 15 percent of our students do not take any American history in high school, and at least 50 percent do not study either world history or Western civilization.

Since 1982 a score of major books and studies, commissioned by such diverse organizations as the Council on Basic Education, the National Commission for Excellence in Education, the Carnegie Foundation, the American Federation of Teachers, and the National Endowment for the Humanities, have called for a more substantial academic core for all students and for more varied and imaginative approaches to teaching that common learning. Documenting the serious declines in

16

achievement in reading, writing, mathematics, and science, they have endorsed the need for more rigorous classroom study coupled with more innovative pedagogical methods.

History is obviously not the only subject that has suffered. The Bradley Commission, however, is the first national group to devote its attention exclusively to history in the schools. Indeed, the case for the importance of history has not been so cogently and powerfully made since 1892, when the National Education Association (NEA) appointed a distinguished Committee of Ten to examine the entire high school experience.

The 1892 subcommittee on History, Civil Government, and Political Economy, chaired by President Charles Kendall Adams of the University of Wisconsin, was to have a major influence on the shape of American education. It recommended that all students, whether or not they were college-bound, should take four years of history on the secondary level. History, it declared, broadened and cultivated the mind, counteracted a narrow and provincial spirit, prepared students for enlightenment and intellectual enjoyment in after years, and assisted them to exercise a salutary influence upon the affairs of their country.

Unhappily, this common, democratic curriculum did not survive the educational changes made during and after World War I. Now the Bradley Commission declares once more that history should occupy a large and vital place in the education of the private person and the public citizen. Unlike many other peoples, Americans are not bound together by a common religion or a common ethnicity. Instead, our binding heritage is a democratic vision of liberty, equality, and justice. If Americans are to preserve that vision and bring it to daily practice, it is imperative that all citizens understand how it was shaped in the past, what events and forces either helped or obstructed it, and how it has evolved down to the circumstances and political discourse of our time.

From its inception, the Bradley Commission set itself two goals:

- to explore the conditions that contribute to, or impede, the effective teaching of history in American schools, kindergarten through grade 12

- to make recommendations on the curricular role of history, and on how all of those concerned—teachers, students, parents, school administrators, university professors, publishers, and boards of education—may improve the teaching of history as the core of social studies in the schools

To accomplish this task, I asked sixteen outstanding scholars and teachers to join me on the Commission. Together they determined the scope of the Commission's work and how it would be done. They represented different political philosophies, geographic regions, academic specialties, and levels of instruction. They shared only a passion for the study of history and a deep concern about its place in the curriculum.

The Organization of History Teachers, the American Historical Association, and the Organization of American Historians have all endorsed the efforts of the Bradley Commission. But in the end, the authority of this report rests upon the reputations of the commissioners themselves. As an examination of the list of members indicates, many of the most honored and respected members of the profession have given their time and energy to this report. Our roster includes former presidents of all the major professional associations in history and winners of the most prestigious prizes for writing and scholarship.

What was remarkable about the Bradley Commission, however, was its inclusion of classroom teachers as full voting and deliberative members of the policy-making group. These instructors were chosen because they had earned, on the front lines of American education, reputations as master teachers. Their contributions have been essential at every meeting and on every point, and they have helped us bridge the gap between the school and the university.

The Bradley Commission recognizes that the most important ingredient in any instructional situation is the individual teacher. It is easy to make pronouncements about what should happen in the classroom. But in truth what does happen in the classroom is determined by the person who daily has to contend with often undermotivated youngsters and an overly crowded curriculum. With too little time and too many students, many teachers still manage to convey the excitement, the complexity, and the relevance of the past.

Such teachers deserve more than our respect and admiration. They deserve our support. For too long, educational reform has been mandated from the top down. This lack of teacher involvement has demoralized many instructors and has meant that many changes have been more cosmetic than real. The Bradley Commission believes that teachers must be partners in educational renewal, and that the quality of history instruction can be no higher than the quality of history instructors.

Precisely because so many history teachers have been inspiring and effective, the Bradley Commission recognizes the importance of careful training and selection. We deplore the practice, unfortunately quite common, of assigning unqualified teachers to teach social studies in our schools. State certification is not a guarantee of competence, if only because in some states it is possible to be certified to teach social studies without ever taking a single college course in history.

Because our resources and time were too limited to become heavily involved in pedagogical techniques or improved teacher training, the Bradley Commission concentrated on curriculum. We were dismayed to learn that the eleventh-grade course in American history is no longer universal, and that many school districts now allow optional classes, sometimes called "area studies" and with little history content, to substitute for the eighth-grade course. Instead, the Bradley Commission asserts that history ought to be an important part of the educational experience of every American. All students need to understand the complexities of the Constitution and of the Civil War, of immigration and Manifest Destiny, and of the struggle against slavery and for civil rights. The need for more curricular time is obvious. Unfortunately, history courses are now commonly so rushed that they remain superficial and/or never reach the twentieth century.

American history is only part of the problem. Our students also need to confront the diverse cultural heritages of the world's many peoples, and they need to know the origins and evolution of the political, religious, and social ideas that have shaped our institutions and those of others. Without studying the history of the West and the history of the world, students remain out of touch with these realities. They will not understand the origins and major tenets of the world's religions, they will not be familiar with the ancient and worldwide struggles for freedom and justice, and they will not know the many roads that nations have taken to conquest or survival.

No commission, whatever its size, membership, or resources, could possibly restructure the entire history curriculum. Nor would such a result be desirable, given the diversity of a continental nation. The Bradley Commission has, however, endorsed nine important resolutions that we think deserve the careful consideration of professional educators. In particular, we depart from current practice in our recommendation that history be a substantial part of the elementary school experience. In addition, and once more, we believe that all children in a democracy—not just the gifted or the college-bound—deserve the knowledge and understanding that history imparts.

We are grateful to the Lynde and Harry Bradley Foundation, especially to the board of directors and to President Michael S. Joyce, Vice-president Hillel Fradkin, and Program Officer Daniel Schmidt, for generously funding this project. We also wish to thank Gilbert Sewall and Lisa Rothman of the Educational Excellence Network; Barbara Russell and Victor Mainente of Teachers College; Patricia Albjerg Graham, Samuel Gammon, and James Gardner of the American Historical Association; Joan Hoff-Wilson and Arnita Jones of the Organization of American Historians; John Agresto and Jeffrey Thomas of the National Endowment for the Humanities; Ruth Wattenberg of the American Federation of Teachers; Salvatore J. Natoli of the National Council for the Social Studies; Arthur Link, Fay Metcalf, and David Katzman of the National Commission on Social Studies in Schools; Christopher L. Salter of the National Geographic Society; and Earl Bell of the Organization of History Teachers. We also want to acknowledge the contributions of the eight hundred classroom teachers across the country who answered our extensive survey. Finally, and most importantly, the Bradley Commission acknowledges the indispensable contributions to its work of Paul A. Gagnon, Elaine Wrisley Reed, and Joseph P. Ribar. Without their devoted and extraordinarily professional efforts, these guidelines would not have been produced.

We do not presume to have said the final word on history in the schools, but we trust that these guidelines will stimulate and encourage those who believe that the study of the past is essential to informed judgment and to democratic citizenship.

KENNETH T. JACKSON

WHY STUDY HISTORY?

History belongs in the school programs of all students, regardless of their academic standing and preparation, of their curricular track, or of their plans for the future. It is vital for all citizens in a democracy, because it provides the only avenue we have to reach an understanding of ourselves and of our society, in relation to the human condition over time, and of how some things change and others continue.

We can be sure that students will experience enormous changes over their lifetimes. History is the discipline that can best help them to understand and deal with change, and at the same time to identify the deep continuities that link past and present.

Without such understanding, the two foremost aims of American education will not be achieved—the preparation of all our people for private lives of personal integrity and fulfillment, and their preparation for public life as democratic citizens.

For the first aim, personal growth, history is the central humanistic discipline. It can satisfy young people's longing for a sense of identity and of their time and place in the human story. Well taught, history and biography are naturally engaging to students by speaking to their individuality, to their possibilities for choice, and to their desire to control their lives.

Moreover, history provides both framework and illumination for the other humanities. The arts, literature, philosophy, and religion are best studied as they develop over time and in the context of societal evolution. In turn, they greatly enliven and reinforce our historical grasp of place and moment.

For the second aim of education, active and intelligent citizenship, history furnishes a wide range of models and alternatives for political choice in a complicated world. It can convey a sense of civic responsibility by graphic portrayals of virtue, courage, and wisdom—and their opposites. It can reveal the human effects of technological, economic, and cultural change, and hence the choices before us. Most obviously, a historical grasp of our common political vision is essential to liberty, equality, and justice in our multicultural society.

As in the case of the humanities, history and geography provide the context of time and place for ideas and methods drawn from the social sciences—anthropology, economics, political science, psychology, and sociology. In turn, the formulations of the social sciences offer lively questions to explore in the historical narrative, and numberless insights to enrich it.

Beyond its centrality to educating the private person and the citizen, history is generally helpful to the third aim of education: preparation for work. It is needed for such professions as law, journalism, diplomacy, politics, and teaching. More broadly, historical study develops analytical skills, comparative perspectives, and modes of critical judgment that promote thoughtful work in any field or career.

COMMISSION RECOMMENDATIONS

In recognition of the critical value of historical study to the education of Americans, the Bradley Commission has adopted the following resolutions, addressed to all citizens who bear responsibility for designing and implementing sources of study in our schools:

1. That the knowledge and habits of mind to be gained from the study of history are indispensable to the education of citizens in a democracy. The study of history should, therefore, be required of all students.
2. That such study must reach well beyond the acquisition of useful information. To develop judgment and perspective, historical study must often focus upon broad, significant themes and questions, rather than the short-lived memorization of facts without context. In doing so, historical study should provide context for facts and training in critical judgment based upon evidence, including original sources, and should cultivate the perspective arising from a chronological view of the past down to the present day. Therefore it follows . . .
3. That the curricular time essential to develop the genuine understanding and engagement necessary to exercising judgment must be considerably greater than that presently common in American school programs in history.
4. That the kindergarten through grade six social studies curriculum be history-centered.
5. That this Commission recommends to the states and to local school districts the implementation of a social studies cur-

riculum requiring no fewer than four years of history among the six years spanning grades seven through twelve.

The Commission regards such time as indispensable to convey the three kinds of historical reality all citizens need to confront: American history to tell us who we are and who we are becoming; the history of Western civilization to reveal our democratic political heritage and its vicissitudes; world history to acquaint us with the nations and people with whom we shall share a common global destiny. It follows . . .

6. That every student should have an understanding of the world that encompasses the historical experiences of the peoples of Africa, the Americas, Asia, and Europe.
7. That history can best be understood when the roles of all constituent parts of society are included; therefore the history of women, racial and ethnic minorities, and men and women of all classes and conditions should be integrated into historical instruction.
8. That the completion of a substantial program in history (preferably a major, minimally a minor) at the college or university level be required for the certification of teachers of social studies in the middle and high schools.

The Commission is concerned by the minimal, frequently insubstantial, state requirements for historical studies in the education of social studies teachers. The kind of historical instruction we believe to be indispensable requires prior study of the subject in depth.

9. That college and university departments of history review the structure and content of major programs for their suitability to the needs of prospective teachers, with special attention to the quality and liveliness of those survey courses whose counterparts are most often taught in the schools: world history, Western civilization, and American history.

The Commission is concerned that the structures and requirements of the undergraduate history major are too frequently in-

choate, and that insufficient attention is paid to courses demonstrating useful approaches to synthesis, selection, and understanding of organizing themes.

HISTORY'S HABITS OF THE MIND

The perspectives and modes of thoughtful judgment derived from the study of history are many, and they ought to be its principal aim. Courses in history, geography, and government should be designed to take students well beyond formal skills of critical thinking, to help them through their own active learning to:

- understand the significance of the past to their own lives, both private and public, and to their society.
- distinguish between the important and the inconsequential, to develop the "discriminatory memory" needed for a discerning judgment in public and personal life.
- perceive past events and issues as they were experienced by people at the time, to develop historical empathy as opposed to present-mindedness.
- acquire at one and the same time a comprehension of diverse cultures and of shared humanity.
- understand how things happen and how things change, how human intentions matter, but also how their consequences are shaped by the means of carrying them out, in a tangle of purpose and process.
- comprehend the interplay of change and continuity, and avoid assuming that either is somehow more natural, or more to be expected, than the other.
- prepare to live with uncertainties and exasperating, even perilous, unfinished business, realizing that not all problems have solutions.
- grasp the complexity of historical causation, respect particularity, and avoid excessively abstract generalizations.

- appreciate the often tentative nature of judgments about the past, and thereby avoid the temptation to seize upon particular "lessons" of history as cures for present ills.
- recognize the importance of individuals who have made a difference in history, and the significance of personal character for both good and ill.
- appreciate the force of the nonrational, the irrational, the accidental in history and human affairs.
- understand the relationship between geography and history as a matrix of time and place, and as context for events.
- read widely and critically in order to recognize the difference between fact and conjecture, between evidence and assertion, and thereby to frame useful questions.

VITAL THEMES AND NARRATIVES

In the search for historical understanding of ourselves and others, certain themes emerge as vital, whether the subject be world history, the history of Western civilization, or the history of the United States.

To comprehend the forces for change and continuity that have shaped—and will continue to shape—human life, teachers and students of history must have the opportunity to pursue many or most of the following matters:

Civilization, cultural diffusion, and innovation. The evolution of human skills and the means of exerting power over nature and people. The rise, interaction, and decline of successive centers of such skills and power. The cultural flowering of major civilizations in the arts, literature, and thought. The role of social, religious, and political patronage of the arts and learning. The importance of the city in different eras and places.

Human interaction with the environment. The relationships among geography, technology, and culture, and their effects on economic, social, and political developments. The choices made possible by climate, resources, and location, and the effect of culture and human values on such choices. The gains and losses of technological change. The central role of agriculture. The effect of disease, and disease-fighting, on plants, animals, and human beings.

Values, beliefs, political ideas, and institutions: The origins and spread of influential religions and ideologies. The evolution of political and social institutions, at various stages of industrial and commercial development. The interplay among ideas, material conditions, moral values, and leadership, especially in the evolution of democratic societies. The tensions between the aspirations for freedom and security, for liberty and equality, for distinction and commonality, in human affairs.

Conflict and cooperation: The many and various causes of war, and of approaches to peace making and war prevention. Relations between domestic affairs and ways of dealing with the outside world. Contrasts between international conflict and cooperation, between isolation and interdependence. The consequences of war and peace for societies and their cultures.

Comparative history of major developments: The characteristics of revolutionary, reactionary, and reform periods across time and place. Imperialism, ancient and modern. Comparative instances of slavery and emancipation, feudalism and centralization, human successes and failures, of wisdom and folly. Comparative elites and aristocracies; the role of family, wealth, and merit.

Patterns of social and political interaction: The changing patterns of class, ethnic, racial, and gender structures and relations. Immigration, migration, and social mobility. The effects of schooling. The new prominence of women, minorities, and the common people in the study of history, and their relation to political power and influential elites. The characteristics of multicultural societies; forces for unity and disunity.

TOPICS FOR THE STUDY OF
AMERICAN HISTORY

History is a great, suspenseful story whose turning points and consequences are best revealed in a narrative that is analytical and comparative. Chronological development is essential, but within it, major topics and questions must make clear the significance of the unfolding story. The following are central to the history of the United States:

1. The evolution of American political democracy, its ideas, institutions, and practices from colonial days to the present; the Revolution, the Constitution, slavery, the Civil War, emancipation, and civil rights.

2. The development of the American economy; geographic and other forces at work; the role of the frontier and agriculture; the impact of technological change and urbanization on land and resources, and on society, politics, and culture. The role and emancipation of American labor.

3. The gathering of people and cultures from many countries, and the several religious traditions, that have contributed to the American heritage and to contemporary American society.

4. The changing role of the United States in the outside world; relations between domestic affairs and foreign policy; American interactions with other nations and regions, historically and in recent times. The United States as a colonial power and in two world wars. The Cold War and global economic relations.

5. Family and local history, and their relation to the larger setting of American development.

6. The changing character of American society and culture, of arts and letters, of education and thought, of religion and values.

7. The distinctively American tensions between liberty and

equality, liberty and order, region and nation, individualism and the common welfare, and between cultural diversity and civic unity.

8. The major successes and failures of the United States, in crisis at home and abroad. What has "worked" and what has not, and why.

TOPICS FOR THE STUDY OF WESTERN CIVILIZATION

As in the case of United States history, the facts and narrative of ancient, medieval, and modern European history must be grouped and taught in relation to significant topics. And particular emphasis should be placed on two aspects of the history of the Western world. First, upon those developments that have so much shaped the experience of the entire globe over the last five hundred years. Second, upon those ideas, institutions, and cultural legacies that have directly influenced American thought, culture, and politics since colonial times. Each of the following meets these criteria.

1. The political, philosophical, and cultural legacies of ancient Greece and Rome.
2. Origins, ideas, moral codes, and institutions of Judaism and of Christianity in all its forms.
3. Medieval society and institutions; relations with Islam; feudalism and the evolution of representative government.
4. The culture and ideas of the Renaissance and Reformation, European exploration, the origins of capitalism and colonization.
5. The English revolution, its ideas, and the practices of parliamentary government, at home and in the colonies.
6. The culture and ideas of the Enlightenment, comprising the scientific revolution of the seventeenth century and the intellectual revolution of the eighteenth.

7. The American and French revolutions, their sources, results, and world influence.
8. The Industrial Revolution and its social consequences, its impact on politics and culture.
9. The European ideologies of the nineteenth and twentieth centuries and their global influence: liberalism, republicanism, social democracy, Marxism, nationalism, communism, fascism, nazism.
10. The new nineteenth-century imperialism, ultimate decolonization, and the consequences of both for colonizers and colonized.
11. The two world wars, their origins and effects, and their global aftermath and significance.
12. The making of the European community of nations; new approaches to cooperation and interdependence.

TOPICS FOR THE STUDY OF WORLD HISTORY

Given the enormous scope of world history and the difficulty of teaching it effectively, even in the expanded curricular time the Commission recommends, it is all the more necessary to make imaginative use of the larger "vital themes" listed above. Facts and narrative must be selected and taught to illuminate the most significant questions and developments.

The world history course should incorporate many of the following topics:

1. The evolution and distinctive characteristics of major Asian, African, and American pre-Columbian societies and cultures.
2. The connections among civilizations from earliest times, and the gradual growth of global interaction among the world's peoples, speeded and altered by changing means of transport and communication.

3. Major landmarks in the human use of the environment from Paleolithic hunters to the latest technologies. The agricultural transformation at the beginning and the industrial transformation in recent centuries.
4. The origins, central ideas, and influence of major religious and philosophical traditions, such as Buddhism, Islam, Confucianism, Christianity; and of major ideologies and revolutions, such as the American, French, Russian, and Chinese.
5. Close study of one or two selected non-European societies, to achieve the interest and power of the good story that narrative provides.
6. Study of at least one society that can no longer be simply defined as "Western" or "non-Western," such as in South and Central America.
7. Comparative history of selected themes, to demonstrate commonalities and differences not only between European and other societies, but among non-European societies themselves.
8. Comparative study of the art, literature, and thought of representative cultures and of the world's major civilizations.
9. Varying patterns of resistance to, or acceptance and adaptation of, industrialization and its accompanying effects, in representative European and non-European societies.
10. The adaptation of both indigenous and foreign political ideas, and practices, in various societies.
11. The interplay of geography and local culture in the responses of major societies to outside forces of all kinds.
12. Selected instances of historical success and failure, of amelioration and exploitation, of peace and violence, of wisdom and error, of freedom and tyranny. In sum, a global perspective on a shared humanity and the common human condition.

Historical study of nations and cultures other than our own must be at the heart of the new movement toward global and international studies. The overriding reason for the Commission's insistence on a minimum two-year sequence for the presentation of Western civilization and world history is that world history is inadequate when it consists only of European history plus imperialism, just as it is inadequate when it slights European history itself. It is imperative that more time, and better ways of preparing teachers to illuminate both European and non-European history, be found if students are to emerge with an intelligent global perspective.

THE PLACE OF HISTORY IN THE EARLY GRADES

In recommending that "the kindergarten through grade six social studies curriculum be history-centered," the Commission underscores the need for decisive change in elementary schools. For decades, historical studies and historical literature have been widely neglected in the earliest grades. The curricular pattern in most states is based on a concept called "expanding horizons," which dictates that young children study themselves (in kindergarten), their family (in first grade), their neighborhood (in second grade), and their city or community (in third grade). As explicated in widely used pedagogical textbooks, expanding horizons as a concept is indifferent to historical instruction, because children are bound by time and place to remain in the present and in their own personal environment—my family, my neighborhood, my community.

Although this approach is sanctified in state guidelines, in teacher-training programs, and in social studies textbooks, it is not grounded in cognitive research on how children learn or in developmental studies of what they are capable of learning. Indeed, there is now a convincing body of research and practice that demonstrates the practicality and desirability of enriching the social studies in the primary grades, reaching far beyond the limitations of the child's own family and community to the exciting worlds of history, biography, and mythology.

Young children are fascinated by heroes, amazing deeds, fantastic tales, and stories of extraordinary feats and locales. History offers a wide range of materials to delight and engage the young learner. Although the use of dates is inappropriate in the early grades, children can begin to develop a sense of time and place ("long, long ago and far away") as they are introduced to historical literature. But as frequently practiced, the expanding horizons pattern discourages imaginative studies of distant worlds, different cultures, and exemplary lives.

In their classrooms, many imaginative teachers are applying two kinds of approaches to achieve the desired change. One is to abandon the expanding horizons curriculum altogether and to substitute a different pattern of historical and literary subject matter. On almost any topic, children's classics and trade books abound: folk tales of different cultures; novels that vividly portray important events and people, and the experiences of ordinary people in extraordinary times; poetry; songs, stories of immigrants; and books that bring complicated subjects such as the U.S. Constitution within the understanding of young children.

The other approach is to infuse as much as possible of such literature into the current framework. An engaging start could be made on family and local history. By introducing more literature, geography, history, and biography, the horizons could be much expanded by readings about the lives of children, families, and communities of long ago and of other lands—together with the legends and heroes that excited them.

Whichever approach is chosen, the Commission is concerned that teachers be left free to choose engaging books with memorable content, and to tap the same vein of curiosity and imagination that popular culture recognizes and exploits for commercial gain. Teachers of young children should be encouraged to be storytellers and dramatists, not just monitors of basal readers or sociologists of the neighborhood.

Historical enrichment of the earliest grades should be followed by courses that are explicitly history-centered. State history is frequently introduced in grade four. An introductory United States history and geography course is fairly common in grade five. For grade six, several options are possible, depending upon the district's curricular pattern for grades seven through twelve. At present, sixth-grade courses vary greatly, including local and family history, state history, ancient and European history, and world history, world geography, or world cultures. Whatever the chosen pattern, every effort should be made to ensure that each course has links to, and avoids repetition of, those courses that precede or follow it.

Suggested Elementary Curricular Patterns

The following are offered as suggestions, possible alternative course sequences by which curriculum-makers might improve the social studies program in elementary grades.

Pattern A begins with the familiar "expanding horizons" approach but adds the historical dimension to the study of children, families, neighborhoods, and communities. History-centered courses begin with state history in the fourth grade. In this sample, the fifth-grade United States history course is not a survey but dwells on the period prior to 1865. Likewise, world history and geography stress the beginnings of civilization.

Pattern B resembles the newly adopted California social studies curriculum, which in the earliest grades, kindergarten to third, represents another kind of adaptation to the expanding horizons sequence, infusing historical, literary, and biographical materials. Grades four, five, and six are similar to Pattern A, but with even greater stress on the very earliest periods of American and world history.

Pattern C represents the sharpest break from the concept of "expanding horizons"; it is a wholehearted concentration on history, geography, biography, literature, and the arts, together with an early beginning on work with primary sources. Obviously, a very great number of different combinations and sequences is possible.

PATTERN A

Grade Course

K   Children of Other Lands and Times
1   Families Now and Long Ago
2   Local History: Neighborhoods and Communities
3   Urban History: How Cities Began and Grew
4   State History and Geography: Continuity and Change
5   National History and Geography: Exploration to 1865
6   World History and Geography: The Growth of Civilization

PATTERN B

Grade Course

K   Learning and Working Now and Long Ago
1   A Child's Place in Time and Space
2   People Who Make a Difference
3   Continuity and Change: Local and National History
4   A Changing State
5   American History and Geography: Making a New Nation
6   World History and Geography: Ancient Civilizations

PATTERN C

Grade Course

K   Children's Adventures: Long Ago and Far Away
1   People Who Made America
2   Traditions, Monuments, and Celebrations
3   Inventors, Innovators, and Immigrants

THE PLACE OF HISTORY IN THE MIDDLE AND HIGH SCHOOLS

The Commission's resolution on the place of history in middle or junior high schools and high schools is based on its stated conviction that "the curricular time essential to develop the genuine understanding and engagement necessary to exercising judgment must be considerably greater than that presently common in American school programs in history."

History should have special relevance for adolescents who are developing a sense of their own past as different from the present, struggling with problems of time's irreversibility in their own lives, searching for meaning and commitment for themselves, and redefining their relationship to society.

Following upon a history-centered social studies curriculum for the preceding grades, the Commission recommends to state and local school districts "the implementation of a social studies curriculum requiring no fewer than four years of history among the six years spanning grades 7 through 12."

Suggested Secondary Curricular Patterns

The Bradley Commission offers the following four patterns of history and related courses as suggestions only, from which curriculum-makers may choose, or upon which they may build, their own sequence of courses. In each of these patterns, the Commission demonstrates its unanimous conviction that a minimum of two years is necessary to teach

United States history to an acceptable level of content and sophistication and, likewise, that two years are required to present the necessary combination of Western and world history, whether within an integrated course or by devoting a year to each.

Whatever the order of courses chosen for any given school or district, the curriculum should:

- be uncomplicated, clear in its scope and sequence, and wholly practicable (as opposed to the overloaded, overambitious curricular instructions common in social studies).
- be explainable to students, in terms directly useful to their comprehension of its aims.
- provide sufficient time to teach significant portions of the substance, and to exercise the habits of mind discussed earlier.
- provide ways to relate each course to the other history courses that precede and follow it, throughout the curriculum.
- provide an ordered developmental sequence of increasing challenge and sophistication, based on current knowledge of learning styles and stages of intellectual development in students.
- recognize that the need for survey courses does not preclude substantial concentration on selected eras and topics.
- provide ways to relate the study of history to biography, to geography, and to other subjects in the social sciences and humanities.
- provide, together with the history-centered courses of grades four, five, and six, a meaningful portrait of the national and civilization past, warts and all, from regional and local history to national, Western, and world history.

Pattern A: This pattern is familiar in its repetition of United States history, grades eight and eleven. Less common is the two-year sequence of Western and world history, which the

Commission considers essential for adequate learning. Each pattern suggests American government, or an equivalent course (civics, problems of democracy, and the like), as a capstone course in social studies in the twelfth grade, when it is hoped that students will have acquired the historical knowledge and habits of mind to profit most from a study of contemporary democratic institutions and their workings.

PATTERN A

Grade Course

Grade	Course
7	Regional and Neighborhood History and Geography
8	U.S. History and Geography
9	History of Western Civilization
10	World History and Geography
11	U.S. History and Geography
12	American Government; Social Studies Elective

Pattern B: This pattern resembles Pattern A except for the two-year integrated course in world and Western history, divided by chronological eras. Putting the two halves in adjoining grades should facilitate teaching the great sweep of such a course, whether it is broken at 1789 or at some other workable date.

PATTERN B

Grade Course

Grade	Course
7	Social Studies Elective; Local History
8	U.S. History and Geography
9	World and Western History to 1789
10	World and Western History Since 1789
11	U.S. History and Geography
12	American Government; Social Studies Elective

Pattern C: This pattern generally reflects the recently adopted *History–Social Science Framework,* in California, continuing the sequence of courses noted above for the elementary grades. Its main feature is the division of American and world history courses into chronological eras, and provision for a full year of social studies electives in the ninth grade.

PATTERN C

Grade Course

7   World History and Geography to 1789
8   U.S. History and Geography to 1914
9   Social Studies Electives
10   World History, Culture, and Geography Since 1789
11   U.S. History and Geography, Twentieth Century
12   American Government; Social Studies Elective

Pattern D: Pattern D puts two two-year sequences together. The history and geography of European and of African, Asian, and Latin American civilizations are studied in successive years. The two-year United States history course is divided in the nineteenth century for flexibility of coverage and emphases.

PATTERN D

Grade Course

7   Social Studies Electives; Local History
8   History of European Civilization
9   History of Non-European Civilizations
10   U.S. History and Geography to 1865
11   U.S. History and Geography since 1865
12   American Government; Social Studies Elective

COURSE STRUCTURES AND PRIORITIES

The Bradley Commission strongly recommends that all social studies teachers be involved, directly and throughout, in the shaping of their school's curriculum, insofar as this can be done at the building level, and that their representatives be similarly involved in whatever deliberations are carried on at the district and state levels. Curriculum-building without the involvement of experienced teachers conversant with their local school conditions, and with their own students, is most likely to be counterproductive.

As the structure, priorities, and content of each course are being decided, certain questions and criteria should be kept in mind:

1. Are the aims of the course and its overall structure readily explainable to students? Is there a good answer to their common question: "What am I supposed to be getting out of this?"
2. Does the course begin with a unit on why study history, and this sort of history in particular? Does it allow time for a free-swinging exchange on the blunt question: "So what?"
3. Is the proposed—and promised—course coverage likely to be achieved in the time available? This is especially important for courses purporting to reach the present day, which they so often fail to do, to the disappointment of students and teachers alike.
4. Has the notion that "less is more" been considered, as themes, topics, and questions are selected? The amount of time required to achieve student engagement and genuine comprehension of significant issues will necessitate leaving out much that is "covered" by the usual text.
5. Has the selection of what to teach considered the content of earlier courses, and the likely content of courses still to be taken by the students? Has the depth and sophis-

tication of topic treatment been similarly considered?

6. Does the course include particular topics and materials that explicitly relate its substance to history courses that precede and follow it?

7. If more than one course surveys the same historical eras at different grade levels, are the courses properly designed to avoid repetition, to be markedly different in style and emphasis?

8. If different historical eras are stressed and taught at different grade levels, are the various courses attentive to needed reviews and continuing, unifying themes and questions?

9. Are there plans to explain to students what is being left out of the course, and why? Again, given the nature of most textbooks, some good explanation will be necessary—and can itself be highly engaging and instructive.

10. Has the selection of what to teach also been made with regard for nourishing the larger perspectives and habits of critical judgment that history helps to teach?

11. Do the selected themes and topics lend themselves to teaching, and using, the relationships between history and biography, history and geography, history and the social sciences, history and the humanities?

12. Has it been decided beforehand, at least tentatively, which topics may be worth extended treatment, perhaps over a week or so, and which may be done more briefly? Which may lend themselves to "active learning" projects? Which could most effectively be taught by use of original sources?

Above all, time must be found for discussion of significant, thoughtful questions. For example, in regard to World War I, narrative of detail should not crowd out such questions as:

• What were the war's origins, long term and immediate?
• What were the roles of individual acts and characters, of the irrational, the accidental?
• How did past actions or inaction limit human choice at the moment of crisis?

- What was the social and psychological impact of the scale of slaughter?
- What was the war's impact on the United States, on colonial societies in Africa and Asia?
- What "lessons" have we drawn from the war of 1914–18? Are they dependable?

HISTORY'S MANY MODES AND METHODS

There are today, as we hope there always will be, vigorous debates over the best kind of history to teach, and the most effective methods by which to teach them. Obviously, teachers of history, whatever their own specialties or levels of instruction, may profit from following these debates and plucking from them new ideas and insights. But just as obviously, they should feel free to choose their own emphases and ways of teaching, according to their own teaching conditions, interests, and talents. And they should be encouraged to apply the axiom that variety is the spice of learning, just as it is of life. Even the most exciting, innovative method loses its effect when it is overused, just as no single mode of history—political, economic, social, cultural—will remain fresh under too much concentration.

Among the popular questions currently under discussion are several that directly pertain to the teaching of history in the schools:

- Should history be taught as activity, as "something you do," or as cultural heritage?
- Should the history curriculum be driven by our cultural diversity as Americans, or by our common, mainly Western, political heritage?
- Should social history, concerned with ordinary people and daily issues, play the primary role, or should political history, concerned with "elites" and decision making?

• Should we stress facts or concepts? Chronology or case studies? Narrative or thematic history?

Experienced teachers will recognize these as false dichotomies, however earnestly they may be debated by various partisans. Good history and good teaching have always encompassed something of each of these modes and methods. There is no right answer, no one best way, but only a sensible mixture put together by each teacher according to circumstances, to the subject and students being taught, and to that teacher's particular strengths. It is hard to imagine not taking advantage of every one of the above approaches, to one extent or other, in teaching the history of slavery, of immigration, of the depression and the New Deal, of the struggle for civil rights. It is hard to imagine not taking advantage of local history, where primary sources can be used to their best effect, and genuine discoveries may be made by students on their own.

Each form of history—political, economic, social, intellectual, cultural, urban, local, labor, family, women—has its own color and texture. Student interest may be sustained, or revived, by shifting from one to the other, explicitly, and explaining to students why each has its own contribution to make in re-creating a usable past. And how each kind of history provides a sturdy bridge to one or more of the social sciences and humanities:

• political, military, and diplomatic history as context for political science
• economic history and geography, for economics
• social, ethnic, family, urban, and local history, for anthropology and sociology
• cultural, religious, and intellectual history, for the arts, literature, religion, and philosophy

Each kind of history offers narrative and case studies to test and illustrate concepts drawn from other disciplines, which in their turn give added meaning to the historical record. History, by its nature, is an interdisciplinary subject. It should never be reduced to a thin recital of successive dates and facts, but carry what has been called "thick narrative," which combines lively storytelling and biography with conceptual analysis drawn from every relevant discipline. Biography in particular reveals the significance of individual lives, both of leaders and of ordinary people, as a way of making historical processes and their human consequences real to students.

Here, two examples may make the point. In teaching nineteenth-century colonialism in Africa and mid-twentieth-century decolonization, the historical narrative simply cannot do without the concurrent study of geography, religion, and culture and their interplay in the several regions of Africa. The force of ideas, both indigenous and foreign, is revealed in memoirs and literature, as are the human effects of technology and economic and military power. Particular examples, such as that of the Congo, or that of Algeria, offer chances to add firsthand accounts, novels, film, drama, and the classroom testimony of recent immigrants to bring historical complexity and controversy home to the students.

Another example is the fateful collapse of the Weimar Republic in Germany and the coming to power of nazism. The chronological narrative of the Republic's problems, failures, and final disappearance is indispensable. Reaching back to German unification, through the great era of progress and pride before 1914 to defeat and humiliation in war, the Versailles Treaty, and the scourges of inflation and depression, the narrative alone is full of adventure, irony, and tragedy. But it is greatly enriched by concepts, insights, and illustrative materials from literature, biography and memoirs, psychology, economics, sociology, culture both high and popular, military and political science, film, drama, music, and philosophy. We cannot stress too much the fruitful combination of narrative with the new, wider range of historical modes and the variety of cultural documents increasingly available in recent years.

CONCLUSION

The Bradley Commission is well aware that most of what we have to say is already known and done by good teachers in schools that encourage them to work at their best. Our aim is to help create those conditions that will enable more of our teachers and students to enjoy the benefits of more history, better taught. We do not underestimate the obstacles to achieving the quantity and quality of historical instruction we believe to be needed in American schools, and we shall address these obstacles in the following pages.

Like the Committee of Ten and all its successors, the Bradley Commission is concerned with the central role of history for civic education. The social studies have always taken education for democratic citizenship, and for the public good, as their primary aim. In the late twentieth century, it is evident that American public life can profit from a grounding of its debates, on all of the major issues of our time, in the knowledge and perspectives that history provides. By its nature, history is not wishful, or partisan, or proselytizing. By grounding us in reality, it sets us free to make our own informed, considered choices. All children, all students, all adult citizens, deserve such freedom. Without it, democracy is wanting.

Decisive changes will be necessary not only in curricular and course design as addressed in these pages, but in every other condition that affects the teaching of history in the classroom. Thoughtful teaching will require better textbooks. Much recent criticism of textbooks is well founded. They are often overstuffed with facts, distracting features, and irrelevant graphics, and they are rarely organized to clarify the larger themes and questions the Commission finds indispensable.

At the other, "innovative," end of the school materials spectrum, many audiovisual and computer-assisted programs are shoddy and shallow in design and content, the products of commercial zeal and misapplied techniques rather than of historical and pedagogical imagination. The Commission is convinced that means must be found for regular critical reviews of textbooks, auxiliary materials, and instructional technology by teams of historians and classroom teachers.

Genuine change will also require more flexible class schedules—to allow the use of seminars, debates, cooperative projects, and extended lecture/discussions—as well as more favorable student/teacher ratios, a significant reduction of the many extracurricular duties and paperwork chores that weary and distract teachers the country over. It will require greater teacher authority in all matters that bear upon instruction, from curriculum making to textbook choice to the design of in-service programs.

Nothing will be more important than the expansion of collaborative efforts among school, college, and university teachers of history, on the model of the American Historical Association–Organization of American Historians–National Council for the Social Studies History Teaching Alliances. College and university departments of history need to assume much greater responsibility than is now common for knowing what is going on in the schools, for knowing what their former students are facing as classroom teachers. Each party has much to tell the other. Only as equal partners will they succeed in producing better texts and materials, designing better courses, and constructing more effective in-service programs. Fully as important, college and university historians will manage to improve undergraduate and graduate preparation of teachers only by becoming sharply aware of the necessities of the kindergarten to twelfth-grade classrooms.

This Commission calls upon college and university history departments to reorder their priorities. All members should be active in the design and teaching of broad and lively survey courses in United States history, the history of Western civilization, and world history. The last, which requires the most ingenuity of all, is also the scarcest. We recommend the establishment of special chairs for distinguished professors of survey history. We cannot overemphasize our belief that history departments fail their students—whether as citizens or as prospective teachers, or both—and they fail themselves no less when they neglect wide-ranging interpretative courses, when they do not concern themselves with the quality of schoolbooks and materials, and when they isolate themselves from the teachers and the very schools from which they must draw their future students.

Long-term cooperation will also be needed not only to keep healthful initiatives alive, but to ward off or reshape those periodic bursts of fashion that threaten the quality, and equality, of American schooling. Among recent trends is the rush to "assessment" and "accountability," which in many instances results in standardized testing of the sort that limits local school autonomy, forbids curricular and methodological flexibility, and discourages the thoughtful, conceptual history we believe to be necessary. Since we cannot simply say no to testing, the triple alliance of classroom teachers, university historians, and faculties of education faces the challenge of devising tests that will help and not hurt the quality of learning.

There are and will be many other challenges, not the least of which will be the continuing review and revision of the guidelines we propose here. There is much work to be done together, and as historians we are the last to deny the difficulties and the need to shape our recommendations in the light of realities. At the same time, we have the responsibility to say clearly what ought to be done. To set forth the ideal place of history in the curriculum of a democratic school system is a goal worth our unceasing effort.

PART II

The Changing Role of History in Schools

CHAPTER 3

The Plight of History in American Schools

by DIANE RAVITCH

Futuristic novels with a bleak vision of the prospects for the free individual characteristically portray a society in which the dictatorship has eliminated or strictly controls knowledge of the past. In Aldous Huxley's *Brave New World*, the regime successfully wages a "campaign against the Past" by banning the teaching of history, closing museums, and destroying historical monuments. In George Orwell's *1984*, the regime routinely alters records of the past; it rewrites newspapers and books to conform to political exigencies, and offending versions are destroyed, dropped "into the memory hole to be devoured by the flames."

If knowledge of the past does in fact allow us to understand the present and to exercise freedom of mind—as totalitarian societies, both real and fictional, acknowledge by dictating what may be studied or published—then we have cause for concern. The threat to our knowledge of the past arises, however, not from government censorship but from our own indifference and neglect. The erosion of historical understanding among Americans seems especially pronounced in the generation under thirty-five, those schooled during a period in which sharp declines were registered in test scores in virtually every subject of the school curriculum.

Based on the anecdotal complaints of college professors and high school teachers about their students' lack of preparation, there was reason to suspect that the study of history had suffered as much erosion and dilution as other fields. To test whether students had a secure command of the "foundations of literacy," the National Assessment of Educational Progress (NAEP) administered the first national assessment of history and literature in the spring of 1986. One object of the test was to ascertain whether students had ready command of essential background knowledge about American history.

The results were not reassuring. Presumably there is certain background information about American history so fundamental that everyone who goes to school should have learned it by age seventeen (and nearly 80 percent of those who took the assessment were enrolled in the second semester of their high school American history course). In *What Do Our 17-Year-Olds Know?*, Chester Finn, Jr., and I pointed out that there had never been a test of this kind on a national basis, and that there was no way to know whether students were learning more or less about history than in the past. Nonetheless, we found it disturbing that two-thirds of the sample did not know that the Civil War occurred between 1850 and 1900; that nearly 40 percent did not know that the *Brown* decision held school segregation unconstitutional, that 40 percent did not know that the East Coast of the United States was explored and settled mainly by England and that the Southwest was explored and settled mainly by Spain, that 70 percent did not know that the purpose of Jim Crow laws was to enforce racial segregation, and that 30 percent could not find Great Britain on a map of Europe.

Since the test had never been given before, critics were quick to quarrel with our judgment that student performance was disappointing. Perhaps, they suggested, students thirty or fifty years ago might have done worse on a comparable test. Others complained that the test should also have been given to a representative sample of the adult population, because if adults don't know such things, then high school students should not be expected to know them either. Still others complained that we should not expect students to know or care about history because our society does not reward people who value learning, whether teachers or professors. And there were critics who insisted that the test relied too much on factual knowledge, which is insignificant compared to learning how to think. The most repeated criticism was that the results were of no importance because the study of history itself was of no importance, of no utility whatever in the world today. Again and again, the questions were posed, "What can you do with history? What kind of job will it get you?"

Polemics can be both endless and frustrating because there is almost always some truth in every assertion and counter-assertion. Everything the critics said was true to some extent. But it was also true that the assessment revealed that students were not learning some important things they should know about American history. Whether their counterparts in the past knew less, and whether adults today know less, is beside the point. Three wrongs don't make a right.

Plainly, a significant number of students are not remembering the history that they have studied; they are not integrating it into their repertoire of background knowledge, either as fact or as concept. In reality, as every student of history ought to recognize, facts and concepts are inseparable. Some information is so basic, so essential that all students must know it in order to make sense of new learning. Nor can students be expected to think critically about issues unless they have the background knowledge to support their reasoning. Insisting that facts have a rightful place in the study of history does not mean that history must be learned by rote. However one learns about the Civil War, however innovative or unorthodox the teacher's methodology, the student should know that it took place in the latter half of the nineteenth century, not because of the singular importance of that isolated fact, but because that fact connects the events to a particular place in time, to a larger context, and to a chronological setting in which it is possible to make judgments about causes and consequences and relationships among events in the same era.

Was there once a golden age in the study of history? There may have been, but I know of no evidence for it. In 1943, the *New York Times* reported the results of a test given to seven thousand college freshmen in thirty-six institutions. It was an open-ended test, not a multiple-choice test. Only 45 percent could name four of the specific freedoms guaranteed by the Bill of Rights; fewer than 25 percent could name two achievements of Abraham Lincoln, Thomas Jefferson, Andrew Jackson, or Theodore Roosevelt; less than 15 percent could identify Samuel Gompers as a leader of organized labor or Susan B. Anthony as an advocate of women's rights; and only 6 percent could name the thirteen original colonies.[1]

Compared to the college freshmen of 1943, today's high school juniors do well; after all, 50 percent of today's sample identified Gompers and 69 percent identified Susan B. Anthony. But our test takers had some critical advantages: first, they took a multiple-choice test, which limits their options and jogs their memory with the right answer; second, Gompers and Anthony are included in their high school textbooks, but were not always included in the textbooks of forty years ago; third, the multiple-choice format virtually guarantees that a minimum of 25 percent will guess the right answer.

The search for comparability may be a blind alley. After all, the historical knowledge that seems most important will differ with each generation, because the salient issues are different for each generation. Today, we expect youngsters to learn about the history of civil rights and minorities, and we stress social history as well as political history. On the NAEP test there were a number of questions about recent history, like Watergate and Sputnik. Such questions obviously could not have been asked forty years ago, and some of them may seem unimportant forty years from now.

The questions we may reasonably ask about history instruction in the schools are whether students are learning what schools are trying to teach them; whether the history that schools are teaching is significant, current, and presented in ways that encourage student engagement; whether enough time is provided to study issues and events in depth and in context; whether students learn to see today's issues and events in relationship to the past; whether events are studied from a variety of perspectives; whether students understand that the history they study is not "the truth," but a version of the past written by historians on the basis of analysis and evidence; and whether students realize that historians disagree about how to define the past.

I first became concerned about the condition of history in the schools while visiting about three dozen campuses across the country in 1984–85, ranging from large public universities to small private liberal arts colleges. Repeatedly, I was astonished by questions from able students about the most elementary facts of American history. At one urban Minnesota campus, none of the thirty students in a course on ethnic relations had ever heard of the Supreme Court's *Brown* v. *Board of Education* decision of 1954. How were they learning about ethnic relations? Their professor described the previous week's role-playing lesson. The class had been visited by a swarthy man who described himself as an Iranian, made some provocative statements, and then launched into a tirade, chastising them for being prejudiced against him (in reality, he was an Italo-American from Long Island, and not an Iranian at all). This "lesson" hardly compensated for their ignorance about the history of immigration, of racial minorities, of slavery and segregation, or of legislative and judicial efforts to establish equality in American life.

As a Phi Beta Kappa Visiting Scholar, I lectured at various campuses on the virtues of a liberal education and its importance to society today. After one such speech at a university in the Pacific Northwest, a professor of education insisted that high school students should concentrate on vocational preparation and athletics, since they had the rest of their lives to learn subjects like history "on their own time." Time and again, I heard people wonder why even prospective teachers should have a liberal education, particularly if they planned to teach below the high school level. The younger the children, according to the skeptics, the less their teacher needs to know; they seemed to think that knowing and nurturing were incompatible.

In my meetings and talks with students, who were usually the best in the education or the history program, I was surprised to find that most did not recognize allusions to eminent historical figures such as Jane Addams or W.E.B. DuBois. As I traveled, I questioned history professors about whether their students seemed as well prepared today as in the past. None thought they were. Even at such elite institutions as Columbia and Harvard, professors expressed concern about the absence of a common body of reference and allusion to the past; most said their students lacked a sense of historical context and a knowledge of the major issues that had influenced American history. As a professor at Berkeley put it to me, "They have no furniture in their minds. You can assume nothing in the way of prior knowledge. Skills, yes; but not knowledge."

Those who teach at nonelite institutions perceived an even deeper level of historical illiteracy. Typical were comments by Thomas Kessner, a professor of history at Kingsborough Community College in Brooklyn, New York: "My students are not stupid, but they have an abysmal background in American or any other kind of history." This gloomy assessment was echoed by Naomi Miller, chair of the history department at Hunter College in New York. "My students have no historical knowledge on which to draw when they enter college," she told me.

"They have no point of reference for understanding World War I, the Treaty of Versailles, or the Holocaust." She expressed dismay at her students' indifference to dates and chronology or causation. "They think that everything is subjective. They have plenty of attitudes and opinions, but they lack the knowledge to analyze a problem." Professor Miller believes that "we are in danger of bringing up a generation without historical memory. This is a dangerous situation."

In search of some explanation for these complaints, I visited social studies classes in New York City. In one high school, where most of the three thousand students are black, Hispanic, and/or recent immigrants, a teacher said to me, "Our students don't see the relevance to their own lives of what a lot of dead people did a long time ago. American studies means more to them than American history."

I observed a class in American studies, where the lesson for the day was state government, its leaders and their functions. When the teacher asked whether anyone knew what the state attorney general does, a girl answered tentatively, "Isn't he the one that says on the cigarette box that you shouldn't smoke because it gives you cancer?" The teacher responded, incorrectly, "Yes, but what else does he do?" The teacher went on, earnestly trying to explain what New York's secretary of state does ("he keeps the state's papers") and to find some way to connect the work of these officials to the students' daily lives. The youngsters were bored and apathetic. Watching their impassive faces, I thought that a discussion of the Crusades or the Salem witchcraft trials or Nat Turner's rebellion would be infinitely more interesting, and relevant, to their adolescent minds.

In another American studies class the topic for the day was the Dred Scott decision. Ah, I thought, I will now see how historical issues are dealt with. The class began with ten minutes of confusing discussion about how students would feel if they were drafted and told they had to serve in Vietnam. The teacher seemed to think this was relevant to the students (since it was relevant to her own generation), although it was not clear that the students had any idea what the war in Vietnam was about. What she was trying to do, I finally realized, was to get the students to wonder who is a citizen and how citizenship is defined.

It was a worthy aim, but the rest of the lesson shed little light on the meaning of the Dred Scott decision. The students were told he was a slave who had been brought into a free territory and then sued for his freedom; they were also given a brief definition of the Missouri Compromise. With this as background, the teacher divided them into groups, each of which was a miniature Supreme Court, where they would decide whether Dred Scott should be a slave or go free. Ten minutes later, no surprise, each little Supreme Court recommended that Dred Scott should be a free man, and the class ended. They did not learn why Chief Justice Roger B. Taney decided otherwise, nor did they learn the significance of the Dred Scott decision in the antislavery agitation, nor its importance as a precursor to the Civil War. Since the course was law studies, not American history, the students had no background knowledge about sectional antagonisms, about slavery, or about anything else that preceded or followed the Civil War.

When I expressed surprise about the complete absence of traditional, chronological history in the social studies curriculum, the chair of the social studies department said, "What we teach is determined by guidelines from the State Education Department. In the late 1960s the state decided to deemphasize chronological history and to focus instead on topical issues and social science concepts. We followed suit." A teacher chimed in to explain, "We don't teach history, because it doesn't help our students pass the New York State Regents examination in social studies." This teacher claimed to have compiled a list of concepts that regularly appear on the Regents examinations; his students prepare for the Regents by memorizing the definitions of such terms as "cultural diffusion" and "social mobility."

*   *   *

What happened to the study of history? Many factors contributed to its dethroning; some relate to the overall American cultural situation, others to specific institutional forces within the schools and changes in the social studies field. Those who claim that American culture devalues history make a strong case. Despite the fervor of history buffs and historical societies, Americans have long been present- and future-oriented. I suspect that it has never been easy to persuade Americans of the importance of understanding the past. Trends in recent years have probably strengthened popular resistance to historical study. Even in the academy, rampant specialization among college faculties has made professors less willing to teach broad survey courses, less concerned about capturing the attention of nonmajors or the general public by tackling large questions.

Within the schools, the study of history has encountered other kinds of problems. During the past generation, history was dislodged from its lofty perch as "queen" of the social studies by the proliferation of social sciences, electives, and other courses. Many in the social studies field say that history still dominates the social studies, since almost all students take the traditional one-year high school course in American history, and about half the students take a one-year course in world history. However, even though the high school American history course may be secure, researchers have found "a gradual and persistent decline in requirements, courses and enrollments" in history at the junior high school level, as well as a reduction of requirements and course offerings in world history in high schools. Indeed, the only history course that is well entrenched in the curriculum is the high school survey of American history.[2]

To some teachers, social studies means the study of the social sciences, and many schools offer electives in sociology, political science, economics, psychology, and anthropology. Some see the field as primarily responsible for the study of current social problems. Others see it as a field whose overriding objective is to teach students the essentials of good behavior and good citizenship. Still others declare that the goal of the social studies is to teach critical thinking, or values, or respect for cultural diversity.

Because of the ill-defined nature of the social studies field, it is easily (and regularly) invaded by curricular fads, and it all too often serves as a dumping ground for special-interest programs. Whenever state legislatures or interest groups discover an unmet need, a new program is pushed into the social studies curriculum. Each state has its own pet programs, but under the copious umbrella of social studies can be found courses in such subjects as energy education, environmental education, gun-control education, water education, sex education, human rights education, future studies, consumer education, free-enterprise education, and a host of other courses prompted by contemporary issues.

This indiscriminate confusion of short-term social goals would have dismayed those historians who first took an active interest in history in the schools. In 1893 a distinguished panel of historians, including the future president Woodrow Wilson, recommended an eight-year course of study in history, beginning in the fifth grade with biography and mythology and continuing in the following years with American history and government, Greek and Roman history, French history, and English history. Criticizing the traditional emphasis on rote learning, the Committee of Ten argued that history should teach judgment and thinking, and should be conjoined with such studies as literature, geography, art, and languages. The historians' recommendations were aimed at all children, not just the college-bound: "We believe that the colleges can take care of themselves; our interest is in the schoolchildren who have no expectation of going to college, the larger number of whom will not enter even a high school."

In 1899 the Committee of Seven, a group of historians created by the American Historical Association (AHA), recommended a four-year model high school curriculum: first year, ancient history; second year, medieval and modern European history; third year, English history; and fourth year, American history and government. It was expected that students would read biographies, mythology, legends, and hero tales in the elementary years, and that this reading would provide a foundation for their subsequent study of history. The Committee of Seven's proposal set a national pattern for American high schools for years to come. Like the Committee of Ten, the Seven believed that history should be the core of general education for all students in a democracy.

This four-year model history curriculum came under increasing attack, however, from the newly emerging field of social studies, whose major purpose (according to a 1918 report known as *The Cardinal Principles of Secondary Education*) was "social efficiency." Characteristic of the progressive effort to make education socially useful, the new report, which for decades has been considered the most influential document in American education, rejected those studies that seemed not to contribute directly to the goal of training students to take their place in society. Moreover, *The Cardinal Principles* broke sharply with the findings and recommendations of earlier committees. It endorsed differentiated curricula, based on students' future vocational goals, such as agriculture, business, clerical, industrial, and household arts programs. Much of the history that had been taught had no immediate social utility and thus its advocates had difficulty claiming a place in the curriculum. In the decades that followed, as the curriculum incorporated more courses that seemed socially useful or were intended to teach social skills, the time available for history shrank. Many schools collapsed their courses in ancient history, European history, and English history into a single, and optional, one-year course called "world history" or "Western civilization."

The new emphasis on short-term social utility also affected

the curriculum in the early grades. The various reform reports of the early twentieth century had recommended that young children read exciting stories about remarkable people and events that changed the course of history. In most city and state curricula, children in the early grades studied distant civilizations and read their myths and legends in addition to learning the stories about heroes and the folktales of their own country. They also celebrated holidays and learned about their local community through field trips, an emphasis called "home geography." But by the 1930s this curriculum began to be replaced by studies of family roles and community helpers. Instead of thrilling biographies and mythology, children read stories about children just like themselves. The new curriculum for the early grades, called "expanding environments" or "expanding horizons," was factual and immediate, ousting imaginative historical literature and play from the early grades. Increasingly, time in the early grades was devoted to this fixed pattern: kindergarten, myself; first grade, my family; second grade, my neighborhood; third grade, my city. There was no evidence that children preferred to read about postal workers over tall tales, stories of heroes, or ancient Egyptians. Nonetheless, the new curriculum gradually swept the country, pushing historical content out of the early grades.

Not until the late 1980s did the social studies curriculum in the primary grades attract sustained criticism. According to leading cognitive psychologists, the "expanding environments" approach has no grounding in developmental research. Indeed, there is good reason to believe that it dwells unnecessarily on what the child already knows or does not need to go to school to learn. In 1987 a content analysis of social studies textbooks for the early grades was conducted at the University of Georgia. One of the investigators, Professor A. Guy Larkins, concluded, "If asked to choose between teaching primary-grades social studies with available texts or eliminating social studies from the K-3 curriculum, I would choose the latter. Much of the content in current texts is redundant, superfluous, vacuous, and needlessly superficial." Larkins also complained that children were reading about taking field trips instead of actually taking field trips, seeing pictures of a generic community rather than investigating their own.[3]

Learning again and again about the roles of family members and community helpers in the primary years may well be extremely boring for children who are used to watching action-packed stories on television and seeing dramatic events on the evening news. The me-centered curriculum fails to give children a sense of other times and places, and fails to appeal to their lively imaginations. Children might enjoy the study of history if they began in the early grades to listen to and read lively historical literature, such as myths, legends, hero stories, and true stories about great men and women in their community, state, nation, and world. Not only in the early grades but throughout the kindergarten to twelfth grade sequence, students should read lively narrative accounts of extraordinary events and remarkable people. Present practice seems calculated to persuade young people that social studies is a train of self-evident, unrelated facts, told in a dull manner.

By mid-century most American public schools had adopted a nearly standardized social studies curriculum: children in kindergarten and the first three grades studied self, home, family, neighborhood, and community; children in fourth grade studied state history; in fifth grade, American history; in sixth grade, world cultures; seventh grade, world geography; eighth grade, American history; ninth grade, civics or world cultures; tenth grade, world history; eleventh grade, American history; twelfth grade, American government. While there have been many variations from district to district, this has been the dominant social studies curriculum for the last fifty years. Most cities and states follow the model for the early grades, teach one year of American history in elementary school and again in junior high school, and require a single year of American history for high school graduation. Most, however, do not require the study of world history in the high school years.

Despite this format's persistent emphasis on social relevance and student interest, surveys have repeatedly shown that students find social studies to be less interesting and less important than their other school subjects. Why is this field, whose intrinsic human interest is so compelling, so often perceived as boring? There are many possible answers, including the compendious, superficial, and dull textbooks students are assigned to read. But the curricular pattern itself must be in some measure at fault, as it forces repetition of courses on the one hand and too little time for study in depth on the other. Both problems are surefire formulas for dullness, and curriculum planners have been thus far unable to resolve either of them.

When the usual curricular model is followed, American history is taught three times: in the fifth grade, the eighth grade, and the eleventh grade. The question is whether to teach a complete survey course (from pre-Columbian times to the present) at each of the three grade settings. If the survey is taught three times, there is no time to go beyond the textbook, to explore significant questions, to examine original sources or to conduct mock trials or debates. Some districts have broken away from the "coverage" survey by instead teaching major topics and themes in American history, but this approach is clearly insufficient when youngsters fail to understand chronology, the sequence of events, or the casual connections among events.

Another alternative to the survey is to devote each of the three years of American history to a different time period. The usual pattern is that the elementary school course concentrates on exploration and settlement and daily life in the colonies; the junior high course emphasizes the nineteenth century; and the high school year carries the student from the Civil War to the present. The advantage of the latter program is that it allows for time to treat issues in depth, without neglecting chronology. The disadvantage is that it allows no time for mature students to examine the Revolutionary era, when the principles of American government were shaped, or to consider the constitutional conflicts that led to the Civil War. It is also problematic in light of population mobility from state to state, as well as the immigrant influx from other countries, which means that newcomers in the middle or later grades will miss out on important events in the life of the early Republic. While there is no easy answer to this problem, the history curriculum adopted in California in 1987 attempts to meld the two approaches; each year concentrates on a different time period, but each course begins and ends with an intensive review of critical issues and events.

In the world history program, the most pressing problem is time. In most districts where world history is taught, it is studied for only one year, not nearly enough time to encompass the history of the world. New York State adopted a two-year global studies sequence in 1987 (though not strong on history), and California adopted a mandatory three-year world history sequence in the same year. Most other states, however, do not require even one year of world history.

Furthermore, the social studies field is divided about whether world history should emphasize Western Europe or global studies. When the course focuses on Western Europe, it is unified by attention to the evolution of democratic political institutions and ideas, as well as to their betrayal by genocide, war, and racism. When the course is global studies (as, for example, in New York State), equal attention is given to Western Europe, Africa, Latin America, Asia, and other regions. The "Western civilization" course has been criticized by some as "ethnocentric," while the "global studies" approach has been criticized by others for superficiality, for incoherence, and for minimizing the importance of the West in world history. No matter which approach is taken, a single year is insufficient to study world history. The difficulty of trying to compress the history of the world into an introductory course is exemplified by one widely adopted text, in which World War II is reduced to a brief summary and the Holocaust to two sentences: "Many millions of civilians also lost their lives. Six million Jews alone were murdered at Hitler's orders."[4]

Does it matter if Americans are ignorant of their past and of the world's? Does it matter if they know little of the individuals, the events, the ideas, the forces, and the movements that shaped their nation and others? If the study of history is to gain public support and attention, historians must directly answer the utilitarian challenge. They must be prepared to argue that the study of history is useful in its own terms. Those who study history learn how and why the world came to be what it is, why things change and why they stay the same. Knowledge of history is both useful and necessary for our society because everyone has the right to choose our leaders and to participate in our civic and social life. All citizens, not just the few, are expected to understand major domestic and international issues. Without historical perspective, voters are more likely to be swayed by emotional appeals, by stirring commercials, or by little more than a candidate's photogenic charisma.

Even between elections, a knowledge of history is vital today for the average citizen and vital for the health of our political system. Politicians and news organizations regularly poll the public to assess their view of domestic and international issues. When public sentiment is clear, the government and the media take heed. When the public is ill-informed or uninterested, policymakers are free to act without the consent of the governed. American today require historical background in order to understand complex social and political questions in Latin America, Africa, and elsewhere.

Writers and editors in national newspapers and magazines assume the presence of a historically literate public by alluding without further explanation to historic events and individuals. Without a historically literate public, readily able to understand such references, newspapers and television journalism will have no choice but to simplify their vocabulary, to reduce their coverage of serious topics, and serve as little more than headline and amusement services, devoid of significant context.

Those who have a professional commitment to the study of history have a particular responsibility to improve the way it is taught and learned in the schools. Organizations such as the American Historical Association, the Organization of American Historians (OAH), and the National Council for the Social Studies (NCSS) have a direct responsibility for the quality of history instruction. The teacher-scholar collaboratives sponsored by these organizations are one valuable means to assist professionals in the schools. There are others. For example, professional associations should lobby to ensure that teachers of history have actually studied history in college; in several states, including New York and California, social studies teachers may be certified without ever having studied any history. Professional associations could assist curriculum planners in enriching the study of history at every grade level. The AHA and OAH could provide invaluable support to state curriculum offices that are pressured by powerful interest groups to rewrite or water down the history curriculum; some kind of review mechanism could fend off unreasonable demands.

In 1932, Henry Johnson of Teachers College, Columbia University, wrote a delightful review of the teaching of history throughout the ages, somewhat misleadingly entitled *An Introduction to the History of the Social Sciences.* Johnson quoted a sixteenth-century Spanish scholar, Juan Vives, to explain why it is valuable to study history: "Where there is history," wrote Vives, "children have transferred to them the advantages of old men; where history is absent, old men are as children." Without history, according to Vives, "no one would know anything about his father or ancestors; no one could know his own rights or those of another or how to maintain them; no one would know how his ancestors came to the country he inhabits." Johnson cited the view of seventeenth-century French oratorians that "history is a grand mirror in which we see ourselves. . . . The secret of knowing and judging ourselves rightly is to see ourselves in others, and history can make us the contemporaries of all centuries in all countries."

History will never be restored as a subject of value unless it is detached from vulgar utilitarianism; it should not be expected to infuse morals or patriotism. Properly taught, history teaches the pursuit of truth and understanding; it establishes a context of human life in a particular time and place, relating art, literature, philosophy, law, architecture, language, government, economics, and social life; it portrays the great achievements and terrible disasters of the human race; it awakens youngsters to the universality of the human experience as well as to the particularities that distinguish cultures and societies from one another; it encourages the development of intelligence, civility, and a sense of perspective. It endows its students with a broad knowledge of other times, other cultures, other places. It leaves its students with cultural resources on which they may draw for the rest of their lives. These are values and virtues that are gained through the study of history, values and virtues essential to the free individual exercising freedom of mind. Beyond these, history needs no further justification.

NOTES

1. *New York Times*, April 4, 1943.

2. Matthew T. Downey, "The Status of History in the Schools," in *History in the Schools*, ed. Matthew T. Downey (Washington, D.C.: National Council for the Social Studies, 1985), pp. 1–12.

3. A. Guy Larkins and Michael L. Hawkins, "Trivial and Noninformative Content of Social Studies Textbooks in the Primary Grades," a paper delivered to the American Educational Research Association annual meeting, Washington, D.C., April 1987; see also Kieran Egan, "Teaching History to Young Children," *Phi Delta Kappan*, March 1982, pp. 439–41; Diane Ravitch, "Tot Sociology," *American Scholar* 56, 3 (Summer 1987).

4. Leften Stavros Stavrianos, *A Global History of Man* (Boston: Allyn & Bacon, 1970), p. 199.

CHAPTER 4

History and Progressivism: A Century of Reform Proposals

by HAZEL W. HERTZBERG

Progressivism occupies a pivotal position in the creation of the modern state and of an urban, industrial society in the United States. Nowhere is this more evident yet more elusive than in education, for beyond its general characteristics, there are many different strains in progressivism, some at extreme variance with each other. Just as the variety and conflict within progressivism make it a phenomenon difficult to define, there are similar difficulties in judging its effects on education, especially in the secondary school. On the one hand, we know a good deal about how progressivism in this period affected some aspects of the public high school, whose spectacular growth in the late nineteenth and early twentieth centuries was shaped by the developing movement of progressive reform. On the other hand, we have paid little attention to its relationship to curriculum itself, either in content or in method.

An important exception here is the literature that generally decries the impact of "progressive education" on the social studies. John Dewey is often depicted as its Great Satan. History, according to this critique, has virtually disappeared from the schools, driven out by the social studies that are the bastion of progressive education. This literature, like much of the writing on the subject, reveals considerable confusion as to just what is meant by progressive education. Often it is equated with an antiintellectual and chaotic classroom where individualism runs rampant and students are encouraged to weave baskets or swing from the chandeliers if that's what helps them to express themselves. Progressive education is held responsible for the classroom as a place where students are served up an unappetizing and brain deadening "stew" called "social studies" from which history has been excluded and where process has triumphed over substance.

However wide of the mark these critiques may often be, they raise an important question: Is there a connection between progressive education and the social studies in secondary education, and if so, what is its nature? One of the main problems of the critique outlined above is that it assumes progressive education in the social studies curriculum began only with the introduction of the term in the 1916 report of the NEA Committee on the Social Studies, whose recommendation supplanted the "traditional" curriculum in which history reigned supreme. Many social studies advocates calling themselves progressives make the same mistake when, from the opposite point of view, they attack "traditional history" in the schools as the enemy of true learning. What neither side seems to realize is that in 1916 the curriculum they hail or decry as "traditional" had been in place for less than two decades, supplanting a truly traditional curriculum in which history had played a merely peripheral role.

Our examination must begin in the 1880s, when the high school was in the process of transformation and the modern curriculum was taking shape. In 1880, history and the other social subjects, whether in high school or college, were either absent or of minor importance. There was, for example, no department of history in any college in the United States; history was usually attached to the classics and ancient languages. The dominant teaching method in both high schools and colleges was the textbook recitation in which students memorized passages from the text and repeated them.

It was in the 1880s that most of the common core of beliefs that characterize progressive education in history and the other social subjects was emerging in the literature of reform. It included a commitment to these subjects as ways of building an informed dedication to the public good; an emphasis on active rather than passive student learning and on the utilization of the student's own experience; an attempt to link the life of the school with the life outside; a belief that the school should offer broad unspecialized as well as specialized knowledge and a consequent interest in putting things together; an affinity with social science; an advocacy of the study of peoples and places far beyond the United States; and a belief in the efficacy of experiment and change. To these was later added a tendency to favor the recent over the more distant past.

One factor for change was that in that decade public high schools became more numerous than private academies, and the pressure for the neglected social subjects began to mount. At the same time, American academicians were having their battle between "the classics"—Latin, Greek, and mathematics—and "the moderns"—history, English, science, and modern languages. In general, the old-time college was the home of the classics, and the new university the home of the moderns (plus, of course, the classics, for the university was open to a wide spectrum of knowledge). With the development of the university and the movement of some colleges toward university status, the paths from high school to college became more problematic since each college had its own pattern of entrance requirements. Although a minority of students actually went to college, the high schools had to provide for them. As the number of high schools, colleges, and universities grew, the problem became more urgent.

Another force for change was the professionalization of

history and the other social subjects. Unlike the situation in other countries, this process in the United States coincided both with the development of the university and with the rapid rise of the public high school. In the latter part of the nineteenth century a generation of young men went to Germany for advanced training in "scientific history," a history based on primary sources. It was critical, interpretative, and concerned with the development of balanced judgment in weighing and evaluating evidence.

The founding generation of professional historians not only valued scientific history but had a deep commitment to history as the conscience of the state and a concern with its role in public affairs. They brought back a knowledge of European secondary education, its weaknesses as well as its strengths. They were well aware that while in autocratic Germany the purpose of schooling was the education of subjects, in the United States our schools were supposed to produce citizens who would participate actively and intelligently in a democratic society. The entwining of history, the public good, and the education of citizens fit well into the historic mission of the public schools. The education of citizens began to be assigned not solely but especially to particular school subjects. In the United States, scientific history and the education of citizens required a new and dynamic curriculum and new methods of teaching in both schools and colleges.

The newly professionalized historians (the American Historical Association was founded in 1884) brought to the task of transforming method and content a sophistication based on their own experience in the schoolroom. Most of the founding generation of professional historians had themselves been schoolteachers or were otherwise closely associated with the schools. Herbert Baxter Adams, whose Johns Hopkins seminar trained the first two generations of American social scientists and who served as secretary of the American Historical Association for the first two decades of its existence, was a former schoolteacher. Passionate commitment to public education was one of the leitmotifs of his seminar. Albert Bushnell Hart of Harvard was a member of the Cambridge School Board who published more extensively in educational methodology than in history itself, while also producing the *American Nation* series, the *Harvard Guide* (with Edward Channing), and school and college textbooks. Frederick Jackson Turner was a high school inspector in Wisconsin and taught courses in the study and teaching of history. These men were typical in their educational experience and commitments.

For the newly professionalized historians, it was essential not simply to establish history in the schools and colleges but to create new methods of teaching suitable for critical history based on inquiry and for educating boys and girls who would be inquiring citizens in a democratic society. The textbook/recitation/memory way of learning was the enemy of such history. It is significant that the first collective statement of this first generation of professional historians was a book published in 1883 entitled *Methods of Teaching History*, edited by the psychologist G. Stanley Hall, leader of the child development movement and future explicator of adolescence.

Thus, questions not only of content but of method were sharply posed in 1892 by the Conference on History, Civil Government, and Political Economy, one of nine subcommittees of the famous NEA Committee of Ten. Set up initially to smooth the path from high school to college, the Committee of Ten, led by Charles W. Eliot, president of Harvard, rapidly moved far beyond this charge to become the first national committee to recommend curricula for all the high school subjects, both classic and modern, focusing not on the needs of college-bound students (whom the Committee believed "could take care of themselves") but on the majority of high school students who did not go to college.

The membership of the History Ten is significant in what it tells us about the links of the social subjects with progressivism. The chairman was the historian Charles Kendall Adams, a former schoolteacher, pioneer of the semi-

nar method at the University of Michigan, and past president
of Cornell, who had just become president of the University
of Wisconsin. Albert Bushnell Hart, the secretary of the
committee, was a friend and Harvard classmate of Teddy
Roosevelt and later an active member of the Bull Moose
party. Woodrow Wilson, the future progressive president,
was a prime mover in the affairs of the committee. James
Harvey Robinson, the future doyen of the "new" or
"progressive" history, was a committee member, while Frederick Jackson Turner, who sat in on its meetings, was probably the first historian to be identified as progressive.

The History Ten's recommendations set the agenda for
what the members considered to be progressive education in the
social subjects in purpose, content, and method. The value of
instruction in the social subjects, they asserted, was that, taught
by the newer methods, they served to "broaden and cultivate
the mind; that they counteract a narrow and provincial spirit;
that they prepare the pupil in an eminent degree for enlightenment and intellectual enjoyment in after years; and that they
assist him to exercise a salutary effect upon the affairs of his
country."[1]

The Committee recommended biography and mythology
for fifth and sixth grades; American history and elements of civil
government in seven; Greek and Roman history with their
Oriental connections in eight; French history in nine and English in ten, both "taught so as to elucidate the general movement of mediaeval and modern history"; American history in
eleven; and a selected historical period studied intensively (a
high school version of the seminar) and civil government in
twelve. In the report of the Committee of Ten, history and civil
government became the backbone of the social studies curriculum, history was firmly linked with geography and economics
and with literature and composition, and the same curriculum
was recommended for all students whether or not they were
going to college.

Informal talks by students as well as teachers rather than formal lectures; probing questions and discussion rather than catechism; reference books, maps, and historical novels and poems rather than sole reliance on a textbook; the use of original sources as a teaching supplement; investigation rather than predigested knowledge—these were to be the hallmarks of the classroom envisioned by the History Ten. The teacher who presided in this lively classroom was to be well trained in both subject matter and methods of teaching it. In order to reassure the public, the Ten pointed out that these recommendations had already proven their worth in many classrooms, but their report was in fact a radical and effective challenge both to the traditional curriculum and to traditional teaching methods.

The History Ten put a good deal of emphasis on methods and active student participation. "How far should pupils be expected to memorize?" the Committee asked:

> "A few things should be learned by heart and, when forgotten, learned again to serve as a firm ground on which to group one's knowledge; without knowing the succession of dynasties, or of sovereigns, or of presidents, or the dates of great constitutional events, the pupil's stock of information will have no more form than a jelly-fish." But those few necessary facts ought to be clearly defined as only a framework to assist the memory. The pupil's stock of information is to be kept in mind not by calling for it in glib recitations devoid of thought but by constantly framing questions which will require for an answer a knowledge of the necessary facts. . . .[2]

In place of rote memorization the History Ten proposed: much more discussion; student reports and investigations both oral and written; debates; actual observation of the workings of community and government; visits to historical places and museums; integration of history and geography; use of a variety of instructional materials including primary materials, historical fiction, and visual aids; creation and expansion of school libraries; and other such measures, which many educators still regard as recent and innovative.

This first recommendation by a national committee for a curriculum in the social subjects represented the first type of educational progressivism—that is, humanistic progressivism. The History Ten sought to nourish the development of the individual in both private and public roles—to cultivate the mind and spirit of each student while helping him or her to participate intelligently in a democratic public culture. The student was an inquirer rather than simply a receiver. The curriculum was linked to both the humanities and the social sciences and was concerned with countries and peoples far beyond the United States in space as well as time. Its central and synthesizing academic discipline was history. An understanding of the past they would study and the present and future society in which students would live required the exercise of judgment and interpretation, not simply the acceptance of facts and received opinions.

At the dawn of the progressive period, therefore, and at a time when the curriculum of the high school was being decisively shaped, people who became major figures in progressivism, both in education and in public life, were helping to fashion the first nationally recommended social studies curriculum. The report of the History Ten was a practical guide to democratic education in the high school. The new historians found ready allies in school administrators of their day, who welcomed the role of history in the education of citizens and the new methods of teaching. They were deeply sympathetic to history; some were themselves historians, either professional or amateur. This informal but powerful alliance, channeled through the NEA, helps to account for history's meteoric rise from a peripheral school subject to a central one between 1890 and 1916.

The second influential committee on the social subjects was the American Historical Association Committee of Seven, reporting in 1899 at the request of the NEA, which was still attempting to resolve the problem of articulation between schools and colleges. Like the Ten, almost all the members of this committee were former or current schoolteachers or principals, or otherwise had experience in secondary education. They were all practicing historians, most of them leaders and shapers of the historical profession. The Committee was headed by Andrew C. McLaughlin of the University of Chicago, the great constitutional historian who was a former high school principal in Michigan and whose father had been a superintendent of schools there. Among its members was the first woman to serve on a national curriculum committee, Lucy Salmon of Vassar, a former student of both Charles Kendall Adams and Woodrow Wilson; she was a clear-eyed and tough-minded woman who had been both a schoolteacher and a normal school teacher, had introduced the seminar method at Vassar, and was a social historian and a suffragist. Charles Homer Haskins, a medieval historian, who had also sat in on the meetings of the History Ten, was a member—one aspect of his lifelong interest in education. So was Herbert Baxter Adams, the AHA secretary. Albert Bushnell Hart provided continuity with the Ten. George L. Fox was the only member currently teaching in high school.

The extraordinarily influential report issued by the Seven was built on the recommendations of the Ten but went into more detail. Like the Ten, the Seven believed that the high school should serve the purpose of "developing boys and girls into men and women" rather than only fitting them for college. History was "peculiarly appropriate for a secondary course." Students would acquire "some appreciation of the nature of the state and society, some sense of the duties and responsibilities of citizenship, some capacity of dealing with political and social questions, something of the broad and tolerant spirit which is bred by the study of past times and conditions." History, the Seven believed, was a synthesizing subject that could give "unity, continuity, and strength to the curriculum" by unfolding over a period of years as the pupils' minds and capacities developed, an enlarging process that could not be achieved by bits and pieces of information drawn from disparate subjects. At the very point when specialization was taking hold in the professions and in the emerging state, the Seven asserted the importance of history as a synthesizing force that would draw together knowledge into a comprehensible and interrelated whole.

For the education of citizens, the study of government was also necessary. But the Seven believed that while the study of civil government was essential, it was not sufficient; it was too static, "too presentist," too concerned with existing institutions. In a time of change, the Seven said explicitly what was only implied in the report of the Ten: that understanding change was one of the basic values of the study of history, and that this understanding would help students make changes in their own times. Students needed to understand that "society is in movement, that what one sees around him is not the eternal but the transient, and that in the process of change virtue must be militant if it is to be triumphant." No advance or practical reform could be secured without knowing "how forces have worked in the social and political organization of former times," the committee argued. This attitude toward change, rooted in an understanding of how change took place in the past and how the present came to be, was an essential element in the humanistic progressivism of the Seven. Eventually it became the object of attack from other kinds of "progressives" to whom the only important change would take place in the future and equally by those who wished to engineer students to fit neatly and permanently into the status quo.

The curriculum proposed for the high school was: first year, ancient history including the early Middle Ages to the fifth century; second, medieval and modern European history from the end of the first period to the present; third year, English history; fourth year, American history and civil government taught together or separately. The Seven recommended that political, economic, and social affairs be taught within the framework of history, with the inclusion of the lives of ordinary men and women as well as the fortunes of institutions, states, and empires.

Like the Ten, the Seven took method seriously and devoted a good deal of attention to teaching and learning. They condemned rote memorization. They advocated inquiry and critical thinking, written work using several books and a variety of narratives and viewpoints, original sources, audiovisual aids, collateral reading, and correlation with other subjects, both the humanities and the social sciences. The Seven's report was another strong statement of humanistic progressivism in secondary education, published just before the new century opened and clearly looking forward to the future. It was in the progressive era during the first decade and a half of the twentieth century that their recommendations were widely adopted—probably more widely than those of any social studies committee before or since. Because they matched the spirit of the age, the Seven's curriculum became solidly entrenched in many schools. In 1911 the Seven's recommendations were somewhat modified by another AHA Committee of Five, which urged more attention to modern European history and separate treatment of American government in grade twelve.

One of the factors that helped the spectacular spread of history in the progressive period was the emergence of a new school of historical interpretation, associated with James Harvey Robinson and soon called "progressive history." Robinson had been a member of the Committees of Ten and Five, and a leader and president of the Association of History Teachers of the Middle States and Maryland. Another famous practitioner was Charles A. Beard, who was also a leader in the middle states and one of the most influential historians of his generation. Robinson and Beard collaborated on a series of widely used textbooks for the schools.

Such men made up the historical wing of the progressive movement. They believed in "history that speaks to the present"—that is, a history that illuminates the present and explains how it came to be, knowledge the progressive historians believed essential for social progress. They favored more emphasis on "recent" (the last two or three hundred years) over ancient history and a history broadened far beyond "past politics," one that investigated the conditions of everyday life, of industry and work, of ordinary folk as well as of princes and presidents, of social and economic as well as political change. They essentially created intellectual history, which they thought necessary to promote the intellectual liberty upon which they believed progress fundamentally depended. They sought alliances with the rising social sciences so recently separated from history, and that suggested new insights and interpretations. Their history, with its belief in social progress, social science, and social education, was just the history that the schools appeared to be seeking in the first decades of the twentieth century.

By 1913, however, the alliance between historians and school administrators had already begun to weaken. In that year a new force erupted among administrators hard pressed to cope with a rapidly expanding school system—more students, more buildings, more teachers. This was the doctrine of "scientific management," borrowed from industry where the work of Frederick Taylor in time and motion studies and other attempts to ensure cost-effectiveness and accountability were rapidly gaining ground. Thus was born a second type of educational progressivism, and one that exercises a powerful, even dominant, influence in our own time. The devotees of scientific management tended to be unsympathetic to history as having insufficient immediate payoff; ancient and medieval history and the classical languages were especially disdained.

Concurrently, a new group of specialists in both administration and curriculum making conducted extensive "scientific" school surveys (the survey being a typical progressive device) that purported to demonstrate the characteristics of teachers judged by supervisors and colleagues to be "good," and to measure the cost-effectiveness of various school subjects. Men like Franklin Bobbitt of the University of Chicago were not only the theoreticians of the new movement, they were also the progenitors of the new "science" of curriculum making. Need I say that what could be measured most easily became most valued?

These new scientific management progressives, like some of their counterparts in government, were concerned primarily with efficient, cost-effective, and orderly administration. Scientific management progressivism sought, and still seeks, accountability and immediately demonstrable results. It is characterized by an abiding faith in "objective" testing as a way of sorting students, enforcing a curriculum, and showing results. It is not surprising that scientific management progressivism favors sociology, economics, current events, and other "practical" and easily tested subjects, and that history is often regarded as impractical and irrelevant.

Another type of educational progressivism, closely allied to and sometimes indistinguishable from scientific management progressivism, developed, one centered on "social efficiency." Sometimes a term becomes popular and powerful both because it suits the spirit of the age and because it can assume very different meanings. Thus different wings of educational progressivism assigned different and often conflicting meanings to social efficiency. To some tendencies in sociology, especially educational sociology, it meant a tough version of social control, a term popularized by the sociologist Edward A. Ross at the turn of the century. A student of Ross's, David Snedden of Teachers College Columbia, for example, took the reform school as the model for the public school. He envisioned the schools as unparalleled instruments of social control, hierarchically organized and scientifically managed, with separate schools for rulers and ruled, or what he called "consumers" (the elite) and "producers" or "the rank and file," selected according to their parents' station in life. Schools were to engineer pupils to fit neatly into the status quo. This was Snedden's version of the education of citizens. I leave to the reader's imagination the depth of Snedden's contempt for history in general and any history without immediate practical usefulness (such as ancient history) in particular. His was an extreme version of social efficiency.

Social efficiency could also mean something quite different. John Dewey's model for the school was an idealized community, permeated with "the spirit of art, history, and science," saturating the child with "the spirit of service" and "providing him with the instruments of self-direction," in a society that would be "worthy, lovely, and harmonious." Dewey wrote that social efficiency in its broadest sense was "nothing less than the socialization of *mind* which is actively concerned in making experiences more communicable; in breaking down the barriers of social stratification which makes individuals impervious to the interests of others."

John Dewey's conception of history was essentially that of the progressive historians, to whom he was linked by ties of friendship and intellectual consanguinity. Dewey's book *Democracy and Education*, published in 1916, is his most extensive statement on the school subjects comprising the social studies. Dewey says that history and geography supplied subject matter that "gives background and outlook, intellectual perspective, to what might otherwise be narrow personal actions or mere forms of technical skill." As we "place our doings in their time and space connections," we understand that we are "citizens of no mean city" and "our ordinary daily experiences cease to be things of the moment and gain enduring substance." The progressive historians and Dewey clearly belong to the humanistic wing of educational progressivism that had been enunciated by the History Ten and further developed by the Seven.

In addition to the three types of educational progressivism that had emerged by the middle of the second decade of this century, there was a fourth, not yet very evident in secondary education. This was child-centered progressivism, in which the development of the individual child is the controlling element according to which the school subjects are tailored, or subordinated. Both the Ten and Seven were, of course, well aware of the necessity of fitting subject and method to the age and developmental level of the student: This was one factor that their own school experience had made vivid. But it would not be until the 1920s that this variety of progressive education became a fashionable and self-conscious element.

These four types of educational progressivism—humanistic, scientific management, social efficiency, and child-centered—were mixed (although by no means integrated) in the 1916 report of the NEA Committee on Social Studies. The report was a progressive document, formed and issued at the height of the progressive era during the presidency of a member of the History Ten, Woodrow Wilson, and published only a few months before our entrance into World War I. There were similarities between the new report and the older ones, and it is as important to understand the continuities as well as the changes. Like that of the History Ten, it was issued by a subcommittee of a larger NEA curricular review body, the Commission on the Reorganization of Secondary Education (CRSE). Again like those of the Ten and the Seven, it grew out of the perennial and still unresolved problem of college admissions and thereafter blossomed into a complete curricular review. The courses proposed were in line with overall trends in the parent social disciplines, although not with the specialization that was taking hold in them. The 1916 committee retained history and civics as the curricular core established by the Ten and the Seven but enlarged the time devoted to civics.

Some of the differences as well as the similarities between the 1916 report and its predecessors can be seen in the life of its chairman, Thomas Jesse Jones. Like them he was a former schoolteacher from the Midwest. But unlike them he was a first generation immigrant who had come to the United States from Wales as an eleven-year-old speaking no English and had settled with his widowed mother in Ohio. Unlike his predecessors, who were historians with conventional religious commitments,

Jones was a sociologist and a minister, a combination less unusual in those days. He was also what might be called a nonprofit career progressive. At the time of the formation of the committee he was an official of the U.S. Bureau of Education and later became a leading foundation executive. In many ways Jones was a model of the upwardly mobile immigrant who retained a passionate pride in his former nationality while committing himself passionately to his new one.

It was Jones who bequeathed the name social studies to the field then known by the ungainly "history and allied [or kindred] subjects." He changed the committee's original title from the Committee on Social Science to the Committee on Social Studies. "Social" was an adjective freely and favorably given to many progressive ideas and institutions of the period, such as in social gospel, social settlement, social efficiency, social control, and socialized recitation. Besides the obvious convenience of an overall name for a field then burgeoning in schools and colleges, the term "social studies" also implied a certain detachment from the increasing specialization of the parent disciplines and even from the disciplines themselves.

The report took care to begin by defining the social studies ("those whose subject matter relates directly to the organization and development of human society, and to man as a member of social groups") and to use the term throughout. Major influences on the document came from sterling progressives of the time: the leading progressive historian, the leading progressive civic educator, and the leading progressive philosopher. James Harvey Robinson, the doyen of the "new history," was the major historian on the committee; Arthur W. Dunn, the committee's secretary, was the best-known proponent of community civics in the country; and John Dewey, while not a member of the committee, was quoted liberally (albeit with a curious omission, as we shall see). Permeating the report was the influence of sociology, in which the chairman and secretary of the committee both held doctorates.

One major difference between the 1916 committee and its

predecessors was that a substantial proportion of its membership consisted of currently practicing secondary school administrators and teachers. The majority, including the two women
members, were active in the regional history teachers associations started by the Seven, where much of the consensus on
which the report was based was worked out. There were fewer
university and college people than in the earlier committees and
instead a sprinkling of normal school and teachers college members. One of the most striking contrasts with earlier committees
was the weight of school administrators, who comprised at least
half the members. The group also had close ties to the government through the U.S. Bureau of Education, of which the
chairman and the secretary were both officials. The 1916 document, unlike those of the Ten and the Seven, was issued as a
bulletin of the U.S. Bureau of Education.

The Committee on Social Studies spoke in the name of their
own version of "social efficiency," one closer to Dewey than to
Snedden. The aims of the social studies were thus announced:

> The social studies differ from other studies by reason of their
> social content rather than in social aim; for the keynote of modern
> education is "social efficiency," and instruction in all subjects
> should contribute to this end. Yet, from the nature of their
> content, the social studies offer peculiar opportunities for the
> training of the individual as a member of society. Whatever their
> value from the point of view of personal culture, unless they
> contribute directly to the cultivation of social efficiency on the
> part of the pupil they fail in their most important function. They
> should accomplish this end through the development of an ap-
> preciation of the nature and laws of social life, a sense of the
> responsibility of the individual as a member of social groups, and
> the intelligence and the will to participate effectively in the
> promotion of the social well-being.[3]

In contrast to the Ten and the Seven, neither here nor elsewhere
in the report is there concern with developing the "personal
culture" of the individual student. This distinguishing feature
of humanistic progressivism was notably absent.

As defined by the committee, secondary social studies would consist of history, geography, and civics taught in two cycles, one in the junior high school and the other in the senior high. The junior and senior cycles coincided "roughly with the physiological periods of adolescence" (a glimmer of child-centered progressivism here) but were based chiefly on the fact that large numbers of children left school at the end of sixth and at the end of eighth and ninth grades. Each cycle was to be capped by a civics course.

The committee proposed two new courses in civics, Community Civics in ninth and Problems of Democracy—Social, Economic, and Political—in twelfth. These courses expressed the committee's zeal for social efficiency. They were also in tune with developments in political science where the formal study of government was being superseded by a functional approach, with a particular focus on the municipality, where so many progressive experiments took place.

Community civics referred not only to the local community, whose accessibility and familiarity made it useful for learning through direct investigation and experience, but also to the "communities" of the city, the state, the nation, and the world. "Humanity is bigger than any of its divisions," the members said. Issued on the brink of our entrance into World War I, the document was firmly internationalist.

Unlike the other recommendations, Problems of Democracy (POD) emerged full-grown from the head of the committee and was one of the report's few revolutionary suggestions. It was an ingenious way of accomplishing several objects. At a time when most high school graduates did not go to college, such instruction provided a way of putting knowledge to work on problems of democracy that they as citizens might be called upon to face. It was also a way of accommodating the social sciences, which had grown mightily since the turn of the century, both in number of separate courses in the schools and in separate professional organizations. Rather than recommending distinct courses in the various social sciences, the 1916 committee urged that their insights be brought to bear on problems of democracy that were to be selected on the basis of their immediate interest to the class and their vital importance to society.

One of the committee's most influential yet unrecognized legacies was its wrongful interpretation of the past of the social subjects themselves. The report identified two deterrents to good secondary education in the social studies. One was the four-year high school curriculum in history, which had been "largely fixed in character by the traditions of the historian and the requirements of the college." Thus was sanctified one of the holiest myths of the history of the social studies, which to this day is devoutly believed by many social studies proponents, who fail to understand both how recently won had been history's secure place in the schools and how revolutionary were the curricular changes so recently brought about. The members of the Ten and the Seven were hardly speaking from isolated ivory towers across vast distances to the schools. And the idea of tailoring the secondary curriculum to the requirements of the college had been firmly and eloquently rejected by both.

In the 1916 report the chief losers in history were ancient and English history. They were collapsed into modern European history, the chief beneficiary of the change. Probably this was due to the widespread demand, as reflected in the 1911 Committee of Five report, for more modern and more European history. No doubt James Harvey Robinson's presence on the committee was an important element in its shift of emphasis.

The section on history took up a problem then widely discussed in the history teachers associations: how to make history more real to students. The 1916 report contains a number of excerpts from Robinson on the new history and the problem of determining, as he put it, "what conditions and institutions in history shall be given the preference, considering the capacity of the student on the one hand and the limitations of time on the other." To this the report proposed that the selection of a topic in history and the amount of attention given to it should depend, not merely upon its relative proximity in time, nor yet upon its relative present importance from the adult or sociological point of view, but also and chiefly upon the degree to which such topic can be related to the present life interests of the pupil, or can be used by him in his present processes of growth.

The report immediately pointed out that by stating this principle the committee did not imagine that it had "solved the problem of the organization of the history course." Instead it had "made the problem more difficult" by raising the new questions, "What history does meet the need of the child's growth?" and, "How may a given topic be related to the child's interest?"[4]

These questions remain significant today. To the first and more profound question there has not as yet been anything but the most cursory attention even after seventy years, beginning with the 1916 report, whose prime example of "meeting the needs of present growth" was inappropriately drawn from an experimental campus elementary school. It remains one of the most difficult, interesting, and neglected areas of research and instruction. The second is quite the opposite. It is almost universally, if often routinely, addressed in most social studies classrooms, including those all too frequent instances where the teacher confuses adult interest with student interest, a confusion that the report explicitly warned against. The emphasis given to these questions points to the "child-centered" progressivism of the twenties.

While suggesting such principles for the selection of topics in history, the committee made clear that it was opposing not chronology but annalistic history, the "what-comes-next" variety. The committee pointed out that the gradual and orderly evolution, step by step, of institutions and conditions "is of the very essence of history" and impossible to eliminate from historical study. It is difficult to see much difference between the 1916 report and those of the Committees of Ten and Seven on this matter. But there is an important difference in what kind of history these groups advocated. The Ten and the Seven, while including social and economic history, basically favored political history in the education of citizens for participation in the political system. The 1916 report, in contrast, favored industrial, social, and economic history as appropriate for the education of citizens for participation in a broader series of institutions. This was in line with the thrust of the new or progressive history of the historians, just as the civics of the report was in line with trends in political science. Yet the deemphasis on political history went further than most progressive historians would have gone.

The report shows a distinct preoccupation with teaching and learning in the elementary grades, despite the fact that it is supposedly directed at secondary education. The quotes from John Dewey are from his work on elementary education and are not necessarily appropriate for adolescent students. Yet the committee must have had available to it Dewey's *Democracy and Education*, which was published early in 1916, well before the report came out. Dewey's discussion of the roles of history and geography in this book, the most extended of his writings on the social subjects, would have been much more appropriate.

The report of the Committee on Social Studies combined the four types of educational progressivism that had emerged by 1916 and that continue to this day. It was primarily a social efficiency document, strongly influenced by humanistic progressivism. This was due, I believe, primarily to the role of history in the schools, and its proven synthesizing power and adaptability, and to the influence of the associations. The committee's recommendations constitute the basic curriculum found today in most American secondary schools. The main casualties have been the courses most beloved of the committee: Problems of Democracy and community civics. The latter began to lose ground in the late twenties, but it was the sixties and early seventies, with the combination of the lack of interest and disciplinary bias of the new social studies, followed by widespread disillusionment about the nation itself, that finished off POD and civics. So fundamental, however, is the need for attention to government in the schools that law-related education began to emerge as POD and civics faded.

If one compares the report of the social studies committee with that of its parent commission (CRSE), one can see in the latter a sterner version of social efficiency progressivism. The commission, whose report appeared during World War I, set forth the "Seven Cardinal Principles" of education that were heavily influenced by Herbert Spencer: health, command of fundamental processes (reading, writing, and arithmetic), worthy home-membership, vocation, citizenship, worthy use of leisure, and ethical character. The contributions of the school subjects were to be judged on the basis of these aims—that is, on criteria largely outside these subjects themselves. The commission urged that the social studies should be taken by all students and thus probably helped to ensure its place in the curriculum. But in fact, the main lines of actual curriculum and classroom development in the social studies reflected the 1916 report rather than that of its parent commission.

Like many reform measures in education, the recommendations of the Committee on Social Studies took root in a period whose character was quite different from the period in which it rose. Following World War I, not only did progressivism fade but the postwar reaction put humanistic progressivism on the defensive while encouraging social efficiency, scientific management, and child-centered progressivism. It was in this atmosphere that the curricular changes of the twenties took place. By the mid-twenties a survey estimated that only about one-third of the schools were following the Committee of Seven curriculum, one-third that of the Committee on Social Studies, and one-third were foundering without clear direction.

Shortly after World War I, two organizations important to the future of progressive education in the social studies were founded. The Progressive Education Assocation (PEA) was established in 1919. Like the Committee on Social Studies, the

PEA bestowed its name on a movement that was in reality much broader than its own interests. The PEA's major emphasis in the twenties was on child-centered progressivism, and it showed little concern with the education of citizens. In this period, "progressive education" found great favor in affluent private schools and public schools in well-to-do suburbs. For the public, unfortunately, the PEA and its interests and constituency seem to have defined and represented the sum and substance of progressive education.

The second organization, the National Council for the Social Studies (NCSS), was founded in 1921 by college and university professors of teacher education who constituted the leadership of the organization. The NCSS was primarily an expression of humanistic progressivism, but from the beginning there were a few social efficiency supporters. The council was sympathetic to history and civics as the core of the social studies. To them, social studies did not at all mean the abandonment of history. But they favored "the social studies" because it meant to them a broader and richer definition of the field, which would include greater attention to the social sciences. They were much concerned about the reaction against the term "social studies" on the part of many academics beginning in the early twenties. Probably most would have agreed with Edgar Wesley's later characterization of the social studies as "the social sciences simplified for pedagogical purposes."

Three national reports appearing in the thirties were signs and signals of what was happening to the various types of educational progressivism. The first represented humanistic progressivism: the AHA Commission on the Social Studies, headed by medieval historian August Krey. The commission was the culmination of a decade of discussion in the AHA and NCSS on the future of the field. The commission began its work in 1929 just before the crash and ended in 1934 in the depths of the depression. It bears clearly the imprint of its times, a sense of immersion in a vast historical transition from an age that was dying to a new age emerging.

The commission brought together historians, social scientists, teacher educators, and curriculum specialists, although, it should be noted, not current classroom teachers. They produced a fourteen-volume report, most of the books being written by individuals but two representing directly the views of the commission itself. The commission's volumes constitute a highly sophisticated series dealing with such fundamental issues as the nature of objectivity, the relationship of science to history and the social sciences, their relationships to each other and to the school subjects, academic freedom, the role of citizens, as well as methods of teaching, the history and current status of the social studies in the schools, and other such matters.

There is only slight evidence of child-centered progressivism, and scientific management gets short shrift. In fact, supporters of "the scientific movement in education," such as J. Franklin Bobbitt, severely criticized the conclusions because of its skepticism about scientific management. The commission favored the judicious use of "new-type" (objective) tests, for limited purposes, such as testing for factual information, but warned that such tests had severe limitations and dangers. But the commission fell afoul of its own venture into a form of social efficiency progressivism. Its *Conclusions and Recommendations* warned that in the United States and other countries the age of laissez-faire in economy and government was closing and a new age of collectivism was emerging. The schools, the commission averred, could and should help bring about the changes in attitudes and knowledge that were needed to make the transition less fraught with difficulties and to retain and fulfill the historic principles and ideals of American democracy. This position seemed to many people, including friendly critics, to put too great a burden on American schools and teachers, and to come perilously close to the indoctrination that the commission elsewhere condemned. Probably the fact that the commission also failed to suggest a scope and sequence, as most schoolpeople had hoped it would, caused an even sharper focus on the commission's accommodation to what it called "collectivism." Boyd Bode saw the main defect of the report in its "attempt to combine an authoritarian 'frame of reference' with its cultivation of effective and independent thinking."

The commission stood for the broad sweep of history, for historical synthesis rather than minute specialization. It is not an accident that its chief intellectual influence, Charles A. Beard, was a European as well as an American historian and was also the last major academic historian to write, with historian Mary Beard, a one-volume history of the United States.

The work of the AHA commission was cited by two other reports. The first, called *The Social Studies Curriculum*, constituted the fourteenth yearbook of the Department of Superintendence of the NEA (1936) and deals with the social studies in both elementary and secondary schools, with somewhat more emphasis on the former. Among other things, it suggests various ways of organizing the curriculum, including the fusion of several subject areas. Its attitude toward history was to take it for granted, simply assuming that it was important in both the elementary and the secondary school. Charles A. Beard was a member of the commission, in fact the only professional historian to serve. George Counts, the social reconstructionist who was a leading member of the AHA commission and served on its staff as well, was also a member of this one, the others being school administrators and professors of education.

The second report, entitled *The Social Studies in General Education*, was issued in 1940 by the Progressive Education Association. It is very different from the reports already discussed in that it gives almost no attention to subject matter; rather, it concentrates on the nature of adolescence in American society and how the social studies teacher might deal with the "personal-social," "social-civic," and "economic" relationships of adolescents, as well as "personal living" and "community living." It contains a few references to the AHA commission and none at all to the NEA yearbook of 1936. Most extraordinary, John Dewey does not exist in this report. The PEA document combines child-centered and social efficiency progressivism.

The historical obscurantism of the PEA report can be illustrated by its references to the Committees of Ten and Seven. Their reports, the PEA said,

> clearly rested on the assumption that the transmission of the cultural heritage—as interpreted by historians—is the dominant function of the social studies. . . . A rational intellectual appreciation of the traditional values in American culture was emphasized, and that appreciation was to be developed in students by a more or less severely didactic presentation of historical facts. The dominant method was, consequently, to be textbook memorization, class recitation, and fact tests. Such methods of instruction were supposed to discipline the mind, provide economy in learning, and establish a proper respect for authority.[5]

The report goes on in this vein for several pages, reconstructing a wholly mythical but convenient past. The 1916 Committee on the Social Studies was much more promising, the PEA asserted. Many of its proposals were "almost revolutionary in nature." But, unfortunately, it did not "solve the problem of education for effective social living." This the PEA report set out to do.

According to the PEA,

> adolescent needs and democratic values set the task and define the role of social studies teachers. *It is the function of social studies teachers to use the resources of the social sciences in meeting adolescent needs so as to develop the desirable characteristics of behavior essential to the achievement of democratic values within the realities of the changing American culture.*[6]

The perspective of the PEA report on how to achieve these goals was unswervingly and relentlessly presentist. It was also indifferent to content except as content served to illustrate these goals. The document represents a strain of thinking about the social studies that has been important ever since, especially among social studies educators in colleges and universities and state departments of education.

World War II represented a great divide in the social studies, as it did in so many other aspects of American life. For almost four decades after the war there were no great commissions in the social studies. It was a time when accurate historical knowledge of the past of the social studies was virtually wiped out. The generations that had fought for history and the other social studies in the school were aging, retired, or dead. With them went their oral tradition and historical memory, which were not replaced by written history of social studies education.

For a brief period after the war the education of citizens was the focus of social studies with a combination of intercultural education and active student participation, representing a reverberation from the war and a continuity of social efficiency and child-centered progressivism. But the war had also greatly increased the pressures for professionalism and specialization in curriculum as well as in research. Professors who once taught the synthesizing survey courses now spent their time working with graduate students on specialized research, not on teaching. The survey course, often taught by those same graduate students, lost prestige and intellectual power in the colleges and universities. Thus the academic bases of the school survey courses began to atrophy. A rising mode of historical interpretation rejected progressive history in favor of an American past in which the reform and conflict of the progressives were replaced by consensus as the central character of American history. Specialized history bloomed and the social sciences became much more powerful and authoritative as they also became more quantitative and specialized. Area studies, a new academic grouping arising from America's position as a world power, was the only place in which any syntheses were even attempted and these were limited to the area in question. Enormous strides were supposedly made in "objective" testing, which was used much more extensively in both schools and colleges and in getting from one to the other. Humanistic progressivism seemed pitifully old-fashioned if not downright wrong. The triumph of scientific management progressivism was at hand.

In the early sixties the movement called the New Social Studies, following the pattern of earlier developments in the teaching of science, based in university social science and fueled by Sputnik, moved still further from humanistic progressivism. Professional historians kept their distance from the movement, from the schools, and from the popular history that the humanistic progressives had believed essential for popular education. What little historical curricula were produced did not engage even the modest level of interest and support from historians that was given to the New Social Studies curriculum projects by the learned societies in the social sciences. The bulk of the funding came from the federal government, with a hearty assist from private foundations.

The New Social Studies focused on the individual disciplines, showing little interest in the education of citizens and even less in either synthesis or the scope and sequence of the overall curriculum. Yet the New Social Studies used, or rather discovered or perhaps reinvented all unwittingly, many of the methods of teaching and learning that humanistic progressive educators had created and popularized. This strain of humanistic progressivism did not save the New Social Studies from the fascination with process that began to drain it of content.

The New Social Studies were overwhelmed in the late sixties and early seventies by a yet newer movement that has never developed a name. This was what I awkwardly called the social problem/self-realization social studies, an updated version of social efficiency. With it history, if not historians, returned as an aspect of reform but in a highly specialized version. The new radical historians were on the whole as disdainful of the schools as their consensus elders had been. The history they produced grew out of the causes in which they participated and was adapted by the schools for their own purposes. Their history, if sometimes narrowly ethno- or even gender-centric, often represented a genuine search for meaning and dignity in their own past. They made an immense contribution to hitherto unknown aspects of history. But what resulted was a coalition of histories rather than the historical integration that the schools needed. The fragmentation of history in the schools continued with minicourses made possible by computer scheduling. At the same time, the enormous power of scientific management progressivism, with its calls for cost-effectiveness, accountability, and back-to-basics, was enhanced by the increasing use of computers throughout public and private administration.

As a historian, a teacher educator, and a citizen I see a great need at the present moment to change the teaching of history. Whatever the statistics may show, as a people we are losing contact with history—not only the history of the United States but of the rest of humanity as well. The problem is not only the quantity of history taught, although that is important. It is the quality. American history is almost universally taught in the schools, yet Americans often seem oblivious to and ignorant of their own history.

In our time, two great institutions in this country educate the young: the public schools and television. Television is, I believe, destructive not only of our sense of history but of the democratic process itself. Theoretically, television should make us better informed; in practice we are rendered numb and dumb. Theoretically, it should extend our knowledge of the world; in reality, it narrows our vision. Television encourages us to react more to visual than to verbal language, to think in short bytes, to become impatient with complexity, to seek instant gratification, to confuse image and reality, to find false heroes and heroines, to turn politics into show business, to become willing accomplices in our own manipulation. On television, the past—even yesterday—is continually being devoured by today, which will be just as quickly discarded tomorrow. Our sense of time and space is being deeply and tragically altered. Television has its good programs and its saving graces (mostly on the public network), but the overall impact is, I believe, to undermine our sense of history and autonomous personal culture.

History in the schools could exert a major countervailing force to this omnipresent educator. Not that students should be told that television is "bad" for them and to avoid it. On the contrary, they have to explore the problem of television for themselves, to understand how it operates and how programs are actually put together, within what constraints and opportunities; how it affects and shapes them and their society; how it changes the political life of the country. Students need to investigate television's impact on other societies and how changing modes of communication have caused change in the past. Their own personal experience of time and space can be linked with that of other people and other cultures in different times and different places. By engaging students actively in investigation and discussion, we can help to counter television's casting of them as passive spectators.

Humanistic progressivism provides the foundation on which we can build. It seeks to nurture the development of the individual while at the same time encouraging students to participate actively as citizens in a democratic society. It has a commitment to change and to the study of change as a major theme in the curriculum. Solidly grounded in history, it has links to both the humanities and the social sciences. More than any of the other varieties of progressivism, or of conservatism, it has the potential to meet the challenge of our times.

We are now at a historical moment when history in the schools is a matter of public interest and debate. That time will pass. If we do not use this moment to help the schools use their enormous potential in strengthening the qualities and knowledge that help democracy to function and function well, we will have failed in our duty as academics and as citizens. Humanistic progressivism's great ally is that American democratic tradition from which it draws its strength, one that is liberal, flexible, and moderate, and concerned with both the individual and the public good.

NOTES

1. National Education Association, *Report of the Committee on Secondary Social Studies* (Washington, D.C.: Government Printing Office, 1893), p. 167.

2. Ibid., p. 190.

3. National Education Association, *The Social Studies in Secondary Education*, Bulletin 28 (1916), p. 9.

4. Ibid., p. 44.

5. *The Social Studies in General Education: A Report of the Committee on the Function of the Social Studies in General Education for the Commission on Secondary School Curriculum* (New York: D. Appleton-Century Co., 1940), pp. 5–6.

6. Ibid., p. 23, italics in the original.

PART III

History
and Liberal
Education

CHAPTER 5

Why Study History? Three Historians Respond

By WILLIAM H. MCNEILL, MICHAEL KAMMEN,
and GORDON A. CRAIG

WILLIAM H. MCNEILL

Why should anyone bother learning about things that happened far away and long ago? Who cares about Cleopatra,
Charlemagne, Montezuma, or Confucius? And why worry
about George Washington, or how democratic government and
industrial society arose? Isn't there quite enough to learn about
the world today? Why add to the burden by looking at the past?

Historians ought to try to answer such questions by saying
what the study of history is good for, and what it cannot do.
They ought to explain to all concerned why the study of history
is worthwhile in itself and necessary for the education of effective citizens and worthy human beings.

Historical knowledge is no more and no less than carefully
and critically constructed collective memory. As such, it can
make us both wiser in our public choices and more richly
human in our private lives.

Without individual memory, a person literally loses his or
her identity, and would not know how to act in encounters with
others. Imagine waking up one morning unable to tell total
strangers from family and friends! Collective memory is sim-

103

ilar. Its loss may not immediately paralyze our everyday private activity, but ignorance of history—that is, absent or defective collective memory—does deprive us of the best available guide for public action, especially in encounters with outsiders, whether the outsiders are another nation, another civilization, or some distinctive group within our national borders.

Sometimes it is enough for experts to know about outsiders, if their advice is listened to. But democratic citizenship and effective participation in the determination of public policy require citizens to share a collective memory, organized into historical knowledge and belief. Otherwise, agreement on whose advice to listen to about what ought to be done in a given situation is difficult to achieve. Agreement on some sort of comfortable falsehood will not do, for without reasonably accurate knowledge of the past, we cannot expect to accomplish intended results simply because we will fail to foresee how others are likely to react to anything we decide on. Nasty surprises and frustrating failures are sure to multiply under such circumstances.

This value of historical knowledge obviously justifies teaching and learning about what happened in recent times, for the way things are descends from the way they were yesterday and the day before that. But in fact institutions that govern a great deal of our everyday behavior took shape hundreds or even thousands of years ago. Having been preserved and altered across the generations to our own time, they are sure to continue into the future. The United States government is such an institution; so are the world market, armies, and the Christian church. Skills such as writing and devices such as bureaucracy are even older than Christianity, and concerns that bother us today can be found in the cave paintings left behind by Stone Age hunters as much as twenty thousand years ago. Only an acquaintance with the entire human adventure on earth allows us to understand these dimensions of contemporary reality.

Memory is not something fixed and forever. As time passes,

remembered personal experiences take on new meanings. A bitter disappointment may come to seem a blessing in disguise; a triumph may later turn sour, while something trivial may subsequently loom large—all because of what happens later on. Collective memory is quite the same. Historians are always at work reinterpreting the past, asking new questions, searching new sources and finding new meanings in old documents in order to bring the perspective of new knowledge and experience to bear on the task of understanding the past. This means, of course, that what we know and believe about history is always changing. In other words, our collective, codified memory alters with time just as personal memories do, and for the same reasons.

When teachers of history admit that their best efforts at understanding the past are only tentative and sure to be altered in time, skeptics are likely to conclude that history has no right to take students' time from other subjects. If what is taught today is not really true, how can it claim space in a crowded school curriculum?

But what if the world is more complicated and diverse than words can ever tell? What if human minds are incapable of finding neat pigeonholes into which everything that happens will fit? What if we have to learn to live with uncertainty and probabilities, and act on the basis of the best guesswork we are capable of? Then surely the changing perspectives of historical understanding are the very best introduction we can have to the practical problems of real life. Then surely a serious effort to understand the interplay of change and continuity in human affairs is the only adequate introduction human beings can have to the confusing flow of events that constitutes the actual, adult world.

Since that *is* the way the world is, it follows that the study of history is essential for every young person. Systematic sciences are not enough. They discount time, and therefore over-simplify reality, especially human reality. Current events are not enough either. Destined to almost instant obsolescence, they foreshorten and thereby distort the time dimension within which human lives unfold and, thanks to the perspectives granted us by memory, are examined and conducted.

Memory, indeed, makes us human. History, our collective memory, carefully codified and critically revised, makes us social, sharing ideas and ideals with others so as to form all sorts of different human groups. Each such group acts as it does largely because of shared ideas and beliefs about the past and about what the past, as understood and interpreted by the group in question, tells about the present and probable future.

But you may say: Suppose we agree that some sort of knowledge of history is essential for an adult understanding of the world, what actually belongs in our classrooms? The varieties of history are enormous; facts and probabilities about the past are far too numerous for anyone to comprehend them all. Every sort of human group has its own history; so do ideas, institutions, techniques, areas, civilizations, and humanity at large. How to begin? Where to start? How do we bring some sort of order to the enormous variety of things known and believed about the past?

Teachers of history have always had to struggle with these questions. Early in this century, teachers and academic administrators pretty well agreed that two sorts of history courses were needed: a survey of the national history of the United States, and a survey of European history. In the 1930s and 1940s the latter course was often broadened into a survey of Western civilization. But by the 1960s and 1970s these courses were becoming outdated, left behind by the rise of new kinds of social and quantitative history, especially the history of women, of Blacks, and of other formerly overlooked groups within the borders of the United States, and of peoples emerging from colonial status in the world beyond our borders. These, and still other new sorts of history, enhanced older sensibilities and corrected older biases; but, being both new and different, did not fit smoothly into existing surveys of U.S. national history and Western civilization. Teachers found it exciting to teach the new kinds of history in special courses that allowed them time to develop the new themes properly. It was less satisfying and much harder to combine old with new to make an inclusive, judiciously balanced (and far less novel) introductory course for high school or college students.

But abandoning the effort to present a meaningful portrait of the entire national and civilizational past destroyed the original justification for requiring students to study history. As specialized electives multiplied, historians could not convince others that random samples from the past, reflecting each teacher's special expertise or interests, belonged in everyone's education. For if one sample was as good as another, none could claim to be essential. Competing subjects abounded, and no one could or would decide what mattered most and should take precedence. As this happened, studying history became only one among many possible ways of spending time in school.

The costs of this change are now becoming apparent, and many concerned persons agree that returning to a more structured curriculum, in which history plays a prominent part, is imperative. But the choice of what sort of history to teach remains as difficult as ever. Clearly, we need to search for and carefully reflect on the enduring patterns and critical turning points of the past; it is these historical facts that everyone needs to know, not what one individual teacher or aspiring specialist thinks is of interest. Whether historians will rise to the occasion and successfully bring old and new sorts of history together into an understandable whole remains to be seen. In the meanwhile, a few obvious suggestions are all that can be offered here.

Amongst all the varieties of history that specialists have so energetically and successfully explored in recent decades, three levels of generality seem likely to have the greatest importance for ordinary people. First is family, local, neighborhood history: something often transmitted orally, but worth attention in school for all that. This would seem especially important for the primary school years, when children start to experience the world outside their homes. Second is national history, because that is where political power and political choices are concentrated in our time. Last is global history, because intensified communications make encounters with all the other peoples of the earth increasingly important. These levels belong to high school and college, in the years when young people start to pay attention to public affairs and prepare to assume the responsibilities of citizenship. Other pasts are certainly worth attention but are better studied in the context of a prior acquaintance with personal-local, national, and global history. That is because these three levels are the ones that affect most powerfully what all other groups and segments of society actually do.

Can such courses be taught and fit into the curriculum? The answer is yes, if teachers and administrators try hard to put first things first and achieve a modicum of clarity about what everyone ought to know. National history that leaves out Blacks and women and other minorities is no longer acceptable, but neither is American history that leaves out the Founding Fathers and the Constitution. What is needed is a vision of the whole, warts and all.

Global history is perhaps more difficult. Certainly our traditional training sidesteps the problem of attaining a satisfactory vision of the history of humanity, since few historians even try for a global overview. Still, some have made the attempt. Moreover, every scale of history has its own appropriate patterns that, once perceived, are as definite and as easily tested by the evidence as are the meaningful patterns that emerge on any other scale. This means, I think, that careful and critical world history is attainable just as surely as is a careful and critical national history that does not omit the important and newly self-conscious groups that were previously overlooked.

But consensus is slow to come, and may never be achieved. In the meanwhile, teachers and curriculum planners have a difficult task. Authoritative models for courses in national and global history are not readily available. Personal and neighborhood history, too, must be worked out independently for each classroom and locality. But questions to be asked and the range of information that can be handled by children in the primary grades are, perhaps, less difficult to agree upon than at the high school and college levels. Serious and concentrated effort is clearly called for. Only in this way can history and historians deserve and expect to regain the central place in the education of the young that once was theirs.

Three points remain. First, the study of history does not lead to exact predictions of future events. Though it fosters practical wisdom, knowledge of the past does not enable one to know exactly what is going to happen in the future. Looking at some selected segment from the past in order to find out what will occur "next time" can mislead the unwary, simply because the complex setting within which human beings act is never the same twice. Consequently, the lessons of history, though supremely valuable when wisely formulated, become grossly misleading when oversimplifiers try to transfer them mechanically from one age to another, or from one place to another. Anyone who claims to perform such a feat is sadly self-deceived. Practical wisdom requires us instead to expect differences as well as similarities, changes as well as continuities—always and everywhere. Predictable fixity is simply not the human way of behaving. Probabilities and possibilities, together with a few complete surprises, are what we live with and must learn to expect.

Second, as acquaintance with the past expands, delight in knowing more and more can and often does become an end in itself. History offers innumerable heroes and villains. Reading about what people did in faraway times and places enlarges our sense of human capacities both for good and evil. Encountering powerful commitments to vanished ideas and ideals, like those that built the pyramids, puts our personal commitment to our own ideals into a new perspective, perhaps bittersweet. Discovering fears and hopes like our own in pages written by the medieval Japanese courtier Lady Murasaki, or reading about the heroic and futile quest for immortality undertaken by the ancient Mesopotamian king Gilgamesh, stirs a sense of shared humanity that reaches back to the beginning of civilization and across all cultural barriers.

On the other hand, studying alien religious beliefs, strange customs, diverse family patterns, and vanished social structures shows how differently various human groups have tried to cope with the world around them. Broadening our humanity and extending our sensibilities by recognizing sameness and difference throughout the recorded past is therefore an important reason for studying history, and especially the history of peoples far away and long ago. For we can know ourselves only by knowing how we resemble and how we differ from others. Acquaintance with the human past is the only way to such self-knowledge.

Finally, for those especially attracted to it, investigation of odd corners and contemplation of the main outlines of history can develop into a hunt for understandings of one's own as new ideas about connections between one thing and another spring to mind. This sort of historical research and creativity is, of course, the special province of graduate school and of the historical profession at large. Reinterpretations and modifications of received notions about what really happened result from such personal venturing; and these new ideas and meanings, tested against the evidence available to other historians, feed into high school and college classrooms and provide teachers with an ever-evolving understanding of the past to set before the young.

In such interaction between research and teaching, eternal and unchanging truth does not emerge, only inspired, informed guesses about what mattered and how things changed through time. That is all human minds can do to unravel the mystery of humanity and of human groups' encounters with one another and with the world. Not very good, perhaps, but clearly the best we have in the unending effort to understand ourselves and others, and what happens and will happen to us and to them, time without end.

MICHAEL KAMMEN

What worth can be found in knowing the past? What is the value of studying history? Do we as Americans encounter unusual difficulty in answering such questions? And have we recently reached a critical juncture in our relationship to history? Abundant signs say yes. To judge by rising museum attendance, increasing book sales, successful television programs, and historical-preservation activities, nostalgia is surely in the saddle. But nostalgia is not the same as knowing the past. Unfortunately, nostalgia appears to be a mindless if not a headless horseman, as newspaper surveys reveal a woeful ignorance of the national past by Americans with above-average educational backgrounds.

For several years now, large and well-established professional groups such as the American Historical Association, the Organization of American Historians, and the National Council for the Social Studies have sought measures that might stimulate historical interest in the schools and enhance historical understanding among laymen. They have met with limited (or, at best, mixed) success.

This problem exemplifies a more general American ambivalence about the past—an ambivalence that has been visible for three centuries. Americans who are policymakers and opinion makers, for example, have had a strangely ambiguous relationship to history.

Let us look at three of the most interesting Americans in our pantheon: Thomas Jefferson, Ralph Waldo Emerson, and Henry Ford. Associated with each is a provocative statement about our need to be released from the burdens of an oppressive or meaningless past. Each statement is actually more complex than a one-line excerpt can reveal, but at least the one-liners serve to jog our memories:

> The earth belongs in usufruct to the living . . . the dead have neither powers nor rights over it. [Jefferson to James Madison, September 6, 1789]

> Our age is retrospective. . . . It writes biographies, histories, and criticism. The foregoing generations beheld God and nature face to face, we, through their eyes. . . . Why should not we have a poetry and philosophy of insight and not of tradition, and a religion by revelation to us, and not the history of theirs? [Emerson, "Nature," 1836]

> History is more or less bunk. [Ford in a newspaper interview, 1916]

The problem with taking any of these pithy remarks too seriously is that they are not only misguided as declarations, in my opinion, but they are not even representative of the three men who uttered them.

Consider the fact that Jefferson, in his *Notes on the State of Virginia*, the only book he ever wrote and a classic of American thought, pleaded for the necessary centrality of history in the curriculum of secondary school students. "History, by apprizing them of the past, will enable them to judge of the future; it will avail them of the experience of other times and other nations; it will qualify them as judges of the actions and designs of men."

Consider the fact that Emerson wrote an 1841 essay entitled "History" in which he declared: "Man is explicable by nothing less than all his history. . . . There is a relation between the hours of our life and the centuries of time."

And consider the fact that emblazoned on an iron sign in front of Greenfield Village and the Henry Ford Museum in Dearborn, Michigan, are these words from a Henry Ford grown wiser than the 1916 curmudgeon: "The farther you look back, the farther you can see ahead."

How are we supposed to make sense of such contradictory utterances?

First, of course, we must recognize that their views were as variable as ours. All lived long lives, witnessed and participated in the making of history, and changed their minds on certain key matters from time to time.

Second, we should appreciate that they distinguished between the desirability of knowing history and the imperative that we not be prisoners of the past.

Third, we must recognize that there is a tension contained within the cliché that we ought to learn from the lessons of the past. Do we learn from the so-called wisdom of the past, or do we profit from the follies of the past? Jefferson made that distinction and preferred the second alternative.

One reason why Americans may frequently recite the negative statements by Jefferson, Emerson, and Ford and prefer to neglect their affirmations of historical study is that we have been—most of us, most of the time—an optimistic and opportunistic people. We want to believe that "it" will all work out for the best.

The problem is that history shows us that "it" doesn't always. History, real history, isn't chock-full of happy endings.

Listen to Walter Lippmann back in 1914: "Modern men are afraid of the past. It is a record of human achievement, but its other face is human defeat." How right he was—all the more reason why we must know and understand the past. We have at least as much to learn from our defeats as from our achievements.

Why, then, should we really want to know the past? Here are a few reasons that I find most compelling:

- To make us more cognizant of human differences and similarities, over time and through space.

- To help us appreciate far more fully than we do the non-rational and irrational elements in our behavior: what James Boswell called, in 1763, "the unaccountable nature of the human mind."
- To enhance our awareness of the complexity of historical causation—the unanticipated intertwining of opinion and events—and their consequences for our understanding of that whirlwind we call social change.
- To acknowledge more fully and critically than we do the consequences of what is at stake when powerful people interpret history for partisan purposes on the basis of insufficient or inaccurate information about the past.
- To avoid the tendency to ascribe equal value to all relationships and events. Worse than no memory at all is the undiscriminating memory that cannot differentiate between important and inconsequential experiences.

It is the historian's vocation to provide society with a discriminating memory.

GORDON CRAIG

Why study history, and what is its use? As historians, we are not surprised when some rather old answers remain among the best. In his plan for a basic reform of the lyceum in Riga, Herder wrote, with reference to instruction in the early grades, "The main objective is to give the child, above all, living ideas . . . in order to set him in his world." Today, more than ever before, we need to be set in our world. We need to provide ourselves and our students with an account of the American past that describes where we came from and how we developed our national identity and particularity, our form of government, and our characteristic institutions; that explains how we differ from other peoples and they from us and why, and what the consequences of this are, but does not neglect to point out how interdependent we all are, despite national and cultural differences.

Whatever this may involve in the way of reform of basic curricula—and it suggests a greater emphasis upon world history than is currently true—it is vital that our emphasis be as much upon thinking about history as describing what happened in it. For above all we need living ideas to correct inherited myths and conventional assumptions about the historical process and to provide a basis for the political competence that so often seems in short supply today. General factual knowledge about the past is not enough, whether we consider the role of history in the schools, or in public affairs of the society at large. Consider the political sector, for example. How many officeholders, congressmen, and policymakers on the national level are "historically literate"? In terms of general knowlege of national history and modern European history, probably a great number. In terms of ability to gauge the relevance of historical experience to the perplexities of the present age, certainly far fewer.

A good number of our politicians, our pundits, and our self-styled experts are great users of history, and adroit in finding spurious historical justification for their own purposes, but they are apt to be too intent on manipulating public memory to use it with either accuracy or understanding. Even the best of them have a tendency to regard history as a vast medicine cabinet filled with patent nostrums for all ills, and when crises arise they rummage about frantically in it until they come up with something that seems to fit the current case, all too often succeeding only in complicating it, and making things worse than they might have been.

In the past fifty years or so, moreover, they have been prone to three particularly dangerous weaknesses. The first has been a fondness for the false analogy, like the Munich syndrome, which led many of them, during the Vietnam War, to argue on the basis of a loose and generalized view of the consequences of the Munich Conference of 1938, that any compromises with, or concessions to, totalitarian adversaries were always ruinous in their consequences and that there was no substitute for complete victory.

The second has been a tendency to universalize particular problems by force-fitting them into overarching historical or dialectical patterns and then using such "patterns" to justify policy and strategy. For example, during the Truman and Eisenhower administrations, the members of the National Security Council were great readers of Thucydides and, seeing the Cold War as another Peloponnesian War, constantly argued for unconditionality, disregard of neutral rights, and a search for the total solution, even though this involved ignoring opportunities for solving individual problems and thus reducing the general international tension.

The third tendency betraying an absence of "living ideas" about history has been to overvalue continuity at the expense of change, so that the government and press are, on the one hand, always being surprised (Czechoslovakia in 1968, the fall of the shah and of Marcos, the fall of the stock market in October 1987) and, on the other hand, repeatedly failing to appreciate the magnitude of new problems such as the environment, the urban underclass, and AIDS, and placing them lower on the list of national priorities than the more familiar problems they find easier to deal with.

These failures of judgment and perspective, and others that might be noted—the persistent belief of many of our legislators, for example, that what works in the United States will work equally well in other countries, given a fair chance, since everybody is basically alike—indicate that, historically literate or not, a large proportion of our political leadership have no feel or sensitivity for history, cannot discriminate between historical cases, are incapable of thinking historically, and so have no real historical understanding. It is safe to say that, to an even greater extent, this is true of the general population.

It would seem to follow, then, that whatever the content or order of the history courses offered in our schools, they will not succeed in contributing to "education for public competence," unless their teachers make every effort to prevent their charges—at the beginning of their education or as close to the beginning as is pedagogically practical—from falling prey to the kind of errors mentioned above.

At the very least, this would involve an earnest attempt to teach students to respect facts, to recognize the distinction between fact and conjecture, and to distrust all facile explanations of historical phenomena—that is, all explanations that cannot be verified by fact. It would require them to inoculate students against the attractiveness of abstract generalizations and to disabuse them of the notion that history is moved by mysterious forces as well as to encourage them to respect particularity and to look for the essential differences that lie behind the superficial similarities. (Herder once wrote: "History is the science of what is there, not of that which, because of the secret designs of destiny, might be there.")

It would be enormously useful if teachers could succeed at an early stage of historical instruction in seeking out and destroying the stereotypical assumptions about and characterizations of foreigners that seem in our society to be handed down from generation to generation. (A rereading of George Jean Nathan's *The American Credo* is a chastening experience. Things really haven't changed much.) Equally important, and surely this could be started in the earliest grades, would be a campaign against the belief in monocausality. I sense, although I don't know the reason for this, that more first-year university students today as compared to thirty years ago believe that historical events have single causes, and that there is a disturbing tendency to ascribe everything that goes wrong either to human error or to some universal Murphy's Law.

Finally, and not unconnected with this last point, it is high time Americans learned that one of the things history teaches us is that not all problems have solutions—indeed, because history is a process of change, what may appear to be solutions today are merely tomorrow's headaches—and that, particularly in the world of foreign affairs, where there is no single sovereignty, one has to learn to live with a lot of exasperating, and intermittently dangerous, unfinished business and to be content with the ad hoc alleviation that one can get rather than brood over the perfect solution that one can't. Americans have always resisted these plain truths, often arguing, not very accurately, that their own history refutes them. In an age that has lost the optimism that produced that kind of blindness to reality, teachers of history are challenged to help their students to see things more clearly and to carry into later life the living ideas about history that will help them recognize reality, however it may change.

CHAPTER 6

History as a Humanistic Discipline

by GORDON A. CRAIG

To my considerable wonder, I find that I have been a professional historian for fifty years, if one counts from the time when I received my first advanced degree. Surprise is not an unusual sensation on such anniversary occasions. Where has all that time gone? one asks fretfully. But in this case it is compounded by the recollection that, a scant six years before taking that degree, when I matriculated at Princeton University, I had decided that, if there was one subject in the college curriculum that I would avoid like the plague, it was history. My early experience with instruction in that subject had convinced me that it was not only unrewarding but, even when comprehensible, which was not often, maddeningly dull.

I don't think this was a willful conclusion on my part. I was a reasonably diligent pupil and generally attentive to what my teachers had to tell me. But whenever they started to talk about history, I never seemed to be able to discover what they were driving at or fit what they said into any meaningful pattern or discern in it any relevance to my own world. During my six years in grade school in Toronto, Ontario, I must have been

119

subjected to a good many sessions on Canadian history. If so, I took away from them only the impression (which even in my state of innocence, I suspect, must be sadly muddled) that a Frenchman named Carshay collaborated with a general called Montcalm-and-Wolf to defeat the Americans at Queenston at a time and for reasons that were obscure. Later, when I finished my grade school education in Jersey City, New Jersey, a city founded by the Dutch and having, by my time, a large Italian population, Peter Stuyvesant and Christopher Columbus took the places of the mysterious Frenchman and the soldier with the oddly cumbersome name, although it was never clear to me why I should be interested in either of them.

The passing of the years brought confusion of a higher order. In high school I was forced to sit through a survey of American history that turned out to be an exasperatingly arid chronicle of names and dates, which disappeared from the mind as soon as they had been memorized and regurgitated in daily quizzes, an endless stream of unaccented events in which continuity and causality were ignored and the differences between the world in which we lived and the world of those other Americas, through which we raced like a scalded cat, went unremarked. The mind was left numb and unreceptive to invitations to build upon this unpromising foundation.

Strangely enough, however, while such experiences warned me to avoid anything that was formally labeled history, they in no way diminished my already healthy interest in the past. Thanks to my passion for reading and my possession of a library card, I had discovered a series of storytellers whose powers were sufficient to shore my curiosity up against the depredations of the schoolteachers and those who prescribed the nature and content of the courses they taught. At an early age, and quite by accident, I had discovered that remarkable man G. A. Henty, who had, with inexhaustible energy and verve, written scores of historical romances for young readers, books whose very titles were invitations to go time-traveling: *Beric the Briton, The Boy Knight: A Tale of the Crusades, Under*

Drake's Flag, By Pike and Dyke: A Tale of the Rise of the Dutch Republic, Bonnie Prince Charlie, A Cornet of Horse: A Tale of Marlborough's Wars, With Clive in India, and many more. Henty was a former soldier, which was apparent not only in his preferred themes but in his old-fashioned patriotism and emphasis upon the martial virtues, but his books always had a strong and exciting narrative line and, because he was a conscientious researcher, gave accurate descriptions of the age in which his stories were set and the historical situations in which his characters were involved. You couldn't get a very systematic knowledge of history from reading his books (you didn't, after all, go to them for that), but you did pick up a lot of fascinating miscellaneous information and, now and then, a desire to know more about something that he had described, and this sometimes led to experiments in reading that had surprising results.

This was true also of the stories of Rudyard Kipling, particularly those in the volumes entitled *Puck of Pook's Hill* and *Rewards and Fairies.* When I first picked these up, I was just old enough to suspect them of being "kids' stuff" and to expect to be repelled by whimsy, but, after Henty, Kipling's style was beguiling, and I was soon caught up in the charm and verisimilitude of his tales of two English children who were enabled by magic to travel back to pre-Roman Britain and later to meet and talk with a young centurion of a legion stationed on the Wall, a knight of the Norman Conquest, a Jewish physician and money-lender in the time of King John, a builder and decorator of the age of Henry VII, and other figures from England's past. I was later to realize that these reconstructions were all highly romanticized, but at the time I accepted them uncritically and thankfully, because they filled the past with real people rather than with the mythological figures of my Canadian days and told me in terms that I could understand about societies that were remote from my own but nevertheless connected with it.

And finally there was Sir Walter Scott, first discovered in high school, where *Ivanhoe* was a prescribed text, but then pursued on my own with mounting pleasure and excitement by

means of tattered library copies of *Quentin Durward* and *Waverley* and *Rob Roy* and *Redgauntlet*.

I had, of course, no inkling in those days that my love of Scott was a pale shadow of that enthusiasm that had swept over a whole generation of readers in the early nineteenth century, had awakened a new interest in historical study, and had served as an inspiration to some who, like Leopold von Ranke, became its most distinguished practitioners. Nor would I have found it easy to explain what I found so compelling in Scott or why I came to sense that his stories were closer to the realities of the historical process than Kipling's impressionistic genre sketches or Henty's often one-dimensional adventures. Many years later, in Georg Lukács's book *The Historical Novel*, I discovered what may have been the key to my instinctive admiration. The central figures in Scott's novels, Lukács pointed out, were not heroes but average persons with whom the reader could identify, persons with "a certain, though never outstanding, degree of practical intelligence, a certain moral fortitude and decency which even rises to a capacity for self-sacrifice, but which never grows into a sweeping human passion, is never the enraptured devotion to a great cause." In the typical Scott novel, this kind of average personality is caught up in the turmoil and confusion of a time of change and transition and finds himself involved in the fortunes of opposed characters and groups whose destinies are at stake. Through his puzzled, uncommitted, but sympathetic eyes, Scott shows us the struggles and antagonisms of history, which are in turn represented by characters who in their psychology and destiny represent social trends and historical forces. "Scott's greatness," Lukács wrote, "lies in his capacity to give living embodiment to historical social types. The typically human terms in which great historical trends become tangible had never before been so superbly, straightforwardly and pregnantly portrayed." Something of this I must have sensed and found attractive.

Since all of this, however, seemed completely alien to history as it was taught in the classroom, I decided when I went to college to continue to feed my interest in the past by private reading. And in this resolve I remained firm until my sophomore year, when my closest friends informed me that if my stubbornness in this regard prevented me from hearing Walter Phelps Hall's lectures on "The Course of Europe since Waterloo," I would be depriving myself of one of the greatest intellectual experiences that Princeton had to offer. Peer pressure was no less powerful in the 1930s than it is today. I told myself that I would be disappointed again and that it would be foolish to yield, but, fortunately for me, I yielded.

"Buzzer" Hall (so-called because he was deaf and used a battery-charged hearing aid that made odd sounds when the batteries were running down) was a graduate of Yale and Columbia who came to Princeton in 1913 at the age of twenty-nine and immediately became a campus legend. He was an inspired teacher and at the lecture podium an electric presence, charging about the platform as if pursued by demons, covering the blackboard with mystifying slogans and drawings meant to represent the course of the White Nile or the insides of the British '79, pouring floods of words over the heads of his audience in a high insistent tone that was sometimes modulated into a keening lament for the inadequacies of humankind or howls of rage at the crimes and follies of their leaders. Always passionate and opinionated and challenging, Buzzer was sometimes wonderfully comic, as in those moments of exasperation or enthusiasm when he rained blows upon the blackboard with an iron-ferruled stick, the thunder of which he could not hear but which often drowned out much of what he was saying. Yet he was also admirably persuasive in his insistence that history was so important and exciting that it required a total commitment from his auditors.

It was this rather than the theatrical aspect of his lectures that impressed me, and also the fact that I found in them, for the first time in an instructional setting, what I had found so attractive in my own reading: an approach to the past in which the emphasis was not upon lifeless figures, such as Carshay and

Stuyvesant, or symbolic names and dates (1066 and all that), but upon real human beings dealing with their own problems in their own time and in their own way. Walter Hall had read Scott, too (although I suspect that it was the romantic aspect of the novels that attracted him rather than the qualities that Lukács admired), and he had gone to college at a time when apprentice historians still read Hippolyte Taine, and a lot of it had stuck. He did not, perhaps, believe, as Taine did, that history was a science like physiology and zoology, a kind of applied psychology, for he was too idealistic to share Taine's materialism. But he was inclined to agree that the study of history should begin with individuals and that its goal should be to inquire into the transformations they underwent under the influence of heredity, context, and time, and he would certainly have subscribed to that passage which Stuart Hughes has cited from Taine's *History of English Literature*, where Taine wrote:

> When we read a Greek tragedy, our first care should be to picture to ourselves the Greeks, that is, the men who lived half naked, in the gymnasia, or in the public squares, under a glowing sky, face to face with the most noble landscapes, bent on making their bodies nimble and strong, on conversing, discussing, voting, carrying on patriotic piracies, but for the rest lazy and temperate, with three urns for their furniture, two anchovies in a jar of oil for their food, waited on by slaves, so as to give them leisure to cultivate their understanding and exercise their limbs, with no desire beyond having the most beautiful town, the most beautiful possessions, the most beautiful ideas, the most beautiful men. . . . A language, a legislation, a catechism, is never more than an abstract thing: the complete thing is the man who acts, the man corporeal and visible, who eats, walks, fights, labours.

In his lectures on European history in the nineteenth and twentieth centuries, Walter Hall began with the assumption that the laws and doctrines and reforms and revolutions of those centuries were made by, and in turn affected, human beings. He taught history, in short, as a humanistic discipline, and so compellingly that in the end I decided to follow his example.

The humanistic studies take their name from the term "humanism," which originally referred to a tendency among thinkers during the Renaissance, like Petrarch, Boccaccio, and Lorenzo Valla, to emphasize classical studies and to seek to return to classical ideals and forms, but has been defined in a more general sense as any system of thought or action that assigns a predominant interest to the affairs of men as compared with the supernatural or the abstract. From this latter definition, it is clear that, among the academic disciplines, history has no exclusive right to be called a humanistic study, for university schools of humanities include others that are concerned with human beings and their activities, philosophy and the literature and arts departments, for example, and, among the so-called behavioral sciences, political science, economics, sociology, psychology, anthropology, and others. These other disciplines, however, are concerned with human beings in a selective and partial way—the political scientists study *zoon politikon* and the economists Economic Man, with scant attention to his other interests and capacities—and some of them are inclined to view men and women collectively rather than in their individuality, divesting them, as the sociologists often do, of personality in order to see them as typical members of groups or classes. Even the philosophers and the students of literature are apt to become so fascinated by the derivations and connections of ideas and the language, conventions and forms of poetry and the novel, that they tend to forget at times that the works they study were the products of real people in specific ages. And sometimes, as in the case of the deconstructionists of our time, this forgetfulness is deliberate. It is the historian alone who is interested in human beings in all of their activities, capacities, and quiddities and is best qualified to declare, with the Roman dramatist Terence, that nothing human is alien to him.

This claim will perhaps seem excessive to anyone who remembers the comparatively narrow scope of historical instruction, even at major universities, fifty years ago, and the predominance of the kind of political history that concentrated on the fortunes of the Great Powers—what the irreverent called "drum and trumpet history"—and the statesmen who charted their courses in world politics that had prevailed for much longer than that. Part of the blame for this must be attributed to the nature of the times, for the whole period from 1860 to 1945 was, in the Western world at least, a period of domestic and international violence and change, and historiography tended to reflect this in its choice of themes. The narrowness of range was to be explained in part also by the fact that, before the invention of mechanical means for the easy duplication of documents, few researchers had the energy to go beyond the political files in archival collections, so that whole areas of human experience went uninvestigated. Finally, lack of imagination, reinforced by the prejudices of the time, had a lot to do with it, making certain lines of inquiry—notably the role of women in history and the role of minorities in national cultures—seem to be unpromising and without significance. It is true that smallness of view was not characteristic of the most eminent of historians. One thinks of the astonishing range of J. G. Droysen's *Alexander the Great* and Jacob Burckhardt's *The Age of Constantine* and Theodor Mommsen's *Roman History*, works that not only presented persuasive assessments of the characters and careers of the main figures in their stories, but gave remarkably detailed portraits of the age in which they lived, which included descriptions of social stratification, trades and industry, agriculture, religion, money, the institutions and economy of war, architecture, art and literature, public morality, crime, cuisine, the overlapping of civilizations, the Jews and other minorities, and other aspects of life in the Mediterranean and Middle Eastern areas. This sort of thing represented historical humanism in the grand manner, but it was not within the competence of the average practitioner of the discipline, whose range, like that of the offerings in the departments in which they taught, remained modest.

In our own time, the scope of historical investigation has

been so greatly expanded that the conscience of historians need not suffer when they describe their calling as truly humanistic. Since the end of World War II, their profession has benefited from a democratization of attitude, caused not least of all by the transformation of sexual attitudes, and a massive increase of research capacity that is largely due to the computer revolution. It should now be recognized more generally than it is that, if it is to make good its claim to be the queen of the humanities, history must focus its attention, both in research and classroom instruction, upon the role, not only of the movers and shakers in history, but upon that of men and women of every class and condition, including racial and ethnic minorities in society, and that, since computerized research techniques now make it possible to digest and analyze statistical and social data that were unmanageable and hence inaccessible to earlier generations of scholars, there are no insuperable obstacles to assigning to these formerly forgotten groups their proper place in the historical record.

One should perhaps linger for a moment over the new vistas opened up for historians by the computer. Bernard Bailyn has written in the introduction to what will be a large-scale work entitled *The Peopling of British North America*, that the movement of thousands of people from the area that stretches from Prussia to the Danube and from the Hebrides to Africa across the Atlantic to the seaboard communities and the forests and valleys of North America was "the greatest population movement in early modern history and yet . . . our understanding of this great westward transfer of people is a blur, lacking in structure, scale, and detail. We know only in the vaguest way who the hundreds of thousands of individuals who settled in British North America were, where precisely they came from, why they came, and how they lived out their lives." How rapidly this situation is now changing as a result of computer analysis of data gathered from emigration records, genealogical sources, local histories, town records, personal diaries, and newspapers can be seen in Bailyn's first volume, *Voyagers to the West*, which not only gives a quantitative and structural analysis of what is now seen clearly as a more complicated population movement than had been formerly imagined but also provides micronarratives in which the fortunes of selected individuals and families are traced from their origins to their final destinations in ways that illustrate the whole range of experiences and frustrations and successes of the emigrants.

New possibilities breed new attitudes. In the recent interest in what the Germans call *Alltagsgeschichte*, or everyday history, one can detect the belief that historians should not believe that the world of great political and economic decisions and of ideological conflict is essentially any worthier of their attention than the way in which ordinary people lead their lives and, indeed, that a knowledge of the songs that are sung in the back streets may throw new light on the structure and cohesiveness of society. This is not to recommend that history teachers, in particular, turn their attention away from the "big questions" of state and class formation, of religion and churches, of industrialism and its human effects, and of the basic causes and results of such movements as national socialism, for the thoughts and behavior of people in even the smallest spaces in society are to a large extent determined by these things. But there is no doubt that everyday history brings a concreteness and specificity to the past that is not always found in the description of longtime trends. As Hans-Ulrich Wehler has written, "a colorful, plastic history of individual and collective experiences, happenings, modes of perception, behavioral dispositions and actions (such as is made possible by the study of workers in specific trades, utopian societies, outsiders in society like beggars and vagrants, and other special groups that have attracted the attention of enthusiasts for *Alltagsgeschichte*) broadens the understanding of the past and stimulates the fantasy as well as the intellect."

The new democratization of attitude has affected even the most traditional forms of historical writing for the better. Military history, for example, until very recently concentrated largely upon the so-called decisive battles, which were always seen from the standpoint of the generals conducting them, and the strategies they had devised, or from that of the posterity that benefited or suffered from their results. How the common soldier felt about all this was left to the novelists and the poets, some of whom proved more successful than the historians in conveying a sense of the realities of modern war, as Stendhal's account of the battle of Waterloo in *The Charterhouse of Parma* and Stephen Crane's masterful story *The Red Badge of Courage* make clear enough. Recently, however, the British historian John Keegan has shown, in his brilliant and exciting *The Face of Battle*, that historical imagination and skill in using sources are perfectly capable of revealing the experiences and feelings of the ordinary man-at-arms at Agincourt or the Somme and his *Mask of Command* is a fascinating and original study of the complex relationship between the commander and his troops, illustrated by the cases of Alexander, Wellington, Grant, and Hitler.

Admittedly, many schoolteachers and course planners will doubt the advisability of including much military history in their curricula, but its total exclusion is hardly advisable in view of the importance of war as an agency for historical change and the undeniable interest that many students have in it. Recently, a German newspaper, the *Frankfurter Allgemeine Zeitung*, has been distributing to writers, artists, and other prominent public figures an elaborate questionnaire that was popular in the nineteenth century and was filled out by such people as Karl Marx, John Stuart Mill, and Marcel Proust. One of the questions was "What military achievements do you most admire?," and many of the recent respondents to the questionnaire either left this blank or used the occasion to say how much they hated war. One respondent, however, wrote, "Building the Roman roads." He was perhaps a historian who remembered the Via Aurelia ran all the way from Rome to distant Gaul—"It's twenty-five marches to Narbo," Kipling wrote in "Rimini," one of his poems about the Roman army, "It's forty-five more up the Rhone"—and that it and the many other roads built by the legions long outlasted the Empire and served as a network of communication between localities that would otherwise have languished in total isolation during the medieval period. Historian or not, his answer reminds us that there is more to war than killing, and that imaginative approaches can make the historical role of military establishments a rewarding aspect of historical study.

Concerning historical instruction, whether written or oral, three special problems are worth at least cursory consideration: the effective mode or style of communication; the question of bridging the gap that lies between the time of the historian or the teacher and that of the events that are his subject; and, related to this, the role of moral judgments in historical instruction.

With respect to the first of these, it goes almost without saying that the story or narrative form has the most attractive appeal to readers and students and is the most effective method of covering large stretches of time, of demonstrating connections, of delineating lines of continuity, and of presenting dramatic illustrations of the disruption caused by change. But this linear form of historical discourse is generally better at explaining how events took place in time than why they did so, and even the most effective practitioners of the narrative form, or perhaps *especially* the most effective, are prone to omitting or minimizing the importance of facts and circumstances that interfere with its dramatic sweep. To guard against this propensity of the storyteller and its own inherent weaknesses, the narrative form must be reinforced by other techniques that facilitate the explanation of the origins of events, the operation of cause and effect, and the similarities and dissimilarities between analogous developments, and which monitor the generalizations that the narrator makes and keeps them within the range of plausibility. Such techniques include the rigorous analysis of contingent and apparently irrelevant factors (useful in any case to correct the persistent human assumption that events have single causes) and the employment of comparative techniques that test the plausibility of notions of singularity and reveal patterns of behavior and development. (Thus, one is apt to be more cautious in making generalizations about nineteenth-century British liberalism if one has also studied liberalism in France, Switzerland, and Italy, and one is likely also to discover things not revealed by absorption in the single case.)

It is here that the historian can often find assistance in the methods of other disciplines, particularly the social sciences. If he is dealing with the inflationary period in the Weimar Republic, for example, he would be well advised to consult what economists have written about the general causes and characteristics of inflationary spirals; if he intends to describe a particularly complicated diplomatic crisis, it may be helpful for him to read what Alexander L. George has written about the anatomy of crises as revealed by comparative case studies of such political phenomena; and in general, he should remember that sociologists can tell him a great deal about bureaucracies and social stratification and psychologists about the behavior of crowds. He has no good reason, therefore, to be parochial or scornful of what others have to teach him. On the other hand, he must guard against becoming so entranced with what the social sciences are doing that he begins to base his approach upon theirs or even adopt their literary style, with its use of nouns as adjectives and verbs and its barbaric inventions, which often defeat the precision they are meant to enhance. The business of the social sciences is different from his own, which, as Siegfried Krakauer once wrote, is "to elude not only the Scylla of philosophical speculations with their wholesale meanings but also the Charybdis of the sciences with their natural laws and regulations" and to seek to deal with "the particular events, developments, and situations of the human past," a formulation in which the emphasis should be placed upon the words "particular" and "human."

In general, the nature of the period being studied, the materials available, and the skill and imagination of the historian will determine the most effective mode of presenting the story to his readers and students. Whatever his ultimate choice, however, he must of course be guided by their knowledge and interests and be prepared to build on the former and motivate and heighten the latter. He must never forget that it is the approval of his audience and not that of his colleagues that should be in the front of his mind. Jacob Burckhardt was surely making a wise decision when he wrote, as an apprentice historian, "At the risk of being considered unscientific by the population of pedants, I am firmly determined from now on to write in a *readable* fashion. . . . Against the sneers of the contemporary scholarly generation, one must armor oneself with a certain indifference, so that one will perhaps be bought and read, and not merely be the subject of bored note-taking in libraries." A humanistic discipline deserves to be presented in a humane way, as a story about human beings in circumstances, told with grace and energy, its analytic rigor heightened by clarity and logic, its argument persuasive rather than strident or bullying.

Special problems are posed by the distance that exists between the historian and the events that he describes. The Hungarian historian Michael de Ferdinandy once wrote that the humanistic nature of historical scholarship was nowhere more strikingly demonstrated than in its subjective character, in the fact that what we call history exists only because human beings think about it. "Without the historian—whether chronicler or reader," Ferdinandy wrote, "without the intelligent (understanding) eye which observes and assesses the past, there is no history, only a *caput mortuum*, the inert mass of data and past conditions of something that has been. Only through this eye does the dead material take on life again and order and articulate itself and emerge again within us as a living picture of the once existent." But it does so, he continued, in a way that is determined by the qualities of the observing eye, by the intellectual and historical situation of its time, and by its view of the future.

It is clear that this relationship can be productive of much confusion and erroneous generalization about the past that really existed long before our generation came along to observe it, and the facile analogies that our politicians are fond of making between present and past situations are not the only form that such error assumes. It is all too easy and too tempting to make the real past a mere backward extension of our own times, peopled by individuals who might wear clothing different from our own but who are essentially like us in their fundamental attitudes and motivations, in the passions that move them and in the ordering of their priorities. It does not, of course, take much reflection to convince us that this could not possibly be true, and that there are vast differences between the thought processes of inhabitants of twentieth-century New Hampshire and those of their forebears at the end of the seventeenth century, who witnessed and accepted without surprise a degree of savagery in their quotidian existence that is scarcely comprehensible to us. But we often forget this, in small and sometimes important ways, when we are talking or writing about the past. To prevent this requires a high degree of caution and self-criticism as we approach the past, the utmost fidelity to existing sources, a determined and imaginative search for new ones, and a plenitude of the quality that we call empathy, which permits us to feel our way, if we are lucky and work hard enough at it, into the culture of the age that we set out to study and describe.

One of the greatest mistakes to which we are prone as we think about the past is the assumption of inevitability of result. In his inaugural lecture as professor of history at the University of Jena on May 27, 1787, on the theme "What is and to what end do we study universal history?," Friedrich Schiller began by saying, "The very fact that we find ourselves here at this moment, that, characterized as we are by this level of national culture, this language, these moral attitudes, these *bürgerliche* advantages, and this measure of intellectual freedom, we have gathered here, is perhaps the result of all previous world events: the whole of world history would at least be necessary to explain this single moment." In a limited sense—namely, the sense that we are the result of the past—the great poet was doubtless correct. But if he was intimating that history necessarily tended to this end, he was of course doing grave injustice to the richness and variety of the past (for surely the evolution of Chinese and Indian culture was not driven by the determination to produce a Friedrich Schiller), to say nothing of denying freedom of will to generations of individuals who made the history of his own country. To forget that the present is the result of many developments that might have taken a different course and of decisions that might not have been made, or not at the same time or in the same way, is seriously to foreshorten our historical perspective and to indulge in linear thinking of the most restricted kind. The duty of the historian, the contemporary German scholar Thomas Nipperdey once said, is to restore to the past the options it once had. To do so, moreover, is a marvelously effective way of teaching history, for few things engage students more than opportunities to argue about the reasons why such and such things occurred in history rather than quite different ones.

More difficult than any of the problems discussed so far is the question of whether the historian is called upon, in his writing or teaching, to pass moral judgments upon past actions or individual actors. This is a question of the utmost delicacy and one capable of arousing the most violent controversy among professional historians. In the nineteenth century, Lord Acton insisted that it was the historian's duty to "suffer no man and no cause to escape the undying penalty which history has the power to inflict on wrong," and said of scholars who passed over crime and injustice without comment that "the strong man with the dagger is followed by the weak man with the sponge." In our own century the general tendency among historians has been either to ignore the moral obligation that Acton called for or to insist that, since moral values change from age to age, the historian is best advised to practice a "value-free" kind of history, being rigorous and objective in his presentation of the facts and letting his readers or students make their own judgments.

Yet, as Gordon Wright said in his presidential address to the American Historical Association in 1978, this kind of argument will probably give teachers of history who live in the age of Watergate (we may strengthen his argument by adding in the age of Irangate and Pentagon defense contract scandals) some twinges of self-doubt about their classroom obligations. Most of the people involved in these escapades were holders of university degrees and must have had some exposure to the humanistic disciplines. If so, they seem not to have derived from them any sense of moral values or civic responsibility, and this raises serious questions about the nature of the instruction they received. Were their delinquencies perhaps in part due to too much "value-free" instruction? With apparent approval, Wright quoted the British historian C. V. Wedgwood's words: "History dispassionately recorded nearly always sounds harsh and cynical. History is not a moral tale, and the effect of telling it without comment is, inevitably, to underline its worst features: the defeat of the weak by the strong, the degeneration of ideals, the corruption of institutions, the triumph of intelligent self-interest." A surfeit of this sort of thing is bound to make it easier for people to rationalize crime and immorality by arguing that that is the way of the world.

If history is a humanistic discipline, is not one of its principal functions to promote humane values? And can it do that effectively without reprobating the crimes against humanity with which history is filled? When the "greatness" of Julius Caesar is discussed, does not the historian have an obligation to point to the needless barbarity of the Gallic Wars—the lopping off of the hands of tens of thousands of enemy warriors; the extirpation of whole tribes of innocent men, women, and children for no other purpose than to enhance the political fortunes of the Roman commander? Granted that the chief end of historical instruction is to make students understand the past, surely it is unreasonable to suppose that to understand is to forgive? After he has explained the circumstances that led so many Germans to give their support to Adolf Hitler in the early 1930s, is not the practitioner of a humanistic discipline justified in finding those representatives of the world of culture and learning who, like the philosopher Martin Heidegger, called upon their colleagues to rally to the Nazi cause and those German scientists who collaborated in Hitler's atrocities especially culpable and worthy of condemnation?

Obviously not everyone will think so, but the question should at least be pondered by anyone who considers himself a humanist. It is clear enough that history teachers should not become preachers of morality. But they must, it seems to me, have a moral instinct that is strong enough to recognize that there are limits to objectivity. Aside from that, the search for historical truth should be suffused with a commitment to deeply held humane values and a warm and instinctive sympathy for such qualities as fortitude, steadfastness, endurance, civic virtue, dedication to the greater good, and service to humanity when they are embodied in historical movements and personalities. The recognition of such qualities in historical instruction can be an effective way of reprobating their opposites.

People of a practical turn of mind—politicians, for example—often ask what are the lessons that history has to offer them. In response to a publisher who wanted him to write a short book on the subject, Charles A. Beard, the Columbia University historian, answered that he could summarize such lessons in four sentences:

1. Whom the gods would destroy, they first make mad with power.
2. The mills of God grind slowly, yet they grind exceedingly small.
3. The bee fertilizes the flower it robs.
4. When it is dark enough, you can see the stars.

This answer does not satisfy the politicians, who are apt to make up historical lessons of their own to fit their private agenda; and it may not satisfy many beginning students of history, who will ask insistently why, if there are no specific and tangible benefits in sight, they should study it at all. For anyone who regards history, not as a practical science, but as a humanistic discipline, the answer is clear enough. You should study history because it is good for you. By telling you about how other individuals and societies lived in history, it gives you a vicarious experience and thus makes you a more complete human being. It is a source of reassurance in time of discouragement, for it tells you that other people before you had problems and perplexities and yet managed, because the human spirit is indomitable, to survive them. It is, as the Roman historian Livy once said,

> the best medicine for a sick mind, for in history you have a record of the infinite variety of human experience plainly set out for all to see, and in that record you can find for yourself and your country both examples and warnings: fine things to take as models, base things, rotten through and through, to avoid.

Finally, it provides you with an extension of your own life and a connectedness that gives it a greater significance in the stream of history, making you a vital link in the great process that connects the remotest past with the most distant future. In this concept there is a grandeur that transfigures the brevity of individual existence. This is what Schiller meant in his inaugural lecture when, answering the question "What is and to what end do we study universal history?," he said:

> History, insofar as it accustoms human beings to comprehend the whole of the past and to hasten forward with its conclusions into the far future, conceals the boundaries of birth and death, which enclose the life of the human being so narrowly and oppressively, and, with a kind of optical illusion, expands his short existence into endless space, leading the individual imperceptibly over into humanity.

CHAPTER 7

History Is Our Heritage: The Past in Contemporary American Culture

by MICHAEL KAMMEN

One of the most curious anomalies in contemporary American culture ought to be a matter of considerable concern to historians and other educators. New museums and historic sites open their doors at regular and frequent intervals. After a decline in the late 1970s and early 1980s, attendance at many historical museums, villages, and other sites is on the rise. Their educational outreach programs have been redefined and the quality of interpretive activities is more thoughtful and candid than it was just ten or fifteen years ago. The bicentennial of the U.S. Constitution provided an occasion for new curricula to be developed for the teaching of civics, history, and the genesis of American government. Consequently, many more students have been asked to think carefully about the evolution and present state of our political system.

Looked at more closely, however, the place of history in modern American life is both superficial and precarious. Recent studies, already referred to in previous chapters, have revealed an alarming degree of ignorance and apathy. Our students know only a fraction of the history that we would like them to know, and much less than they would need to know as informed voters, decision makers, or simply as persons able to comprehend the complexities of daily news, both national and international.

The problem is not confined, however, to our young people. Abundant evidence indicates that amnesia concerning the American past afflicts those who are responsible for policy at all levels. Public polls and extensive interviews confirm the realization that we are moving forward at an accelerated pace without having the advantage of a first-rate rearview mirror. The variety of topics affected by this amnesia, moreover, is alarmingly broad. It ranges from the origins and nature of New Deal measures designed to combat the Great Depression, to the changing historical circumstances of native Americans, the civil rights of Afro-Americans, and the prolonged series of national anxieties concerning potentially "conspiratorial" threats to overthrow our government. The "Big Red Scare" that followed World War I, and then McCarthyism in the wake of World War II, do not linger as meaningful object lessons for a society so long prone to periodic spasms of nervous apprehension about threats of ideological subversion.

How can we best comprehend and come to grips with this anomalous pattern of historical indifference and ignorance in an age of escapist nostalgia? Have we perpetrated upon ourselves a form of self-deception? I believe that we have, in fact, and that highly selective, sentimental, and sanitized versions of American history have produced a severely simplified vision of how we came to be the society we now are.

Underlying this pattern is a tendency that I call the "heritage phenomenon." If we can understand the distinction between history and heritage, we may be able to explain the anomaly of historical ignorance on the part of a people that appears to share a widespread enthusiasm for the past. The dynamics of that "heritage phenomenon" can supply us with a context for coming to terms with the peculiar status of history in our society as well as in our schools today.

I

For approximately a full generation now, beginning in the mid-1950s, "heritage" has been one of the key words in American culture. The frequency of its usage has also increased markedly in Great Britain and the Commonwealth, to be sure, and in some of the same ways;[1] but the popularity and pervasiveness of this "buzzword" in the United States is becoming utterly astounding. Therefore the phenomenon requires our attention for various reasons but particularly because it can illuminate the complex (and often self-contradictory) transformation of historical consciousness among Americans who come from diverse backgrounds: diverse in terms of region, ethnicity, class, and level of education. Notions of "heritage" in American popular culture are richly revealing for anyone interested in the status of history and historical understanding in contemporary society.

Before getting to the "how" and the "why" of this trend, however, we must start with the seemingly simple, basically descriptive "what." Ultimately we want to specify the implications of a cultural trend, but first we must describe it, exemplify it, and, precisely because it is so ubiquitous, try to break it down into comprehensible categories.

At the national level, for instance, one immediately thinks of the National Trust for Historic Preservation, established at the end of the 1940s. Its current introductory brochure, which makes an attractive appeal for membership, has three carefully chosen words placed on the cover: "Guarding America's Heritage." A major report, co-sponsored by the National Trust and Colonial Williamsburg in 1965, carried the title *With Heritage So Rich*. One also thinks of the Museum of Our National Heritage, which opened in Lexington, Massachusetts, on April 20, 1975, under the auspices of the Scottish Rite Masonic organization.

At the state level we find that "heritage" has gradually

broadened its meaning. In 1957, for example, five organizations jointly sponsored an elegant Virginia Heritage Dinner in order to celebrate "the 350th Anniversary of the Founding of Our Country." That really meant the first permanent English colony, established at Jamestown. The occasion also seemed to use heritage as a near synonym for history.

In 1974, after eight years of developmental planning, the Wisconsin Department of Natural Resources established an outdoor historical park on forty-three acres of land at the edge of Green Bay on the Fox River. It is called Heritage Hill State Park, and the cover of its big brochure defines its mission as "preserving our heritage through 'Living History.' " The four illustrative sections of that brochure are designated as Pioneer Heritage, Heritage of Growth, Military Heritage, and Religious and Small Town Heritage.

The increasingly ecumenical nature of "heritage" is exemplified by New York, which observed an Architectural Heritage Year in 1986 (promoted by the Preservation League of New York State), and had 1988 designated (by Governor Mario Cuomo) as Community Heritage Year. The latter is occasioned by the bicentennial of the 1788 Town Laws, which brought new towns into being and defined the responsibilities of all existing communities in the Empire State.[2]

At the local level, "heritage" is most notably hooked up with historic preservation, although the chosen sites may vary considerably in character. In northeastern Massachusetts, for instance, Heritage Park in downtown Lowell, run by the National Park Service, is a nineteenth- and early twentieth-century industrial restoration. It offers quite a sharp contrast to rustic Historic Deerfield, Inc., located near the Berkshires and founded in 1952 as Heritage Foundation by Mr. and Mrs. Henry Flynt in order "to promote the cause of education in and appreciation of the rich heritage of the early colonies."

Architectural preservation is the primary mission of the Heritage Foundation of Oswego, New York; the Naperville Heritage Society in Illinois, which received its impetus in 1968 when a venerable mansion was on the verge of destruction; the Athens-Clarke Heritage Foundation, which has maintained the Church-Waddel-Brumby House (1820) as a Welcome Center for Athens, Georgia, since 1971; and Texas Heritage, a private organization that is restoring the home built by a Fort Worth cattle baron back in 1912.

The Dallas County Heritage Society was formed in 1966 to prevent the destruction of Millermore, the largest surviving antebellum home in Dallas (built 1855–62). Most of the structures in Old City Park are Victorian, however, and the Society's leaflet makes the following claim: "Walking across their floors, peeking into their rooms, using their tools and toys and trivia . . . [sic] People are history. How people have lived is the basis for how we see life."

Houston's counterpart is called the Harris County Heritage Society, a private, nonprofit organization that also maintains a cluster of nineteenth-century buildings "Where Houston Remembers." Members of the Society serve as docents in Sam Houston Park, "work in the Yesteryear Shop and Tea Room, organize and host lectures and workshops, and stage the annual Heritage Ball, Candlelight Tour and other special events."

Various structures located at Heritage Square in Los Angeles began to undergo restoration in 1968 owing to the joint auspices of the Cultural Heritage Foundation and the city's new Cultural Heritage Board. The endeavor has proceeded at a snail's pace, however, because the city contributes *no* money to the project and volunteers come and go, but mostly go. As the *Los Angeles Times* remarked in 1976, this reflects "the sluggish historical consciousness for which the region is noted."[3]

Pasadena, on the other hand, which has a Cultural Heritage Commission, adopted a cultural heritage ordinance in 1976 that requires permission in order to demolish buildings that are more than fifty years old. The commission is then allowed thirty days to determine if the building in question has historical or cultural significance and whether it can be saved.[4]

Heritage is not inevitably used as a codeword for the salvation of old structures. Sometimes it signifies the struggles for survival that various groups and subcultures have undergone. In 1982, for example, the Indiana Committee for the Humanities, the Indiana Historical Society Library, and the Muncie Public Library produced a striking photographic exhibit entitled "This Far by Faith: Black Hoosier Heritage." The display was accompanied by a booklet with the same title, and a brochure that began: "Our heritage stares out at us from each photograph in this exhibit." It ended with a passage from Langston Hughes's poem, "History."

> The past has been a mint
> Of blood and sorrow.
> That must not be
> True of tomorrow.

A long-neglected Georgian mansion in Philadelphia became the subject of considerable controversy in 1987–88 after the American Women's Heritage Society (a predominantly Black organization) spent more than $50,000 on repairs, fitting out period rooms that range from early American to contemporary, and sponsoring frequent exhibits "that emphasize Black history and achievement." Several civic groups strenuously disapprove of what has been done with the Belmont Mansion (overlooking the Schuylkill River and Fairmount Park), however. A report prepared by a charitable foundation declared in 1987 that "this current use may not be the best use. This house may be a property of such consummate value to the city that it should be more open to the city, possibly as a reception center for dignitaries." Philadelphians are presently fighting over the most appropriate use and presentation of their urban heritage.[5]

For certain groups, "heritage" has become an ideologically useful or meaningful label. The Heritage Foundation headquartered in Washington, D.C., serves as a conservative think tank and political action group. It also publishes a fair amount of literature to promote and explain its causes, which include a vigorous defense of the free enterprise system. Yet another

Heritage Foundation, based in Trumbull, Connecticut, displays on its letterhead a screaming eagle perched upon an open Bible, below which a dozen words from Psalm 61 appear: "Thou hast given us the heritage of those that fear thy name." Nationalism and fundamentalism can comfortably complement one another.

The heritage emphasis has also become valuable, however, to entrepreneurs offering safe havens in a world that is commercial as well as secular, self-indulgent, and intensely concerned with social status. Heritage Hills of Westchester, New York, offers condominiums in a thousand-acre "country setting of beauty, woods, ponds and streams." Where is the heritage?

> The recreational opportunities are the best. Heritage Hills offers a private golf course and health club with gym, saunas and whirlpool. There are swimming pools, tennis courts and a jogging path. The homes are the best. Fine craftsmanship and quality are evident throughout these beautifully designed homes. . . . There's even a private shuttle service to the nearby commuter train station.

A much more lavish set of homes, located near Morristown, New Jersey, is offered by New Vernon Heritage at prices starting at $1.2 million. Where is the heritage? According to one advertisement, "the architecture, reflecting a return to the classic, will include English manors, French chateaus, and Irish country houses." A rather eclectic heritage, if you will, and if you are willing to live with mixed manors.

In the world of business, "heritage" seems to connote integrity, authenticity, venerability, and stability. Hence the Heritage Federal Bank in Franklin, Tennessee; Realty World-Heritage Realty for vacation sites in Maggie Valley, North Carolina, snuggled along the edge of the Great Smoky Mountains; the Heritage Building, a large office complex in downtown Dallas, Texas; and Heritage Hall Gallery in Lansdale, Pennsylvania, the home of Heritage Collectors' Society, which specializes in restoring, framing, and selling historic documents for "interior accent." A decorator's delight: cover your walls with "original documents signed by those who shaped our nation's destiny."

As for achievement recognition, in 1982 the National Endowment for the Arts created a program of National Heritage Fellowships, "the country's highest award for accomplishment in a traditional arts field." Three years later the recipients included a Hawaiian quiltmaker from Honolulu who has hand-stitched more than one hundred quilts and designed more than four hundred quilt patterns; a Lakota Sioux from Grass Creek, South Dakota, who has worked to preserve the Indian craft of porcupine quill decoration; and a working cowboy who "has told more tall tales and sung more cowboy songs than anyone in Mountain View, Arkansas, can count."[6]

These $5,000 fellowships are awarded on a one-time-only basis by the Folk Arts Program at N.E.A. For our purposes they fill out the heritage spectrum, ranging from institutions to individuals, from the public sector to the private, from statements of purpose to advertisements, and from identity to destiny. The question yet remains, however, what does heritage actually have to do with history and social memory?

II

Basically, I suppose, the essential answer must be "everything and nothing." In some situations, such as Heritage Hills condominiums, the word-concept bears absolutely no relationship to the past. It is simply a euphonious phrase that portends a sheltered if not sybaritic life-style.

In other situations, heritage seems to be very nearly a euphemism for selective memory because it means, in functional terms, what history has customarily meant: namely, that portion of the past perceived by a segment of society as significant or meaningful at any given moment in time.[7]

In still other situations, heritage is virtually intended as an antonym for history, or else it passes as sugar-coated history. But that really means more than mere palatability. It involves an explicit element of anti-intellectualism—the presumption, for example, that history experienced through sites and material culture must be more memorable than history presented on the printed page. An advertisement for New Jersey's *Heritage Guide* shows a winsome modern lass seated at a Chippendale game table from the Revolutionary era. Above her flaxen hair are two lines with a didactic imperative: Let Your Children Experience American History Instead of Just Reading About It.[8]

Many of those who run outdoor museums and similar sites make strident claims about the authenticity of what they have to offer. They also tend to make pejorative statements about the perils of historical imagination—as though that were an *undesirable* quality to encourage in adolescents. And the promotional materials of such administrators are likely to claim that hands-on heritage-as-history guarantees enjoyment, unlike the deadly dull sort of history that is dispensed in the classroom, the library, and via the medium of print. Take, as one representative illustration, these exuberant assertions from the initial page of a booklet produced by Heritage Hill State Park in Green Bay, Wisconsin.

> You don't have to imagine how life was in northeast Wisconsin 100 years ago! When you leave Heritage Hill's Visitor Center, you will actually experience the past through living history. . . . The people who "live" in Heritage Hill's historical structures eat, work, dress and talk exactly as though they were living in bygone days. To them, modern conveniences and language patterns do not exist. . . . Living history brings an added dimension to the historical museum which allows you to learn about your "roots" and enjoy it![9]

When we ask why the heritage rubric has sustained such remarkable appeal, we must start with nostalgia. The nation has been hankering after various imagined golden ages—for more innocent and carefree days—ever since the early 1970s. There is nothing necessarily wrong with nostalgia per se, but more often than not the phenomenon does mean a pattern of selective memory. Recall the good, but forget the unpleasant. And that is just what has happened. The 1965 report published by the National Trust, "With Heritage So Rich," articulated the problem succinctly: "A nation can be a victim of amnesia."[10] The spate of reports that appeared in 1987 indicate that cultural amnesia has overwhelmed the American populace with unusual force.[11]

The heritage syndrome, if I may call it that, almost seems to be a predictable but certainly nonconspiratorial response—an impulse to remember what is attractive or flattering and to ignore all the rest. Heritage is comprised of those aspects of history that we cherish and affirm. As an alternative to history, heritage accentuates the positive but sifts away what is problematic. One consequence is that the very pervasiveness of heritage as a phenomenon produces a beguiling sense of serenity about the well-being of history—that is, a false consciousness that historical knowledge and understanding are alive and well in the United States.

Although American knowledge and understanding of history are *not* altogether healthy, neither is the outlook quite so grim as it may sound. An up-beat emphasis upon heritage can serve as a stimulus to prudent public policy and enhanced concern for a more meaningful relationship between past and present. As a *New York Times* editorial phrased the matter in 1975, referring to New York City's landmark legislation and the campaign to "save" Grand Central Terminal, repercussions of that legislation "are already being felt in other places where the problem of the preservation of a city's and a nation's heritage meet the problem of economic hardship and the rights of property."[12]

One of the more welcome features of the heritage surge involves the development of contacts, even enduring relationships, between popular and academic history. Scholars have been writing for *American Heritage* ever since it began to appear in its present guise during the mid-1950s. Energetic and creative teachers of history and social studies in our secondary and primary schools are presently publishing essays with such titles as "Planning for Local Heritage Projects." Staff members at the Smithsonian Institution, assessing the forthcoming quincentennial of Columbus's arrival in the Western Hemisphere (1992), have observed that "historic anniversaries are even more important to us as a time to focus on our civic heritage and in the case of Columbus, on our world heritage."[13]

Precisely because the heritage phenomenon has become so strong, and because some of its features may seem superficial or self-serving for assorted groups or individuals, there is a genuine risk that critical observers may conclude that "real" history must be 180 degrees removed from the tainted stuff that parades as heritage. What nonsense! Hasn't serious history *always* contained elements of national mythology? Bernard DeVoto once reassured Catherine Drinker Bowen (with a touch of irony) that it was okay to be "romantic about American history. . . . It is the most romantic of histories. It began in myth and has developed through three centuries of fairy stories."[14]

It can be too easily overlooked that, for generations, scholarly students of American history have been motivated by a passion to describe and explain the national heritage. In 1953, Samuel Flagg Bemis wrote Van Wyck Brooks a paean of praise for "all of those high-minded things of our heritage and the goodly currents of our life which you have done so much to hold up before the American people."[15]

Moreover, high-minded creative writers and artists who were neither professional historians nor conservative white males like Bemis, and whose past presented a saga of punishment rather than praise, nonetheless felt compelled to contemplate their heritage and communicate their apprehensions and ruminations. Hence Countee Cullen's long poem, called "Heritage," written in the 1920s.[16]

One three centuries removed
From the scenes his father loved,
Spicy grove, cinnamon tree,
What is Africa to me?

Cullen's wistful lines, along with comparable works by members of many other ethnic groups and subcultures, remind us to acknowledge the presence of multiple heritages—surely no shock in a nation of immigrants. Cullen's poignant poem also reminds us that heritage need not be a mindless affirmation of congenial memories. It has become commonplace to say that one sound reason for studying history is to enrich the understanding of identity—my own along with those of the several groups with which I identify. That, too, is a legitimate preoccupation of those intrigued by heritage.[17]

There are, in addition, events and anniversaries that inevitably remind us that history as heritage has not been free from tension, conflicting value systems, or even violence. In 1983, for example, the Gettysburg National Military Park, Gettysburg Travel Council, Gettysburg College, and the Mason-Dixon Civil War Collectors Association began to sponsor Civil War Heritage Days—more than a week of living history encampments, a reenactment of part of the Battle of Gettysburg (July 1–3, 1863), and a Civil War Collector's show. In 1986 the fourth annual Civil War Heritage Days were attended by more than fifty thousand people.[18]

The unfortunate thing about this heritage boom is that it can lead, and has led, to commercialization, vulgarization, oversimplification, and tendentiously selective memories—which means both warping and whitewashing a fenced-off past. Any or all of those processes provide a disservice to the groups affected. We are better off without heritage than with it when it causes self-deception.[19]

The redeeming virtue of heritage, however, is that it can also serve as a powerful stimulus to the popularization, and hence to the democratization, of history. Heritage that heightens human interest may lead people to history for purposes of informed citizenship, or the meaningful deepening of identity, or enhanced appreciation of the dynamic process of change over time. American responses to "progress," for instance, have frequently followed patterns of ambivalence or rejection rather than mindless approval[20]—a lesson that history can teach whereas "heritage" is less likely to do so.

III

What specific implications does the heritage phenomenon have for classroom teachers and their work? The good news, obviously, is that opportunities for extramural enrichment are rapidly expanding. Class trips to historic sites, farms, factories, and villages are increasingly accessible, and such visits can bring the past alive and make it fascinating in ways that are difficult to achieve in the classroom or library alone.

The more challenging news, however, is that such trips require careful preparation and thoughtful follow-up. I have accompanied interpretive tours where I happened to join a high school class. The guides (from the National Park Service, for instance) did an excellent job of explaining their particular site, but I learned from conversations with the students that they had been given scanty prior background reading to help them understand the context of, in one instance, the onset of American industrialization and development of the factory system. At this particular site, fortunately, the tour began with a very fine twenty-minute film. But most sites are not so well set up, and at many the docents are experts on the particulars of their place—the genealogy of a structure and its inhabitants, for instance—not on the larger pattern or trend of which it is a part. Consequently, it is essential that those patterns or trends be adequately included in the formal learning process. The best history teaching takes into account "how" and "why" along with "what," "when," and context.

Heritage can be used to explain the importance of ethnicity

and religion in shaping American pluralism, for example; but in order to do so successfully the teacher must transcend the chauvinism that characterizes associations formed by hyphenated Americans, or the particularism of denominational or sectarian pride. Heritage can also be used to teach the history of work, professionalization, and economic change in the United States; but in the process teachers must make clear just how different eighteenth-century agriculture and nineteenth-century medical practice were from their late twentieth-century descendants. The heritage phenomenon sometimes has a tendency to overemphasize continuity at the expense of transformation. Teachers need to be as knowledgeable about the interpretive biases of the sites they visit as they are familiar with the orientation of the textbook they assign.

We must also recognize that the heritage phenomenon tends to be up-beat and affirmative in an unqualified way about the American past. Without minimizing what has truly been a remarkable saga of achievements, teachers should be sure to take into account the human and environmental "costs" of many of those achievements. We will not adequately prepare our students for the future if we do not communicate the history of failure as well as the history of success: the failure of rebels with and without a cause, the failure of the framers to resolve all the vexing political problems they faced in 1787, the failure of subsequent reform movements to solve entirely the social ills they responded to, and so forth.

Our heritage phenomenon has the great virtue of accentuating the common core of values, institutions, and experiences that Americans have shared, and to which newcomers have accommodated in the process of becoming Americans. Undeniably, many aspects of the heritage phenomenon provide the glue that holds us all together.

Appropriate attention to those aspects, however, should not cause us to neglect those wonderfully symbolic nay-sayers who seemed out of tune with their times yet may have been prophetic of changes in the American value system. Such figures as Roger Williams, John Woolman, Sojourner Truth, Elizabeth Cady Stanton, Henry David Thoreau, and Frederick Douglass come quickly to mind as examples. One of the marvels of American history is the way certain deviant visionaries subsequently came to be regarded as prophetic leaders; and conversely, the way some popular figures subsequently seem to have been demagogues, do-nothings, or just plain disappointments.[21]

The heritage phenomenon *can* be a potent pedagogical device. It may be used to transmit with memorable force the most attractive and altruistic American values, such as equal justice, full participation in public affairs, broadened economic opportunities for all segments of society, religious toleration, regionalism and the significance of a sense of place, the value of intergenerational connectedness, and so forth.

This highly visible heritage phenomenon is less likely, however, to inform our students about those forces that have undermined our ideals, such as excessive physical mobility, or present-minded hedonism, or commercial opportunism that may be destructive to the environment and our natural resources.

Nor is the heritage phenomenon as I have described it likely to inculcate the need for a discriminating memory—the inescapable fact that not all sites and structures, heroes and heroines, events and objects are equally important. Nor does the heritage phenomenon lend itself very well to the integrative habit of mind that we call synthesis: understanding how discrete but contemporaneous or sequential occurrences are connected to one another.

Nor does it ordinarily help us to recognize and account for differential rates of social and political change, or the ways in which patterns of intergroup conflict emerge and later are reconciled over extended periods of time. Precisely because these are all fundamental aspects of historical experience, it is essential that we teach historical habits of the mind that will enable young people to cope with such matters as component parts of the civic culture.

Although history is surely heritage simply because all of the known past is our legacy, there is more to history than heritage alone. In fact, the heritage phenomenon provides us with vivid reminders that teachers, texts, and classrooms remain indispensable. At the end of June 1988, for example, more than seventy thousand people converged on Gettysburg, Pennsylvania, to spectate and participate in a seventeen-day observance of the 125th anniversary of the Battle of Gettysburg. Presumably this was a self-selecting audience. Why go to Gettysburg if you aren't *some* sort of history buff? Nevertheless, one of the participants in the elaborate reenactment of the battle, a blue-clad man from Michigan, remarked that "I can go into McDonald's wearing my uniform, and people will ask me which side I'm on."[22]

In the last analysis, it seems to me that two conclusions are inescapable. First, that schools and museums, historical organizations and textbooks have a responsibility to package and present "heritage" contextualized rather than in vacuo. They must acknowledge that heritages (plural) sometimes compete with one another (as the Italian-Americans and Scandinavian-Americans did a century ago when the four hundredth anniversary of Columbus's voyages approached), and that tensions among ethnic groups or communities have sometimes been creative, sometimes corrosive, sometimes benign, at other times scarring.[23]

My second conclusion should by now be quite clear. "Heritage" as we have known it is not necessarily history, but the *whole* of history, whether we like it or not, is heritage. The great imperative, therefore, for schools and teachers, textbook writers and curriculum developers, docents and educators at museums and historic sites, is to remember that heritage—this remarkably pervasive notion in American culture during the past three decades—really isn't an alternative to history, or a surrogate for it, but a prologue and a preparation for the pasts (wars and all) that produced the present (warts and all).

Stephen Dedalus once stated, courtesy of James Joyce, that "history is a nightmare from which I am trying to awake." Perhaps; but heritage in its many guises can be a beguiling daydream. We must elude the soothing self-satisfaction that it induces. Heritage as an enticement, however, could conceivably bring us to history as enchantment, as mental exercise, and as a source of self-knowledge that points toward enlightenment if not wisdom.

NOTES

1. See Robert Hewison, *The Heritage Industry: Britain in a Climate of Decline* (London: Secker & Warburg, 1987); and *British Heritage*, a popular magazine that began publication in 1979. Scotland offers The [Robert] Burns Heritage Trail (Alloway to Dumfries); Linlithgow Heritage Trail; and Dunfermline Heritage, which includes the burial place of Robert the Bruce and the birthplace of Andrew Carnegie. Examples in Canada include Heritage Park in Calgary, and Heritage Collection at the Whyte Museum of the Canadian Rockies in Banff, both located in Alberta. See also Siegfried Lenz, *The Heritage: The History of a Detestable Word* (New York: Hill & Wang, 1981), a German novel whose original title (1978) literally translated as "The Homeland Museum." The book's principal theme is the huge chasm between Germany's perception of past and present, a gap caused by the Nazis' warped use of the concepts of "homeland," heritage, and history to legitimize nationalistic xenophobia and the doctrine of racial purity.

2. See *Preservation News*, September 1986, pp. 7, 11; proclamation issued by Governor Cuomo on December 18, 1987.

3. *Los Angeles Times*, December 23, 1976, p. 6.

4. Ibid., p. 4.

5. *New York Times*, November 8, 1987, p. 62.

6. Ibid., September 8, 1985, p. A78.

7. See Carl Becker, *Everyman His Own Historian: Essays on History and Politics* (New York: F. S. Crofts & Co., 1935), pp. 247–48.

8. *Smithsonian*, December 1985, p. 143.

9. *Preserving Our Heritage Through "Living History"* (Green Bay, Wisc., n.d.).

10. Michael Wallace, "Reflections on the History of Historic Preservation," in *Presenting the Past: Essays on History and the Public*, ed. Susan Porter Benson, et al. (Philadelphia: Temple University Press, 1986), p. 177.

11. See Lynne V. Cheney, *American Memory: A Report on the Humanities in the Nation's Public Schools* (Washington, D.C.: National Endowment for the Humanities, 1987); Merrill Peterson, *The Humanities and the American Promise: Report of the Colloquium*

on the Humanities and the American People (Austin, Tex., 1987); Diane Ravitch and Chester E. Finn, Jr., *What Do Our 17-Year-Olds Know?* (New York: Harper & Row, 1987).

12. *New York Times*, December 20, 1975, p. 26. See the 1987 prospectus for the Minnetrista Cultural Center in Muncie, Indiana: "Preserving the Heritage of East Central Indiana." The Center is scheduled to open in December 1988.

13. Claudia J. Hoone, "Planning for Local Heritage Projects," *Hoosier Heritage* 3 (March 1986); Joan R. Challinor and Wilcomb E. Washburn, "Five Ways We Can Hail Columbus," *Washington Post*, October 11, 1987, p. H5. See also "The National Park Service and Historic Preservation," a special issue of *The Public Historian*, 9 (Spring 1987); Betty Shaw, "Interpreting Our Outdoor Heritage," *Museum News* 44 (June 1966): 24–28.

14. The letter is undated. Wallace Stegner, ed., *The Letters of Bernard De Voto* (New York: Doubleday, 1975), p. 285. See also George Jean Nathan and H. L. Mencken, *The American Credo: A Contribution Toward the Interpretation of the National Mind*, 2nd ed. (New York: Alfred A. Knopf, 1921), pp. 69–70; John Higham, "Beyond Consensus: The Historian as Moral Critic," *American Historical Review* 67 (April 1963): 615–16.

15. Bemis to Brooks, June 12, 1953, Brooks Papers, Van Pelt Library (Rare Book Collection), University of Pennsylvania, Philadelphia. See also Perry Miller, *Errand into the Wilderness* (Cambridge, Mass.: Harvard University Press, 1956), pp. viii–ix.

16. Countee Cullen, *On These I Stand* (New York: Harper & Brothers, 1947), pp. 24–28. It may be instructive, though not entirely attractive, to contemplate a letter that Herbert Hoover wrote in 1912: "In these days of stifling struggle our people need something to bring back to them the heritage, not only of the combat of immediate fathers in the upbuilding of the West, but also to bring to the people that they have a heritage of race." Quoted in Robert W. Rydell, *All the World's a Fair: Visions of Empire at American International Expositions, 1876–1916* (Chicago: University of Chicago Press, 1984), p. 208.

17. See Herbert G. Gutman, "Historical Consciousness in Contemporary America," in *Power & Culture: Essays on the American Working Class*, ed. Herbert G. Gutman (New York: Pantheon, 1987), pp. 395–412; Henry F. May, *Coming to Terms: A Study in Memory and History* (Berkeley, Calif.: University of California Press, 1987), esp. pp. xi, 146; William Maxwell, *Ancestors* (New York: Alfred A. Knopf, 1971).

18. *U.S.A. Weekend, Ithaca Journal*, May 23, 1986; and a personal visit by the author in July 1986.

19. See Ron Powers, *White Town Drowsing* (Boston: Atlantic Monthly Press, 1986), esp. pp. 19, 69, 108, 111, 206, 257, 267, 271–72, 274, 277, 287. For the failure of a Mark Twain Heritage Theme Park to develop, as planned, near Hannibal, Missouri, see pp. 115, 128–37.

20. See Merritt Roe Smith, *Harpers Ferry Armory and the New Technology: The Challenge of Change* (Ithaca, N.Y.: Cornell University Press, 1977); Richard N. Current, *Northernizing the South* (Athens, Ga.: University of Georgia Press, 1983), pp. 85, 97, 103–105; Neil Harris, "Cultural Institutions and American Modernization," *The Journal of Library History* 16 (Winter 1981):43; and T. J. Jackson Lears, *No Place of Grace: Antimodernism and the Transformation of American Culture, 1880–1920* (New York: Pantheon, 1981).

21. See "Overrated & Underrated Americans," *American Heritage* 39 (July 1988):48–63.

22. William K. Stevens, "National Trauma Played Out Again at Gettysburg," *New York Times*, June 27, 1988, p. A10.

23. See Michael Kammen, *Selvages & Biases: The Fabric of History in American Culture* (Ithaca, N.Y.: Cornell University Press, 1987), pp. 287–89.

CHAPTER 8

How History Helps Us to Understand Current Affairs

by WILLIAM H. McNEILL

Memory guides human action to a very great extent, and because different people have different memories their actions
vary, sometimes in ways that surprise ignorant outsiders. The
study of history can reduce such surprises, for history is neither
more nor less than a record of the memories that affect public
behavior; and when historians study different peoples, what
most concerns them is the kinds of memories that inspire
action—or, in some cases, inspired it in ancient peoples who no
longer exist. Knowledge of history, therefore, is a supremely
useful tool for understanding current affairs, minimizing misunderstandings and facilitating wiser decisions than are possible for those who lack historical knowledge.

In personal encounters this is self-evident. Everyone acts
and reacts to others on the basis of memories of what happened
before—trusting or distrusting, as the case may be, on the basis
of what one remembers from the past. Without memory we
would be unable to distinguish parents and siblings from
strangers; friends from foes; colleagues and allies from opponents and rivals. We simply would not know how to behave and

would blunder into costly and embarrassing errors over and over again.

Ignorance of the public memories and living past of other peoples has quite the same effect. If we do not know who they are and how they are likely to behave in particular circumstances because of the memories they carry around with them, we will blunder and provoke unexpected responses, just as an individual, deprived of private memory of past relationships with other persons, would do.

In actual cases, short-term memory of past relationships is often enough for managing everyday affairs. One simply assumes, in such instances, that the way things have been going lately will continue, and in most circumstances that is a valid assumption. But once in a while a crisis erupts. Established patterns of behavior come under stress, and may change, sometimes abruptly and in violent, revolutionary ways. Knowledge of the deeper past then becomes useful, for when an established pattern of conduct ceases to satisfy a people, in trying to get rid of whatever bothers them they are compelled to draw on their memories and on traditions that define what can and ought to be. It is, therefore, not an accident that successful revolutions always appeal to the past—often to an idealized and more or less fictitious past—to justify and guide public efforts to make things different. French revolutionaries in the 1790s looked back to the Roman Republic as well as forward to the Rights of Man; Russian revolutionaries in 1917 invoked a Garden of Eden vision of primitive communism while looking ahead to a future in which government would simply wither away.

Discontented peoples also draw on more specific, local memories to give shape to their hopes and define their fears. This was true of the French and Russian revolutionaries who had much to deplore in their respective national pasts. A more recent illustration may be found in the Iranian Revolution of 1979. That revolution was the work of the Ayatollah Khomeini and a host of followers and collaborators who objected to Shah Mohammed Reza Pahlavi's government, which was using vast oil revenues to hasten the modernization of the country. The shah and his henchmen believed that the headlong importation of machinery, skills, and ideas from Western lands, and particularly from the United States, was the way to become rich and powerful. From their point of view, Islamic customs and institutions were an obstacle to be overcome, because they had prevented Persia from keeping up with the advanced peoples of the West and maintaining its ancient greatness—greatness dating back to the Achaemenid empire of Darius and Xerxes (546–330 B.C.).

Khomeini and his followers also wished to see their country great and powerful, but they believed the way to achieve that end was to adhere scrupulously to the will of God as revealed to Mohammed and applied to everyday life by experts in the Sacred Law who adhered to the Shi'a tradition. From such a viewpoint, most of what the shah and his officers were trying to do was sacrilege, and the United States was nothing but a "Great Satan," which was tempting God's people and leading them astray.

Only when one knows something about the history of Iran and of the Persian people is it possible to understand how such diametrically opposed views of the public good could arise and gain popular support—though, as it turned out, Khomeini's followers were more numerous and a great deal more fanatical than the shah's. The cardinal points in that history were those upon which the rival parties fixed in their respective visions of the past. The Persians emerged into recorded history with the rise of the Achaemenid empire in the sixth century B.C. and the establishment of the greatest military state of the age. More than a thousand years later came the revelation of Islam to the Prophet Mohammed, and the conquest of Persia by Arab Muslims. The Persians soon accepted the religion of their conquerors, and in due course became cultural leaders of the entire Islamic world after about A.D. 1000.

Yet Persian leadership in the Islamic world did not last forever. In the sixteenth century a sectarian religious leader and warrior, Isma'il Safavi, won control of most of the Persian lands, and used his military power to enforce conformity to a Shi'a version of the Muslim faith. Thereafter Persia was inhabited by only one kind of Muslim, and the Shi'a experts who flocked from other parts of the Islamic world, to the protection Shah Isma'il offered them, soon established their own authority, even daring to oppose the shah's government on some points of law. The result of this religious revolution of the sixteenth century was to set the Persians in doctrinal opposition to the majority of Muslims elsewhere; and in subsequent centuries, when efforts to reform and purify Islam took root in other Muslim lands, reformers regularly set out to get rid of what they felt were Persian corruptions of the pure, original Arabic expression of the faith.

Persia's religious isolation within the Realm of Islam was eventually followed by military disaster, when dynastic instability invited first Afghan and then Russian and British intervention. By 1907 the country was partitioned into Russian and British "spheres of influence," and European ideas began to challenge Persia's religious and national faith. Reform seemed vital. The only question was what kind. In 1925 an emphatic answer to this question was offered by an upstart military commander who seized power and proclaimed himself Reza Shah. He set the country on the path of modernization, seeking to restore past greatness by borrowing skills and techniques from the all-powerful peoples of the West. His son, Mohammed Reza Shah, accelerated and broadened the process of Westernization after World War II, acting very largely on strategies for national "development" believed in by American economists. He met enormous success, transforming agriculture, building industry, equipping the armed forces with new, sophisticated weapons, and increasing the Gross National Product many times over.

Yet the people were not with him. The actions of the shah's government changed nearly everyone's daily life, and not all changes were agreeable, especially for the hundreds of thousands who left their native villages to live in overcrowded cities. These displaced villagers provided the tinder for Ayatollah Khomeini's revolution. His demand for a return to religious truth and governance struck them as good, right, and necessary; and in due course it was they who constituted the crowds that attacked the American embassy in Tehran and drove the shah into exile.

American advisers and development experts were taken aback at what happened, and the American public was appalled when revolutionaries treated our country as "the Great Satan." The trouble was that American help to the shah's government had been extended with little or no understanding of the country's peculiar past. Americans assumed, as a matter of course, that whatever seemed good to Americans would seem good to the people of Iran, too. And for a long time Americans on the spot and in Washington simply refused to pay attention to the religious preachers who were mobilizing the city crowds against the shah. Their ideas seemed too outlandish, too absurd, too contrary to the Persian people's material needs and economic self-interest to matter. If the Americans responsible for policy in Iran had known more about the country's past, they might have been more sensitive to what the religious leaders had to say and been less surprised by what happened.

This does not mean that knowledge of history would necessarily have allowed Americans or anyone else to foresee what happened. Timing, personalities, and accidents have much to do with political events, everywhere and always, and such crucial superficialities cannot be predicted on the strength of familiarity with a past that necessarily differs in all the details of timing, personalities, and accidents.

A decent familiarity with Persian history might not even have made American policy toward Iran very different. After all, the headlong pace of transformation in the post–World War II decades reflected the will of the shah and his intimate circle of advisers, not the influence of Americans or any other foreigners. Yet we might have been at least partway ready for the sort of sudden upheaval that actually took place, and a few prudent adjustments ahead of time might have made Americans less exposed to the crowds of Tehran than was in fact the case. Even slight knowledge of the country's history would have helped, but that knowledge was almost wholly lacking. We are still paying the price.

Other examples of how a knowledge of history might help us to understand current events are easy to find. An example with overtones that are far more agreeable to Americans is the confusion currently prevailing in Poland, where an intensely unpopular Communist government presides over a population that knows very well what it dislikes but is unable to agree upon, or fully believe in, the feasibility of any alternative to the existing regime.

To understand the Polish situation, one must again know something about the deeper past, since the national and cultural tensions that lie behind contemporary strikes, demonstrations, and other public manifestations of dissatisfaction have their roots in long-standing national rivalries of a religious and political nature. These rivalries are in turn exacerbated by the geographical position in which the Poles find themselves, located, as they are, on a broad and fertile plain with no natural boundaries between themselves and their German and Russian neighbors.

Key events that defined the ethnic alignments and affinities that dominate Polish history date back to the Middle Ages, when the Polish kingdom accepted Christianity in its Latin, Roman Catholic form, whereas farther east the neighboring Slavic lands of White Russia, the Ukraine, and Great Russia were converted to the Greek Orthodox form of Christianity. While this associated Poland with German lands to the west, a religious split with the Germans arose in the sixteenth century. When the parts of Germany abutting on Poland became Lutheran, the Poles, after initial attraction to Reformation doctrines (and some striking experiments with radical sects), turned instead toward a reformed and militant version of Roman Catholicism. From that time on, their religion marked Poles off from Germans on the west and from Russians on the east. Loyalty to the nation fused with loyalty to the Roman Catholic church, each reinforcing the other.

For a while, Catholic Reform and Polish national ambitions combined to extend Polish rule over much of the Ukraine, and some Ukrainians abandoned their traditional Orthodox faith by accepting the headship of the pope. But Ukrainian peasants resisted religious innovation and when given a choice they regularly preferred Orthodoxy. This meant that the Russians, when they began to challenge Polish control of the Ukraine from their capital at Moscow, could count on mass support against the more narrowly aristocratic appeal of Polish culture, religion, and (noble) liberty. Eventually local liberty for nobles in Poland went so far as to weaken the kingdom fatally. After a bitter Time of Troubles (1604–13), during which the Poles occupied Moscow for a short time, poor and backward Russia, by submitting to an oppressive autocracy, was able to create a formidable military power, far superior to what Polish nobles could put into the field. Poland's German neighbors also developed superior armies over the seventeenth and eighteenth centuries.

The result was the extinction of the Polish state in 1795, when a third and final partition of Poland divided Polish lands between Russia, Prussian, and Austria. But Polish national consciousness was not snuffed out. Instead, it intensified, thanks largely to the nurturing support of the Roman Catholic church and to the fact that the Catholic Hapsburgs found it prudent to favor Poles against other, more discontented nationalities of their empire. When World War I led to the simultaneous collapse of the German, Austrian, and Russian empires in 1918, a new Polish state emerged with ambitions to rebuild the Great Poland of the past by liberating part or all of the Ukraine from its Muscovite masters.

A few Ukrainians responded to the Polish vision of liberation, but as before the majority preferred Russians to Poles, if given a choice. This preference survived even the fact that the new Russian regime was Communist and atheistic, consciously opposed to traditional Christian Orthodoxy. When fighting finally ended in 1921, the new Russo-Polish border simply ratified the existing military demarcation line, leaving some Ukrainians and White Russians under Polish rule. Eighteen years later, Poland collapsed under German and Russian attack at the start of World War II. At the close of that conflict, the victorious Russians revised Poland's frontiers, pushing them back westward. Moreover, the Russians imposed a Communist government on Poland and have maintained garrisons in the country since 1944.

Memories of the distant and recent past dominate and direct both Russian and Polish behavior. Neither side trusts the other. Poles who collaborate with the Russians are like the Ukrainians who once collaborated with the Poles: a small minority, viewed as traitors by many, perhaps nearly all, of their fellows.

Yet from a Polish point of view, their German neighbors are just as threatening. In medieval times, the Polish kingdom took shape through wars against German knights. In modern times, Prussian expansion at Polish expense hurt almost as much as Polish losses to Russia, since the territories involved, although smaller in extent, were more vital. That was because efforts to establish a land link between Berlin and East Prussia meant cutting off Poland's access to the Baltic and to the wider world across the sea. Germans never accepted the borders defined in the Versailles Treaty of 1919, which restored Poland's access to the sea, thereby isolating East Prussia from the rest of Germany once again; World War II began when Hitler set out to reverse that settlement. The Polish armies collapsed under Nazi attack and the subsequent German occupation was brutal, though not much more brutal than the first phase of the Russian occupation that succeeded it, for the Communists could make their power secure only by destroying the Polish Home Army, a secret but well-organized resistance organization.

Caught between such powerful, threatening neighbors,

Poles have survived by cultivating a strong sense of their own difference from both Germans and Russians. The idea that Poland was a special sort of sufferer among nations, a Christ figure on the international scene, appealed powerfully to nineteenth-century patriots, who had no independent Polish state of their own. This idea still survives. So does a sense of cultural superiority over the Russians. But how to give these feelings effective public expression is a puzzle that confounds and frustrates Polish patriots.

Poland's contemporary dilemma is that any actual attainment of genuine freedom for the nation requires withdrawal of Russian control. But this is hard to conceive without a simultaneous Russian withdrawal from East Germany and overthrow of the Communist regime there, allowing German reunification with all the dangers that a strong Germany means for Poland's continued independence and freedom. This makes the Polish conundrum insoluble in any short run. The fact is that the majority of Poles see no safe and believable alternative to their present unsatisfactory dependence on the Russians, and this is what allows the unhappy stalemate between the Polish Communist regime and Polish popular feeling to persist.

Knowing more about European than about Persian and Muslim history, Americans have been friendly to the protesters without being willing to encourage real revolutionary action that might actually topple the government. For Americans, too, find the threat of a united Germany's power difficult to cope with. While our interest in keeping the lid on in Eastern Europe is real, our sympathy for the plight of the Poles is no less real. Knowledge of history, in this case, tends to put Americans in the same limbo that the Poles occupy. Drastic action is too risky to try, for us as for them. Slow, small improvements in the way the Polish government behaves toward its people, and parallel development toward a more liberal regime within the USSR seem the best hope for the future, both from an American and from a Polish patriot's point of view.

This sort of judgment, carefully balancing risks and gains

against each other, is a very common consequence of historical knowledge. Ignorance often makes simple solutions attractive. But in human reality, abstract principles and desirable goals always have to be fitted to local circumstances, and as that happens, the costs of sudden and especially of violent change often seem nearly equal to the defects of existing situations, however deplorable actual governments and ongoing social conflicts may be.

Current events in Central America and the Caribbean illustrate this difficulty well, though similar problems confront men and women of goodwill in Africa and Asia, too—and, for that matter, at home within the United States. Let me conclude, therefore, with a few remarks about our Latin American neighbors and some glances at domestic frictions.

Since the proclamation of the Monroe Doctrine in 1823, the United States has claimed a privileged position in Latin America. For a while, the United States was sporadically aggressive, defeating Mexico in 1846 and annexing vast though thinly inhabited domains of California, and the desert southwest. We also defeated Spain in 1898, annexing Puerto Rico and securing a naval base in Cuba. In 1903 the United States provoked a revolution in Panama in order to establish a regime that would allow the construction of a canal across the isthmus, and as recently as 1916 the U.S. Army invaded Mexico in pursuit of Francisco Villa. Even after 1936, when a "Good Neighbor" policy became official, United States armed forces have intervened occasionally in trouble spots, most recently in Grenada (1983). Short of direct and public dispatch of U.S. armed forces to the scene, policies and actions aimed at overthrowing unfriendly governments and at helping friendly regimes continue to the present. Some are conducted in secret, others quite openly.

Within the United States, memories of these and other aggressive actions in the past are usually glossed over. Good intentions in the present and beneficial material results of our past interventions seem to justify what was done. Look at what we have made of California! And at the usefulness of the Panama Canal! But in Mexico, Central America, and the Caribbean the same past looks very different. Distrust of the United States, even when best intentioned, seems fully justified by what we have done and continue to do in pursuit of our real or supposed interests.

Two other factors exacerbate relations. One is the cultural difference between Spanish-speaking (Latino) and English-speaking (Anglo) versions of American society. Latinos combine cultural and racial heritages from both the Indian and Spanish past, and in some parts also embrace an African heritage as well. At one time, Spain was the greatest power of Europe, and Spanish pride in their empire, their Church, and their culture was proportionate. Until well after 1776, Mexico City was a far grander capital than any city of Anglo America, and even after the industrial and commercial transformations of the nineteenth century had raised the United States far above Mexico or any other Latin American country, the old Spanish pride remained—all the pricklier for the comparative weakness and poverty that put Latinos so much at the mercy of Anglo America.

The second factor that makes our relations with the countries to the south especially difficult is their very rapid rate of population growth. This means that in many parts of Latin America and in the Caribbean islands old ways of making a living on the land by subsistence farming are running into crippling difficulty. There is just not enough cultivable land on which young people can live in the old way. Migration to town is one reaction to unacceptable village prospects, but life in overgrown towns, where innumerable similarly situated rural folk are also trying to make a living, is exceedingly difficult. Just as in Iran (and many other parts of the world), this creates a mass of potentially disaffected citizens, who are ready to respond to a variety of revolutionary ideals, sometimes Marxist, sometimes not. Indeed, revolutionary forms of Christianity have a considerable hold in Latin America today, much to the distress of more conservatively minded clergy, from the pope on down. And almost everywhere, national feeling carries an anti-U.S. edge.

Divergent popular memories of past relations between the United States and the peoples of Latin America make for a difficult and potentially dangerous future. Citizens of the United States, however ignorant of details, cherish a generally positive view of our past encounters with the peoples to the south. They, on the other hand, have a pervasive political distrust of their neighbor to the north; conservatives fear cultural contamination, while revolutionaries regard the United States as their principal foreign enemy. Such divergences of outlook make all relations at least potentially awkward. Greater knowledge of the facts of the past—on both sides—might reduce frictions a little. But the situation is sure to remain volatile far into the future, because, until population growth has somehow been checked, satisfactory lives for millions of poor people in Latin America and the Caribbean will remain out of reach; and the possibility of sudden political upheaval, expressing mass frustration, will continue to trouble public life.

Migration to the United States offers another possibility for Latinos, Haitians, and others, but the arrival of large numbers of such immigrants in turn creates new social problems within the borders of the United States. In this fashion, foreign and domestic politics merge into one another. What the United States does to admit or exclude immigrants, and what it does to help the peoples to the south to manage the population crunch ahead, will be important for our own domestic history as well as for what happens in Latin America and the Caribbean. Economic interests, ethnic feeling, and moral principles pull both ways—and on both sides of the borders. What we do and what others do will be colored by what we know of the past and believe about the future. In such a delicate and potentially damaging situation, the more we know about ourselves and those with whom we share the Western Hemisphere, the better.

Yet even with an exact and dispassionate understanding of history, nasty problems will remain that are quite insoluble in the short run. Knowledge will not save us from difficulties and dangers, nor will it prevent angry confrontations and violence. It does make us less likely to provoke such collisions unknowingly and unnecessarily. But national and other sorts of group rivalries will not dissolve by mere wishing. In an inflamed situation such as that in Latin America, it is always best to have a clear idea of what others think, feel, and believe before we act so that unpleasant surprises like those that have lately beset U.S. policy in Asia, the Middle East, and Latin America will be fewer, and the world will be a bit safer for everyone.

It is a goal much to be desired, and the way thither is clear: better education in our schools, and careful teaching about the history of countries with cultural traditions and public memories different from ours. The mistake Americans make is to assume that everyone is, or at least wishes to be, just like ourselves. They cannot conceive of the idea that other peoples wish to remain different, even though they would like to be as rich and powerful as the United States has been. Indeed, the closer they are to us geographically, the more energetically they wish to maintain existing differences.

Getting used to that sort of pluralism and managing that kind of difference asks for sensitivity and forbearance on all sides, but especially on the side of the richer and more powerful partner. That puts a special responsibility on the American public and on our schools. Thoughtful exploration of history— global as well as national and local—is the only way to begin to cope with the task. The need is urgent. We can meet it only if we really try to improve teacher training and upgrade the way we teach history and the social studies.

PART IV

New Wine, New Bottles

CHAPTER 9

Returning History to the Elementary Schools

by CHARLOTTE CRABTREE

Returning history to the elementary school curriculum is one of the decade's major movements for school reform. This movement is not, of course, without its critics. Certain school folk, wedded to assumptions that have dominated the elementary school curriculum for over fifty years, strongly protest the change. Children, they argue, cannot attain the perspectives of historical time and therefore are incapable of understanding the past. The immediate surroundings and present-day world that children daily experience are rich enough, these critics maintain, to serve as the subject matter of their curriculum. Forays into distant times they cannot understand, or studying about people they cannot place in historical perspective, are a poor and irrelevant curriculum alternative for the young.

Such objections to the teaching of history must be addressed by those who speak for history in the education of school-age children. Fortunately, these objections yield in the face of what we know from contemporary studies of childhood learning and development, and from tested practices in a good number of forward-looking schools, public and private. This chapter will explore such evidence and consider its implications for building an appropriate curriculum in history for the elementary school years. It will also refer to certain institutional constraints that for so long have effectively barred history from most years of the elementary school and that must be challenged if history is to reemerge as an important study in elementary education. At issue is the long-lived and sacrosanct "near to far" or "expanding environments" curriculum model. This is the curriculum adopted over the past half century by virtually all school systems in the nation and strongly sustained by the nation's textbook industry. Up to grade five, this curriculum has little or no historical content; instead, it emphasizes the sociological and economic aspects of children's lives in the family, the school, the neighborhood, and the community. Only recently have some important curriculum alternatives emerged, offering promise that long-needed change is indeed under way.

The most comprehensive and so far successful challenge to the constraining assumptions of the near-to-far curriculum model is the recently adopted *History–Social Science Framework for California Public Schools, Kindergarten through Grade Twelve (1987).* The framework committee that drafted this document included classroom teachers and curriculum leaders from the schools and historians, social scientists, and learning and curriculum specialists from universities and from research and development centers. Every issue that arises when considering change in the elementary school curriculum was soundly debated by this group. One by one the arguments barring history from childhood education fell, and the curriculum that emerged reflects the accord achieved within the committee for a history-enriched and, in four years out of the seven from kindergarten through grade six, a history-centered program of studies. The most enthusiastic proponents for this change were, in the end, those best qualified to judge: the experienced elementary school classroom teachers on the framework committee.

What arguments rallied the forces for change? First among

them was the evidence that the monolithic march from near to far in the customary expanding environments curriculum model is supported neither by developmental psychology nor by research in children's learning. Through circulation of correspondence received by committee member Diane Ravitch from four eminent educators, each a seminal thinker in his field, the committee was provided searching appraisals of the validity of the expanding environments model.

Philip Phenix, philosopher and Arthur I. Gates Professor Emeritus of Teachers College, Columbia University, wrote on May 24, 1986:

> The self/family/community/region progression is presumably based on the notion that learning must proceed within the context of the known and familiar and only gradually move out into the larger domains of the unknown and unfamiliar, as the child expands his or her experience. But such a view seems to me a recipe for boredom and sterility, doing poor justice to the expansive capacities of the human mind. Although teaching must obviously take account of where the student is, the whole purpose of education is to enlarge experience by introducing new experiences far beyond where the child starts. The curious, cautious, timid presumption that the limits of expansion are defined in any one grade year by the spatial boundaries defining the expanding boundaries dogma is wholly without warrant. Young children are quite capable of, and deeply interested in, widening their horizons to the whole universe of space and time and even far beyond that into the worlds of the imaginary. And all this from kindergarten years or even before! The concentric circles of the expansion dogma appear to be nothing more than a very adult conceit designed for administrative control through neat curriculum packages unrelated to the realities of human learning.

Joseph Adelson, director of the Psychological Clinic at the University of Michigan, wrote on June 2, 1986:

> I have never understood the logic presumably informing the "expanding environments" approach, since it did not seem to me to be based on anything we knew about cognitive development in

that period. . . . Let me assure you that there is nothing in cognitive science, or in developmental research, which supports the present way of doing things. In fact, I'm quite convinced you could turn the sequence on its head, going from the community to "myself," without its making much of a difference. Furthermore the current curriculum is quite vapid and seems to induce a considerable degree of boredom.

Bruno Bettelheim, the distinguished psychoanalyst and professor of education who for twenty-six years directed the University of Chicago's residential school for highly disturbed children, wrote on May 7, 1986:

> . . . the presently taught curriculum in the social sciences in the early grades is a disservice to the students and a shame for the educational system. Children of this age are sufficiently surrounded by the realities of their lives. The texts I have seen do not explain [their] sources or meaning to the child, and only repeat in tritest form a reality with which they are all too well familiar. . . . What children of this age need is rich food for their imagination, or a sense of history, how the present situation came about. . . . What formed the culture of the past, such as myths, is of interest and value to them, because these myths reflect how people tried to make sense of the world.

Jerome Bruner, a cognitive psychologist long recognized for his distinguished contributions to the field of instructional psychology and to the study of thinking, included in his correspondence of May 12, 1986, the following analysis along with references to his recent book, *Actual Minds, Possible Worlds,* for its treatment in depth of the reasons behind his comments.

> There is little beyond ideology to commend the Hanna [i.e., expanding environments] program and its endlessly bland versions. Whatever we know about memory, thought, passion, or any other worthy human process tells us that it is not the known and the settled but the unknown and the unsettled that provokes the use of mind, the awakening of consciousness. . . . Starting kids off with the familiar and then going out to the unfamiliar is

altogether in violation of this deep principle of thought and of narrative.

These are stinging comments from four of education's most erudite and respected scholars. With one accord, all judge the expanding environments model to be the offspring of unsupported dogma, and in violation of known principles of learning. Phenix, in a final passage, concludes his indictment of the model with the judgment that it is both "irrelevant to the child's growth and unduly limiting of normal development of thought and feeling," strong words indeed.

By contrast, three of these four scholars address the question of alternatives, and specifically propose history and literature as developmentally appropriate studies for the young child. "History and literature," Phenix wrote, ". . . are essentially concretizing presentations of human experience and are therefore best suited as a basis for social studies. These forms of symbolizing enlarge the child's experience as interesting unanalyzed wholes, from which as he grows older abstractions can be developed." Among the virtues of history for children, Phenix noted its ability vicariously to provide "a sense of personal involvement in exemplary lives and significant events, and to supply an appreciation of values and vision of greatness, all this within the context of moving narrative and dramatic appeal."

Parents, children's librarians, and teachers of the young have long known the power of superbly written biographies, myths, legends, folktales, and historical narratives to capture children's imagination and to hold their interest. Incorporating enduring themes of conflict and personal choice; of sacrifice and responsibility; of power and oppression; of struggle, failure, and achievement, sometimes against overwhelming odds, these stories connect in powerful ways with these same impulses and conflicts in children's own lives. They engage children vicariously in the experiences and perspectives of others, expand their ability to see the world through others' eyes, and enlarge their vision of lives well lived and of their own human potential. By helping children transcend their present moment, such studies allow them to understand that they are neither the first to confront these problems nor are they alone in making the human journey.

Whether these biographies, stories, and narrative histories are drawn from the recent past or from some long-ago reaches of human history is not the critical factor in their accessibility to children. Rather, it is the nature of the story told, its power to capture children's imagination, to draw them into the historical event or human dilemma, and to speak to children on matters of enduring worth that should determine its selection for inclusion in the curriculum.

The continuing appeal of Aesop's fables, the tales of Robin Hood, or the frontier adventures of Wilder's *Little House* series speaks to this point. So, too, does the extraordinary success of the Odyssey and Aeneid programs for elementary schools that are sponsored by the American Philological Association through teacher institutes supported by the National Endowment for the Humanities and operating today in individual schools throughout the United States. Reporting on the success of these programs in their schools, one group of teachers commented that the *Aeneid* addressed universal questions as it recounted particular events. Students who are so frequently uprooted themselves can identify with the Trojans in their wandering. Those who have lost a parent or a friend can mourn with Aeneas as he returns to Sicily for the funeral games. When students discuss the merits of the Trojan journey—asking whether Aeneas should remain with Dido, whether he can choose his fate to any degree, or whether the Trojan women were justified in burning the ships—they participate as actors in the past. They come to understand circumstances and character, to begin to grasp their own part in the spiritual civilization that continues into the present moment.

Observing how children's involvement in the adventures of Aeneas had spread throughout all levels of one elementary school, one observer from the National Endowment for the Humanities asked why children found these programs interesting. "They're so exciting," came one child's eager answer, immediately echoed by the rest. One is reminded of Paul Hanna's 1935 indictment of the history-centered programs he was seeking to displace. He objected to them, he said, because they provided children a "happy life for the few hours they spend in school"! Given the terrible strains of the depression years, children should, he argued, be engaged instead in community studies of the great social and economic ills then facing the nation. Without passing judgment here on the quality of those history programs of the mid-1930s, we can nonetheless be impressed by the depth of pleasure and personal meaning children have found in history when it is presented in ways they can relate to and understand.

But can these programs really be historical if children have not yet grasped the structure of time and chronology necessary for placing long-ago events in their proper historical context and relationship to each other? The answer, of course, lies in understanding and working with the developmental sequence through which children achieve such higher powers of historical thinking. Truly revealing accounts of the human story, rendered memorable for children through the organizing power of the narrative, address first things first. By vicariously enlarging children's own experience and deepening their understandings of human experience in general, good and true stories furnish the intellectual foundations upon which subsequent historical analyses may be built.

It matters not that young children have no well-developed mental maps of time for placing people's adventures in temporal relationship according to years, decades, centuries, or eras. For young children it is enough to know that they happened "long ago." "Before I was born?" younger children may ask. "Oh, yes." "Before my mother was a little girl?" they may continue. "Yes, even before that. Long before that." "Oh, long ago," they may solemnly conclude. And soon more refined time concepts take shape, as teachers help children to differentiate today, yesterday, long ago, long long ago, and reaching back to the beginnings of recorded history, long, long, long, long ago. The concept of time, children quickly learn, is a spatial one, involving the mental construction of a continuum of time along which events can be arranged. Historical dates are irrelevant in these early stages, and do not belong in the primary classroom, for the mathematical understandings that make their relationships meaningful are not yet formed. But the *spatial* learnings that allow these critical insights to develop are under way.

Within their first five years of life, young children, we now know, develop ordered sets of causal, spatial, and temporal relationships that render their world not a "buzzing, booming confusion," but a causally ordered, comprehensible, and meaningful environment. This process starts in early infancy. Infant cognitive development is now found to be surprisingly abstract, with infants even in their first year of life using rules for dealing with time, space, and causal relationships. "Well-mothered" infants, interacting with a caring adult, repeatedly play out motion-time-and-space patterns that test their environment and disclose its regularities. Interacting with their environment in this manner, and then "turning over in their minds" what they have discovered, infants develop their sense of order and their rules for operating within the regularities of their world.

As infants gain mobility, their exploratory world widens, and with it the complexity of their temporal, spatial, and causal understandings. Depending upon the richness of experiences available to children and the nurturing they receive from supportive and interested adults, the years of later infancy can be a time of increasing problem solving, creative play, and abstract symbolization. By ages three and four, well-nurtured children regularly produce "mental maps" or cognitive patterns of time and spatial relationships that they have abstracted and detached from the specific activities that brought them forth.

So important are the growing networks of spatial understandings developed during these early years, that psychologists who have studied their development suggest that "spatial knowing" may in fact be paradigmatic for the ways children come to know. Spatializing the nonspatial, their findings suggest, may in important ways facilitate learning even in nonspatial fields.

This notion is intriguing and brings to mind two down-to-earth examples of teachers who have had good success developing in young children some early understandings of historical time. One, an inner-city supervising teacher, constructs with them a temporal sequence of events using a clothesline and clothespins that together create a visual representation of the passage of time. The children first tie a knot near one end of the clothesline to represent "today," and then clip at that place a recent photo of themselves. They then move back a little distance along the clothesline to attach a baby picture brought from home. After the teacher read a biography of Martin Luther King to the class, the children made drawings illustrating the Reverend King's life and clipped them to the line farther back in time. The Reverend King, they then understood, lived earlier, a contemporary of their grandparents. A "long, long ago" story is similarly illustrated and attached to the time line still farther back, a process repeated as each new historical story is read to the children. Inevitably, in this classroom, dinosaurs are brought up, and children decide that these precursors of the human story should occupy a place on the time line long, long, long, long ago.

Spatially displayed on this clothesline's representation of time, these historical moments become easily accessible to children in terms of their "before" and "after" relationships, and establish a sense of historical continuity that lays a foundation for deeper historical analysis in coming years. Another teacher, this one of somewhat older children, lacking bulletin board space, converts the classroom windows along one side of her room into a time line. Then, as her third graders' study of their local history unfolds, they paint pictures to illustrate specific historic events and tape them to the windows, in succession, to represent each succeeding period of their study, from prehistoric to modern times.

By the middle elementary school years, mathematical understandings are sufficiently developed to allow children's meaningful identification of years, decades, and centuries on the basic time line, and their accurate placing of events according to the date of their occurrence. By this age, children's intellectual development also makes possible some kinds of historical analysis that link events in terms of their antecedents and consequences, and support early stages of causal analyses.

One should not, of course, overreach the limitations of children's thinking in this regard. Analyzing the multiple causes of an event (the Revolutionary War, for example, in a fifth-grade study of American history) is a developmental achievement in preadolescence and requires strong instructional support. It is important to remember that in history, as in mathematics, science, or any other field of learning, the process is developmental. Children will not approach all at once the intellectual complexity demanded by historical analysis. It is folly, however, to suggest for that reason that history should not be taught in elementary schools. Leaving all such instruction to later secondary years, when the adolescent mind has emerged "recognizably adult," would be incomprehensible in other fields of school learning. We do not defer all instruction in mathematics to the senior high school, and then rush students through textbooks of a thousand pages or more in a forced march to "cover" the material for which no prior foundations or deep personal interests have been established. Only in history are such approaches seriously contemplated and applied. The unhappy results are widely evident in the displeasure high school students take when a meaningless parade of facts, dates, and hurried events is imposed upon them.

Historical thinking, including causal analysis, takes many years to acquire, but its foundation is rightly laid in the elementary school. One approach being developed for older children in our work with experienced Teacher Associates in the National Center for History in the Schools incorporates striking a balance between (1) rich narrative history that moves the chronology of events along in a compelling and interesting manner, and (2) specific "dramatic moments" in the narrative that the students plumb, looking for deeper meanings of the selected landmark events and turning points in the historical narrative.

In this approach, the continuing narrative provides the historical context in which the dramatic moment arises. This helps children to think about the specific event in terms of the choices presented to the people caught up in that event, and the consequences set in motion by the decisions they then reached and acted upon. The dramatic moments chosen are those that best bring the period vividly alive for students out of the problems and actions of real men, women, and children who were caught up in the forces of their time. Selections from historical documents, artifacts, journals, diaries, newspapers, and literature provided by the Center's historians help to create for children a sense of being there and help to foster historical empathy, the ability to see the world through the eyes of others and to sense what it must have been like to confront their problems without our present-day understanding of how things were eventually to turn out.

We want children to realize that events were not inevitable, that uncertainty is the nature of the human journey, that the choices people made (and make today) carry consequences and that those consequences, good or ill, limit and influence the choices available to those who follow. We would have children come to understand that none of them is an island in this great human journey, but that we are all linked in individual and corporate responsibility for the quality of life our judgments and decisions bestow upon those who follow. The crowning achievement of historical study—a growing wisdom in contemplating the complex web of human affairs and judgment in charting one's own path—will not, of course, be reached in elementary school, but proper approaches to the early study of history are critical stages in that quest, important beginnings for lifelong learning that must continue to develop.

In developing analyses of "dramatic moments," we use history as the great integrative and synthesizing discipline of the social studies. For example, understanding historical events requires geographic analysis. History occurred in specific places, and knowing the influences of geographic factors upon events is often essential to students' understanding of them. Studying why societies developed when and where they did reveals the critical geographic relationships among site, resources, people's technological skills, and settlement patterns. Studying human movement, a dominant theme throughout all of history, must include the motivations that drove such migrations as the European conquest and colonization of the Americas, the enforced transport of millions of Africans to these regions, the westward movement of American settlers into the trans-Appalachia and trans-Mississippi territories, and the northward movements of Mexican settlers into their vast territories in present-day Western and Southwestern United States.

Similarly, dramatic moments often call forth economic analysis, for the course of events within American and world history is frequently related to a society's ways of production, exchange, and consumption. Fifth-grade studies of European exploration, colonization, trade, the development of labor systems, national expansion, war, and peace settlements during the colonial and early national periods of American history are all topics requiring economic perspectives. World history, too, requires economic perspectives: studies of the development and diffusion of agriculture by early peoples, urbanization and the rise and fall of ancient city-states, and how trade and economic expansion in the ancient world shaped cultural life and changing patterns of dominance among ancient societies.

Elementary school studies of U.S. and world history, necessarily centered in the lives of people in order to motivate and sustain children's interest, also provide fruitful opportunities to explore with children the important role of ideas, religion, and the arts in shaping individual behavior and group culture, and in instituting or restricting change. No adequate understanding of human history is possible, we believe, without examining people's most dearly held religious and secular beliefs and the influences of those beliefs upon their ethical and moral commitments and choices, and upon their actions in political, economic, and social life.

Upper elementary school studies of early America are meaningless, for example, if children have not considered the important roles of religious belief, tolerance, and intolerance in the lives of seventeenth- and eighteenth-century colonials. Why did the Puritans come to America and how did the covenant theology they espoused influence the character and course of early American history? Why did Anne Hutchinson come to trial, and why did life in Jamestown, Philadelphia, and Plymouth differ so fundamentally in social organization and practices? Such questions clarify for children how religious beliefs, values, and assumptions helped to explain the actions and consequences that followed. In the colonial and revolutionary period, and throughout their studies of the new nation, and the continuing immigrant experience, it is important for children to consider instances when belief, tolerance, and/or intolerance interacted to influence change. The drafting of the First Amendment religious freedom clauses in the Bill of Rights is such a case, and one that should be examined with children in light of expanding religious pluralism throughout our history and in their own communities today.

By later elementary school years, children are also ready to examine polytheism and animism in the ancient world; the historical foundations, spread, and teachings of the great monotheistic religions of the world—Judaism, Christianity, Buddhism, and Islam—and their influences on the lives of people and on the societies of which they were a part. Dramatic moments in the history of early Mesopotamia and Egypt, Israel, the Middle East, Rome, India, and China will provide the context. Historic records, sacred texts, art, and architecture from these moments disclose to children what societies revered, aspired to, and feared, and somewhat explain why some major beliefs have endured across much of human history into our present day.

Finally, historical analysis can open to older elementary school children some important perspectives on political leadership, institutions, processes, and change. While certain political abstractions may be beyond children, well-selected dramatic moments in American and world history, on the other hand, can provide them with concrete examples of political decision making, and illustrate for them how leaders and institutions function under different governmental forms. For this approach to succeed, children need clearly written materials that bring complicated subjects like the U.S. Constitution within their understanding. They will also benefit if they can enter actively into the issues of the time by debating, dramatizing, or role playing. Out of these experiences children can begin to develop some understanding of democratic and non-democratic politics and institutions, the values on which those institutions are based, and their impact on the lives of citizens, whether in ancient Athens or Sparta, Rome or Han Dynasty China, colonial Massachusetts or the newly established American nation under its Constitution and Bill of Rights.

It should be obvious from the foregoing that a history-centered curriculum for elementary school children can be a rich curriculum indeed, drawing widely upon learning in the social sciences and the humanities and deeply involving children through activities that are developmentally appropriate. It remains, then, to consider how such a curriculum might best be organized for learning across the elementary school years. The California curriculum framework offers one approach by beginning each year of instruction from kindergarten through grade two in the child's immediate present and then moving outward in space and back in time to enrich children's geographical and historical understandings. The model is sometimes termed the "here-there-then" approach to widening children's horizons and expanding their universe into realms far beyond their immediate surroundings. With the middle grades the curriculum becomes history-centered and adopts a rich narrative approach in grade three studies of local history, grade four studies of state history, grade five studies of American history through 1850 (and of the immigrant experience 1850 through the present day), and grade six studies of the ancient world, in which children will have developed interests through the lively literary selections in mythology, folktales, narrative histories, and literature provided throughout the preceding grades.

A second approach, also recommended by the Bradley Commission's 1988 guidelines for history in schools, follows the conventional "expanding environments" curriculum but includes yearly historical and literary studies that connect with that year's topics of family, neighborhood, or community, thus wrenching them free from the narrow presentism from which they now suffer. By incorporating literary selections and historical studies of children, families, communities, peoples, and nations throughout the grades, this modification opens for children far richer and more engaging materials than most now enjoy.

A third pattern recommended by the Bradley Commission centers around yearly instruction in literature and primary documents that are then studied in relation to the historical times they bring to life. The pattern is, essentially, a child's version of the "Great Books" approach to curriculum making, with literature used to take children into adventurous excursions through historical periods.

Are teachers ready for such changes? Are they eager to enliven and enrich the historical and literary curriculum for children? Our wide experiences with teachers in the field strongly suggest that this is the case. The elementary curriculum has become so thin, so skills-driven, so intellectually sterile and boring to teachers and students alike, that teachers are reaching out with enthusiasm for a curriculum that returns to classrooms the pleasures of stories worth telling, of ideas worth pursuing, of adventures that capture and hold children's attention and lead them into the historical perspectives that help each find his or her place in the long sweep of human history.

CHAPTER 10

Public Culture: Inclusion and Synthesis in American History

by Thomas Bender

History has become much more difficult to teach in the course of the past generation. The reasons are many; some lie within the discipline of history itself, others spring from changes in our general culture. Certain problems can be remedied rather easily by public policy, assuming a political will to do so—for example, restoring chronological history to a central place in the social studies curriculum. But such political remedies can succeed only if they are preceded by the solution of deeper intellectual problems in the field of history itself. Schoolteachers, students, and citizens alike suffer from the serious deficiencies to be found in contemporary historical writing.

To begin with, helpful textbooks are hard to find. The teacher looking for a compelling narrative synthesis of American history will look far and wide—and without success. Not since Charles and Mary Beard's *Rise of American Civilization* (1927), written for the general public, and David Saville Muzzey's texts for secondary schools—*An American History* (1911, 1925), *A History of Our Country* (1936, 1948, 1950, 1955), and *Our Country's History* (1957, 1961)—have there been, as

Frances FitzGerald pointed out in *America Revised* (1979), the authoritative, storytelling texts earlier generations read.

FitzGerald's enormously illuminating work leaves one with the impression that the problem is with textbook writing and publishing. What she tells us about the way textbooks are "developed" by teams of consultants and editors rather than written by historian-authors is disturbing, but there is also a prior problem. It is not simply that the story is not being told in a compelling way. It is that we historians are not sure how to frame and tell the story. We are no longer confident about what constitutes the veritable story of American history. Few if any leading historians today are ready to propose the terms of a new synthesis of American history. The vast and rich historical literature produced in the past quarter century has not, alas, fallen into a coherent story. We have many wonderful pieces but little sense of how they form a national history that can be narrated in a connected, compelling way.

Teachers and citizens, then, are stuck in a situation in which professional historians and the discipline itself are incapable of providing the kind of historical writing that would satisfy either pedagogical or civic purposes. And because publishers have accepted the necessity to respond to various and diverse group demands for inclusion, the American history narrative has been further dissolved by the practice of "mentioning" or even featuring various groups in an ad hoc manner, without integration or synthesis. The result is the fragmentation of the American story. Instead of a clear notion of a national past, historians are giving us many partial pasts, the history of many groups, often in splendid isolation, with little suggestion of how or whether they make up a nation or a society beyond themselves.

On one level, there seems to be a conflict over whether history is about representation or about meaning. Is the primary task of historical writing to confer legitimacy on every group through representation, or is it to achieve interpretive understanding of the whole society and its past? Is it possible to have the latter without sacrificing the former? I propose that it is, and

I propose that we can acquire interpretive understanding only by relating the parts to the whole, by integrating them and not, I emphasize, by ignoring them or obscuring them. Here John Dewey serves as my guide. In a chapter on "Meaning" in *How We Think* (1909), Dewey explained that all knowledge and all science is aimed at grasping the wider meaning of particular objects and events. In elaborating, he observed that the "process always consists in taking them out of their apparent brute isolation as events, and finding them to be part of some larger whole suggested by them, which, in turn, accounts for, explains, interprets them," and renders them "significant."

The tendency toward fragmentation and dissolution of national history is most apparent in the writing of American history, but it is evident in other national histories as well. Few people have historically possessed more nationalistic self-confidence than the French and historians of France, whatever their own nationality. Yet Theodore Zeldin's recent two-volume contribution to the Oxford History of Europe, *France, 1845–1945* (1973–77), offers not a unified narrative but a series of forays into disparate topics that undermine any notion of narrative or nationhood, producing what the anthropologist Claude Lévi-Strauss, in another context, called *bricolage*. In similar, though not precisely analogous, ways it has become more difficult to conceptualize the history of Western civilization or the history of the world. How can one any longer write or teach about traditions of our inheritance, whether it is the "progress of Western civilization" or the "rise of the West," without devaluing the "margins" where most human beings have lived? To do so would remarginalize the very groups being rediscovered in current historical writing and rightly added to our sense of the past.

For some commentators the dilemma is easily solved. They would simply return to the old story. It was good for us, they say. It will be good for the next generation. Hence the call for a return to the "classic" texts of American and Western civilization, with a few exceptional women and minorities tastefully thrown in. Of course, that could be done, but much would be lost in the process, and much potential gain would be sacrificed.

First of all, it is doubtful that the story as we once studied it in school could retain its old compelling force. Second, so much that is important to our children's understanding of the world they inhabit would be omitted, distorted, or obscured. The easy way will serve us badly. It amounts to a refusal to face the circumstances of contemporary life. Who would want to build the education of our children upon such a refusal? We must seek the solution to the problem of synthesis on terms that are at once contemporary and compelling, on terms that will best incorporate our best historical scholarship, old and new, and that will best illuminate the way our society has worked. Only then shall we clarify the present as well as the past.

What we seek is not merely strong and vivid writing, though surely we want that. Nor is there any question about whether or not we need narrative history. We do. But what we must yet determine is how to locate a narrative principle, a focus or a plot into which we can incorporate the vast body of new and diverse historical knowledge about individuals, groups, and social practices heretofore slighted or invisible in written history. How can we make all of this new historical knowledge hold together as narrative explanation of national and, for that matter, international development?

Before we can address the problem of new syntheses for history in the schools and for our civic discourse, we must inquire more deeply into developments both within and without the discipline of history that have made it peculiarly difficult in our time to write narrative American history that is at the same time lively, honest, and coherent. Put briefly, the twentieth century has seen a remarkable extension of the territory of history—moving beyond governments and battles, presidents and generals—to the lives of ordinary people. Thus public life, the traditional subject of history, has been dramatically extended in twentieth-century historiography. And beyond public life, in the past two decades historians have delved deeply into the private dimensions of the past, into home and family life, health, sexuality, and more. (In France, a multivolume history of private life is currently engaging many of the country's finest historians, and the volumes are being translated and published in the United States as quickly as they come out in France.) The inventiveness and creativity of much of this scholarship ranks with the finest achievements of the historical intelligence, but no one has yet figured out how to incorporate this vast mountain of fascinating and important work into a general synthesis, at least not into one that is explanatory and interpretive rather than merely descriptive and enumerative.

Especially in the American context, the transformation in historical writing has been associated, sometimes directly, sometimes indirectly, with a "rights revolution" of unprecedented scale. And it has been a rights revolution organized on a group basis, with Indians, women, the elderly, Blacks, the handicapped, and others establishing individual rights within the context of group politics. Hence the resonance between developments in the wider culture and in the discipline of history. Both exhibit a strong tendency to focus on particular groups in society at the expense of a wider civic or societal view. I would not wish to be misunderstood. For both history and society, great benefits have been achieved through this particularistic perspective. But now both our civic life and our historiography are clearly in need of some principle of unity, one that nourishes and respects difference even while laying out a common ground for individual and group relations, a common ground for civic education and civic action.

Our task is not simple, because over the past generation historians have to varying degrees rejected traditional elites and core institutions as the proper, or central, subjects of history. The reasons are various, but two stand out. First, the already mentioned "rights revolution" sensitized historians as well as others in our society to the exclusions that marked much of our earlier history writing. Second, that revolution, along with the disaster of Vietnam and the Watergate scandal, undermined many people's respect for the core institutions and traditional elites in American society.

It is important, however, to remember that this was not an exclusively American shift in historiography. In Europe as well, writers and readers have been drawn to studies of ordinary folk, rather than to the established elites and institutions of power and authority. One cannot help thinking that this tendency marks our generation's own cultural moment in the West, which is characterized by a deep ambivalence about political and economic power and by an interest, at least partly compensatory, in the dignity and distinctiveness of ordinary people whose voices have been lost, repressed, or simply not attended to.

Let us look at two European examples. In the 1950s the prominent French historian Emmanuel LeRoy Ladurie wrote a massive book on the vast subject of the condition of the peasantry through the medieval and early modern periods, treating peasants always in the aggregate. But in the 1970s he wrote a very different kind of book, one that became an immediate best-seller in France and, after its translation in 1978, in the United States. *Montalliou* is an account of the religious, sexual, and material life of a medieval mountain village, explicated almost entirely from the diary of one man. The reader is drawn close to the daily life of a half dozen medieval villagers, close enough to suspect that much of the book's popularity arose from the voyeurism its sexual detail encouraged.

At about the same time, Carlo Ginzburg, the brilliant Italian historian, achieved international acclaim for his reconstruction of the mind of an extraordinary, yet very ordinary, Friulian miller in the fifteenth century. We learn in *The Cheese and the Worms* (English edition, 1980) what books passed into his hands, but also how in the context of the Reformation and Counter-Reformation he interpreted the words on their pages. It is an astonishing experience to be so close to the mentality of a common man who lived half a millennium ago. Again, the traditional institutional subject, the Reformation, is pushed to the background, even if crucial to the book in providing a stage for the central character.

The recent work of Ginzburg, LeRoy Ladurie, and many other historians reveals a novel assumption: "local knowledge," as anthropologist Clifford Geertz calls it, is inherently general, if not always universal, in its significance. A heightened concern for the texture of culture and experience has encouraged close study of very limited historical phenomena to achieve an ethnographic account, or, in another of Geertz's phrases, a "thick description." Again, the results are exciting, but how does one work them into narrative synthesis of national history—or, even more difficult, Western or world history?

Within these general historiographical developments, we must consider the somewhat peculiar American emphasis on the study of particular groups in American society, groups defined by class, ethnicity, race, age, and sex. This focus on groups may in fact provide certain advantages for the historian and teacher who would synthesize our history. For one mode of synthesis would be to find a common frame for considering the relations among groups (as well as among individuals in groups) as they contribute to the shaping of individual, group, and national life.

Such synthesis is more easily proposed than accomplished. In the past few decades an astonishing amount of work has been devoted to the study of immigrants, workers, the poor, Blacks, and women. Although this scholarship has brought into our historical consciousness groups that had been excluded or insufficiently considered by traditional narrative historians, the results are only the raw materials for synthesis. We know more today than seemed to be possible twenty years ago about immigrants, workers, women, and slaves; but this has given us surprisingly little added understanding of the interrelations of race, class, ethnicity, and gender in the formation of American society and culture—or even in the making of individual lives. We have not studied these segments of American society in ways that are relational and thus helpful to an interpretation of the whole.

Our circumstance is an ironic result of the success of American historical writing in this century. In the process of reaching out to incorporate more territory for historical narrative, historians seem to have turned historical writing inside out. Since the time of Thucydides, history has usually meant the history of public life, the doings and sayings of the governing classes. One of the great achievements of American historical writing, something accomplished with a deep awareness of the distinctive qualities of modern democratic life and politics, is the vast expansion of historical concern to embrace all of society. When Charles A. Beard and James Harvey Robinson advocated, in Robinson's phrase, a "new history" at the beginning of this century, they sought to enrich the understanding of public life by expanding its dimensions. It never occurred to them that the effort to reach out to all of society could eclipse or render more difficult a narrative interpretation of public life itself.

The circumstance in which we find ourselves has, therefore, been developing for some time. Its full dimensions and implications, however, have until recently been obscured. The Progressive synthesis identified with Beard (and which provided the structure for Muzzey) exhausted itself in the 1940s. The image of society, the principle of synthesis, embedded in Progressive historiography, as Lionel Trilling pointed out in *The Liberal Imagination* (1950), was easily grasped and was of a piece with American middle-class beliefs. Society in that view was moved by the conflict of material interests, with the "people" on one side and with various and nefarious "special interests" on the other. Most important of all, there was a direction to that history. Progressives, predictably enough, believed in the idea of progress. That belief and commitment gave movement and significance to their narrative, and hope to their readers.

We can no longer believe in that narrative as it used to be spun. The bipolar array of conflicting interests seems too simple to capture the complications of identity and contention in modern society. Nor is the relatively simple psychology of human motivation the Progressives assumed any longer compelling. Their idea of progress did not survive the Holocaust and the bomb. After World War II the teleological belief undergirding the Progressive narrative as well as the usual configuration of dramatic action in history were both undermined. Historians found themselves unable to generate a narrative. The history of the 1950s, often called consensus history because it no longer stressed conflict of interest in the manner of Progressive history, was one response to that emerging difficulty. Without being too explicit about it, historians abandoned narrative development, emphasizing continuity, particularly of the liberal tradition, rather than dramatic story. It was a synthesis, but more structural than narrative.

In the late 1950s, John Higham, writing in *Commentary* magazine, observed that the drift of historical writing in that decade revealed a tendency to homogenize our past. While historians had been fascinated since the 1930s with the different interest groups making up American society, the differences that defined such groups now seemed to be without consequence. Just why historians and Americans generally were hesitant to acknowledge the divisive possibilities of difference is not entirely clear. To a considerable extent, it was assumed by historians and social scientists that for all our apparent economic and social differences, unity was real, to be found in a set of common and democratic American values, values that clearly and permanently distinguished American democracy from Fascist and Communist totalitarianism.

The rise of the subfield of intellectual history supported the assumption that a cluster of core values unified the American experience over time and across groups. The significance of economic and social difference seemed to pale. Social diversity was subsumed into a "consensus" of American democratic values. In historical studies of the American past and in sociological studies of the American present, difference was everywhere, but it did not lead to conflict. Rather, it seemed to nourish a pluralistic equilibrium. Different groups were absorbed into a pattern of static, settled American values; assimilation was simple, direct, and apparently totally successful.

The obvious tension between heterogeneous social elements and homogeneous intellectual ones made the search for a workable narrative plot daunting. Yet Richard Hofstadter, the most distinguished of that generation of American historians, had embarked before his premature death on a prospective synthesis on the order of the Beards' *The Rise of American Civilization*. It is hard to know whether Hofstadter could have overcome the obstacles to this ambitious task. There is some reason to believe he might have. He shared Beard's concern with the history of public life, with politics, but at the same time he was impressed by the many significant groups making up American society. He once characterized his own work as a "literary anthropology" of "groups and classes." In his major works, most notably *The Age of Reform* (1955), he had balanced in a single narrative the center, the public and political life of the nation, and at least some of the groups that were still working out their relations to that center.

During the late 1960s and 1970s, the number of groups embraced by historical writers was multiplied, while respect for the public life and political institutions of the United States was shaken. The result was that the historical center, in Yeats's famous phrase, did not hold. Groups and classes were increasingly studied on their own terms, not in relation either to the center or, for that matter, to other groups, and certainly not subordinated to a set of common American values.

The most innovative work done in the past fifteen years, whether by social or intellectual historians, has explored the diverse cultures of groups in American society. But this work differs fundamentally from that of the older "new" history of Beard or Hofstadter in that it is not concerned, at least not mainly, with the relations of those cultures to the larger public world. Rather, it is devoted almost exclusively to the private worlds of trade, occupation, profession, and locality; of sister-hood, race, ethnicity, and family. If the elites were too much in the past studied in isolation from the masses, the compensatory shift all too often results in the study of laborers in isolation from capitalists. It is a history of parts that assumes each part somehow to be autonomous. One gets no image of the whole, whether of a single life or of the society. Studies of workers, for instance, too often may forget that the individual who is a worker is also a Catholic, female, German, mother, and still more—all categories that invite a new and different specialized inquiry. How, then, can one assess the relative salience, at any given moment, of all the elements of such multiple identities? And how can such current work reveal how various social groupings relate to each other and to elites, either in real life or in historical narrative? The relational sense is missing, and at a moment when it is most needed. Perhaps an image of the whole is too far from our grasp at this point, but surely a sensitivity to the various relational experiences of groups is possible and it would be illustrative of the historical process.

At the present moment in historical writing and in civic life, the most promising prospect for a principle of synthesis seems to be a focus on what I have elsewhere called "the making of public culture." I think it is possible to begin to move, both in writing books and in teaching in classrooms, to a notion of a national synthesis, but with "the nation" understood in a new way. It is not a given, a fixed container into which everything and everyone must be fitted. Rather, the nation needs to be understood as the ever-changing, always contingent outcome of a continuing contest among social groups and ideas for the power to define public culture—and thus to define both themselves and the nation as a whole.

What is the notion of public culture and how might it work to pull together the fragments of history that inundate us? The answer requires that something first be said about the politics of synthesis. It is no secret that the recent tendencies in historical writing, often oversimply called social history, have been much criticized by both academic and political conservatives. It has been conservatives who have most loudly lamented the decline of good, old-fashioned narrative history. My reservations should not be associated with that conservative campaign against social history and the supposed politics of its practitioners. Nor would I want readers to assume that a commitment to synthesis implies a desire to wash out conflict and oppression in the American past that social historians have been so anxious to reveal. It is both a mistake and unjust to identify all calls for synthesis with antiradicalism or with a refusal or inability to appreciate either the methodological achievements or the political significance of social history. If my criticisms of social history find support among some political and methodological conservatives, my way of achieving synthesis will, on the other hand, probably disappoint them.

What is needed is a strategy of synthesis that enables historians to go beyond partial analysis, that allows them to reclaim the public realm, where groups interact to make national politics and culture. A useful principle of synthesis must create a vivid sense of the way American society works. That, more than names and dates, is what readers carried away from *The Rise of American Civilization*. Names and dates are means to the end: critical historical thinking and a genuine *explanatory* understanding of the development of the nation and society in which we live. Not long ago, a retired professor of literature recounted for me his memory of reading the one-volume edition of *The Rise of American Civilization* in high school in 1930, the first year it was available in a one-volume edition. The central interpretive issues of the book remain clearly in his mind—as do its literary qualities—more than a half century later. Who could retain for as long as a week the point of even a single chapter of today's textbooks, which enumerate so much and give causal explanations of so little?

By placing the making, and remaking over time, of public culture at the center of a narrative, one can, I believe, incorporate into a new narrative synthesis the rich social history available to us in a way that will illuminate the relation of groups to each other and to the prevailing definitions of public culture. The study of public culture is more than conventional political history. Rather, it embraces the wider, general subject of power, whether political, economic, social, or cultural, in public life. The notion of public culture embraces a wide range of manifestations of power in society—from the institutional power of the state through the more subtle power of various cultural phenomena, not least the power of citizens to establish terms of public debate, for example, new definitions of poverty or class.

To describe the public culture of a society is to explain how power in all its various forms, including tradition itself, is contested, elaborated, and rendered authoritative. The public world, in other words, is not a given. It is historically constructed, the product of a contest waged, not necessarily fairly, among various social groups and also between inherited conditions and the desire for change. What individuals and groups seek in public life is, at a minimum, legitimacy and justice. At times, of course, one group or other will seek domination by defining the nature of public culture and of American nationality in ways favorable to itself and unfavorable to others. Narrating such searches—for legitimacy, justice, and advantage—is one approach to a needed synthesis.

The advantage of a focus on our evolving public culture is that it allows us to bring together the many elements of society (and of historiography) that otherwise stand in isolation. The point is not to homogenize the experience of various groups, but rather to bring them, with their defining differences, into a pattern of relationships. Once they are in such a relational frame, it is possible to get beyond the parts to a sense of the whole, and of the larger issues of the American society.

In our own lives, we are intensely aware that we are constantly appraising the relation of our private feelings, interests, and experiences to the standards of public culture—whether it is presented to us in school, in newspaper and television, in political debate, in public spaces, or in advertisements. To write or teach about the public culture without attending to the private dimensions of life at the same time is inadequate to the way we live and interpret our own lives. To ignore such dimensions is to cast aside some of the most insightful matter that historical scholarship is now producing. What is presently so exciting is the emerging prospect of a new synthesis that will bring together the public and the private dimensions of history in a single compelling narrative.

At the center of such a synthetic narrative, both as a focus and as an analytical device, we must develop a historical notion of public culture, at once the arena for the play of groups and cultures and interests in society and the product of that play, not infinitely malleable or responsive but not absolutely resistant either. It is this always-changing public culture, and not a series of distinctive group experiences, that reveals and establishes our common life as a people and as a nation. Understanding our peoplehood demands not an assumption of sameness but, rather, a relational sense of the differences that mark and make our society.

Such an approach invites some hard questions about our society, but they are questions citizens and students not only ought to ask but want to ask. Why have some groups and some values been so much—or so little—represented in public life and in mainstream culture and schooling at any given moment in our history? How have the lives, values, and politics of particular groups affected the larger public world? And how, in turn, were they affected by the prevailing patterns of public culture and state authority? With the public center thus restored, it becomes possible to ask whether the interests and values of particular groups are, or were, justly represented in society and to ask, as well, whether the public culture unjustly denies, or denied, the legitimacy of certain groups' most deeply held beliefs, whether about morality, art, or politics.

These are questions that students can be drawn to explore. What are the various motives and forces behind the underrepresentation or denial of such beliefs? Are they all unjust, or does the larger society have legitimate reasons to resist certain group interests and beliefs? Through such questions teachers may bring students to the central analytical and moral issues in the making of public culture. And they may open a way into the study of particular groups and of their relation to the whole, and to the dominant ideas, practices, and institutions of their time and place. What teachers can do is to focus student curiosity by showing that the central American story is an unending historical process, for which students may find causal explanations and on which they may come to their own moral judgments. Again, history teaching of this sort does not mean that we stop studying particular groups. What it does mean is that we consciously and explicitly relate them to the larger historical process of human interaction in the formation of public culture.

In time, one hopes, teachers in the schools will have textbooks that do this work of synthesis. But even now one can begin using the materials provided by historical scholarship to start asking the kinds of questions that will initiate exploration of how various groups have worked at shaping and being shaped by the public culture of their time. A synthetic approach to American history does not always require a complete work of synthesis. Rather, it requires only the willingness to think about and to present particular material in relational terms. So we return to John Dewey's injunction to seek "significant" meaning.

The progress of historians and teachers in thinking about our society as a whole, in thinking about the shape of a synthesis that incorporates groups and dimensions of experience previously omitted, is directly related, I think, to our chances for success in renovating and reinvigorating our civic life. Our ability to reassert a civic purpose as a people, as a nation, will be achieved only in tandem with the work of rethinking our history in terms of an inclusive synthesis. The work of political incorporation in our contemporary life will press us to think about the task of historical interpretation—and vice versa.

CHAPTER 11

Old and New Patterns for the History of Western Civilization

by THEODORE K. RABB

Teachers of Western civilization could be forgiven if they have reached the conclusion that their subject has become fragmented beyond coherence by new historical methods and subjects that were unknown a mere fifty years ago. Certainly their predecessors did not have to concern themselves with the experiences of beggars or criminals, wetnurses or wives, printers of almanacs or keepers of parish registers. The history of the West was a magisterial progression, often violent and oppressive, but basically exemplary. It revealed how democratic freedoms had developed, how great cultural achievements had been shaped, and how increasingly sophisticated economic and social structures had been formed. The chief actors were unmistakable: great political leaders, prophets of revolution, creative geniuses in the arts and sciences, and masters of entrepreneurship. The emphasis might change, and the story might become more complex, but its contours remained clear. The essential materials that students were asked to master did not vary widely from year to year or school to school.

The first cracks in this comfortable assurance appeared in

the years after World War II. During the 1950s, there began to be felt the effects of a revolution in historiography that was under way in France. The members of the so-called Annales school were focusing attention on the material conditions— terrain, resources, food, and disease, among others—that, as they demonstrated, have influenced societies profoundly. At the same time, the related pioneers of historical demography were revealing unsuspected patterns in age at marriage, life expectancy, and other fundamental features of daily life. Within a few years other new subjects had come to be recognized as essential means of understanding the past: magic and superstition, poverty and crime, attitudes toward children and death, gender roles, psychological states, climate, popular belief, and a whole collection of topics known by their French name, *mentalités*. Not only was the content of this historical work unfamiliar, but so, too, was its form. Instead of concentrating on such traditional sources as ambassadors' reports, attention was being given to folktales, doctors' records, tree rings, and similarly esoteric materials. And they were being interpreted with the help of techniques learned from anthropologists, psychoanalysts, demographers, climatologists, linguists, and other previously remote colleagues. The result was the writing of articles and books that Leopold von Ranke might not have recognized as belonging to his discipline.

A closer look, however, suggests that the ties binding recent research to the great themes that have occupied historians since Thucydides are not so strained as they may at first appear. It is true that scholars no longer stand quite so directly on their predecessors' shoulders, but in the final analysis they turn out to be surveying essentially the same terrain. What links even the most unexpected results of current work with the preoccupations of earlier generations is a set of fundamental themes and questions. They may take on new guises or emerge from new types of inquiry, but the continuities are visible nonetheless. All historians are still drawn to a small cluster of central issues and problems that, however approached, remain at the heart of the discipline, and will probably continue to fascinate our successors as long as the field is studied and taught.

It would be impossible to draw up a comprehensive list of those issues and problems that would be acceptable to every member of the profession. And yet one can certainly identify a number of representative examples that will suggest how recent innovations can be related to the efforts of centuries of scholarship, for the most notable exponents of the Western historiographic tradition, ever since it was created by the ancient Greeks, have always sought to understand the past in terms of questions that persist precisely because they are ultimately unanswerable. The ten that follow are indicative.

1. How and why do societies change?
2. When societies compete with one another, what makes for success or failure?
3. How does a society cohere, and how do some groups within it gain and retain authority over others?
4. At what point, and why, does political and/or social conflict erupt, and how is it resolved?
5. What are the causes and consequences of economic success?
6. Why does a distinct outlook or "culture" arise in a society, and why does it change?
7. How are religious beliefs related to political, social, intellectual, and economic developments?
8. Are individuals as important as underlying structures in bringing about change?
9. By what arguments or presentations of evidence does a historian most effectively explain the events of the past?
10. Are there general lessons to be learned from history?

In some form or another, every one of these questions is addressed by either Thucydides or Herodotus, and they can be found, too, over the centuries that followed, in writers as diverse as Guicciardini, Gibbon, and Burckhardt. Despite claims that the new directions of the past half century have transformed the field beyond recognition, it is significant that the very same questions still animate the craft's current practitioners. Indeed, the last question, the lessons to be learned from history, remains as salient as it has ever been. When presidents justify their policies, or new problems arise, the past is still the natural point of reference. For instance, a major part of the effort to understand the climatic change, especially the global warming, of recent decades is an effort to learn lessons from the past: to discover how previous societies have dealt with catastrophic environmental changes, and how we can adapt their effective remedies to our own situation. Even when historians are not lending their skills to such practical pursuits, and are solely concerned with finding new ways of investigating their subject, they remain close to the classic questions of the field. An example taken from a newly minted and innovative subdiscipline that seems unconnected to older traditions, the so-called history of popular culture, will make the point.

Even scholars who had doubts that "popular culture" really existed, let alone had a recoverable past, and therefore dismissed its students as followers of "kitchen sink" trivialities, had their eyes opened by an extraordinarily persuasive representative of the genre, Carlo Ginzburg's *The Cheese and the Worms*. This attempt to reconstruct the world view of an ordinary miller named Menocchio, who lived in a small northern Italian town during the sixteenth century, unearthed a set of beliefs and attitudes that most previous generations would have ignored as insignificant. Using the records of two Inquisition trials—the second time the tribunal did not realize it had examined Menocchio already—Ginzburg was able to recover the strange mix of semi-pagan and magical ideas that were combined in the writer's fantastic cosmology. The solid earth, he believed, had coalesced like the butter and cheese that form out of milk, and human beings had appeared spontaneously, like the worms that suddenly materialize in fruit. Eventually Menocchio was condemned for heresy, and his hometown was rid of an embarrassing nuisance who had loved to press his ideas on his neighbors. It was a charming, though sad, little story, but how could the tribulations of this bizarre character, in his obscure hometown, throw light on any long-standing issues of historical research?

The answer is that Ginzburg's book is a work of history, and not of anthropology or antiquarianism, precisely because it connects with some of the great themes that have animated research into the age of Reformation and Counter-Reformation. By asking how average Europeans reacted to the struggles over faith that swirled about them, Ginzburg is extending, not replacing or ignoring, the standard concerns of sixteenth-century historians: Why was religion so important in people's lives? How did the authorities react to unorthodoxy? What was the relationship between belief and other aspects of life? Each of these issues is central to Reformation research—for instance, to the many shelves of scholarship on Luther. And they can also be linked to such persistent questions as the ten listed above, especially to number seven, the linkage between religious and other developments, in that Menocchio's career helps us to understand much more clearly the limits of political and intellectual authority in the sixteenth century. Ginzburg's research may be highly original, and cause us to look at the past in fresh ways, but it still fits naturally into the ancient traditions of the field.

That realization—that history has not lost the outline familiar to previous generations, but is instead filling in the outline and adding new colors and dimensions—is crucial to the effective teaching of Western civilization. The old monuments have not disappeared, but they have been both reshaped and surrounded by landmarks hitherto unknown. Although political chronologies are still the bedrock of the discipline, more levels now have to be considered, and the issue for the teacher is not whether to abandon the standard accounts, but how to enlarge them in a fashion that will reflect current research.

For some, that process seems so complicated that they have abandoned it entirely and given themselves up completely to one of the proliferating alternatives. Thus, the history of Western civilization is reduced to urban history, the history of women, the close study of "the totality" of just one period, to self-history (where the students conduct community research), and so forth. Alternatively, the subject is taught, not for the information it offers, but for the mental processes it requires and promotes: the ability to synthesize disparate information, to assess plausibility, to produce coherent narratives, or to define values when making comparative judgments. All of these approaches have their merits, and none is irrelevant to the task at hand. The real concern is that, on their own, they offer so partial a view—in both senses of that phrase, since they are one-sided in implying that, say, the urban experience can embody all of history, and at the same time they are limited because they restrict the scope of historical inquiry to just one context (such as urban life) for analysis. The result is to leave students without a full sense of the field and its place in humanistic education.

The responsible teacher must therefore try to find a balance between the ancient verities and the exciting innovations. What the developments of recent years have demonstrated is that there is no single way to achieve that balance. Yet it is also clear that there is an inherent logic in introducing students to Western history through the progression that the discipline itself has followed—that is, by starting with the high political and intellectual achievements of each major period, and then grafting other forms of analysis and understanding on to that solid base. The most effective way of conveying the sweep and perspective that provide the classic reasons for studying the past, without at the same time neglecting the many topics and approaches that have come to the fore in recent years, is to enliven the basic chronology with case studies like Menocchio's. And that is the approach adopted in the presentation of the patterns and themes in Western civilization that follows.

The first prerequisite is to give students a sense of the major eras into which Western history is appropriately divided. The principal divisions and subdivisions are most usefully presented as follows:

I: The Ancient World (to 400)
1. The Ancient Near East
2. The Greek City-States
3. The Hellenistic World
4. The Roman Republic and Empire

II: The Middle Ages (to 1300)
1. The Dark Ages
2. The Carolingian Era
3. High Middle Ages and Crusades

III: The Early Modern Period (to ca. 1750)
1. Renaissance and Reformation
2. Overseas Expansion
3. The Birth of the Modern State
4. Scientific Revolution and Enlightenment

IV: Modern Times
1. The Age of Revolutions
2. The Nineteenth Century
3. The World Wars
4. The Contemporary World

Although each of these periods has its special character, and teachers will vary in their emphasis (many courses, for example, omit the earliest segments), it is important that there be consistent attention to a number of basic questions so that continuity can be maintained and distinctions more sharply drawn. In every period, the major political, economic, and cultural landmarks are the essential foundation for more particular questions. There is no point in reading about Menocchio unless one has some understanding of the nature of the Reformation and Counter-Reformation, or of the conflicts and authorities that have elevated or crushed other Menocchios at other times.

What are the fundamental questions? The list of ten given earlier is a reasonable place to start—all are relevant to each of the periods just outlined. And they will enable a number of

patterns and themes to emerge that are faithful to recent work
yet still echo the achievements of earlier generations of historians. The outlines of those themes can now be presented in the
context of the four main blocks of time into which the subject
naturally divides.

In discussing antiquity, it is important to establish the basic
characteristics through which societies are understood: their
institutions, their politics, their economies, their class relations,
their beliefs, and their intellectual and artistic creations. What
makes the ancient world so effective a starting place is that these
six structures took such different forms in the chief Mediterranean civilizations of the period: the Egyptian, the Assyrian,
the Hebrew, the Persian, the Greek, and the Roman. As a
result, students can perceive the wealth of choices available to
any organized society, and they can learn how the contrasts
provide both perspective and a means of analyzing the nature
of distinct cultures. Why, for example, are the Greeks remembered principally for their political ideas and esthetic achievements, while the Romans excelled primarily in such practical
skills as warfare, engineering, and the law? Why could Athens
and Sparta defeat Persia, but Carthage could not defeat Rome?
Why did civil war in some places (e.g., Athens versus Sparta)
lead to political decline, while internal conflict in other (e.g.,
Rome during the late Republic) encouraged political consoli-
dation? It is the constant comparison that leads to understanding, and is one of the main lessons to be gained from a survey
course.

It should be easy for the teacher to bring to life the great
figures of each period and context, from Moses to Hannibal,
because they have inherent appeal. Less simple to grasp are the
analytic approaches historians use. Yet here, too, antiquity
offers ideal material, for the striking divergences among history's different civilizations allow one to identify ways of judging
the relative strengths and weaknesses of various political, economic, and social systems. One can see a society as a coherent
whole, in which all aspects—from preferences in sports to taste

in building—relate to one another, and thus to characterize, compare, and assess individual historical developments. Why do some cultures encourage political freedom, while others do not, and what can we learn from their experiences? Can we relate our answers to the kind of art these cultures produced? And so on. Laid out for exploration are both the narrative sweep and the specific problems of interpretation that have formed the grist for traditional as well as contemporary historians' inquiries.

When we move on to the Middle Ages, the tempo and the content change dramatically. Many of the questions will remain the same—why do empires rise and fall, (e.g., the Carolingian); how has the West related to its neighbors (Byzantium and Islam); and why do certain political, religious, economic, social, and intellectual systems take hold, lose their grip, and connect to one another?—but the materials with which they are answered will be more monochrome, less kaleidoscopic. During the eight centuries after the fall of Rome there is a uniformity to the features of Western civilization, and the issues its people faced, that sets the period apart from the dramatic disparities of antiquity. The task of the student is not so much to contrast and compare as it is to focus on coherence and change over time.

It may be that a teacher will want to emphasize the persistence of certain questions throughout history. If so, medieval Europe will provide a new and distinct context in which to investigate such issues. As in antiquity, the role of religion, struggles over political authority, the relationship among classes, the rise of cities, and the forms of creativity are central topics, and afford the opportunity to study both continuity (from antiquity and within the Middle Ages) and new directions. Yet the Middle Ages can also stand on their own as a source of traditions and commitments essential to Western civilization—such as university education and common law— and as an abundant mine of materials (chronicles, biographies, legislation, contracts, and sermons, to name but a few) that reveal not only the nature of historical processes but also the ways in which they can be analyzed. From the classic problems, such as the appeal of the crusades, the reasons for the papacy's ascendancy and decline, or the aims of Gothic art, to the newer questions, like the position of women, the influence of magic, and the effects of climatic change, it is a period rich in issues that can appeal to students even as they learn how to understand their past.

By the end of the Middle Ages the foundations should have been established. At this point, a history class should have a basic comprehension of both the substance and the techniques of the historical enterprise. What it must now come to terms with is a series of great movements that shaped Western society into configurations that begin to seem familiar to denizens of the twentieth century. The essential topics, though their order can be changed, are as follows.

At the outset, the Renaissance was the first (and far from successful) deliberate attempt in Western history to make a clean break with the past. Its advocates, the humanists and their patrons, from Petrarch, Machiavelli, or the Medici, to Thomas More, Henry VIII, and Montaigne, spawned revolutions in politics, literature, international relations, warfare, and scholarship, and all of these changes—both the progressive and the regressive—deserve some attention. The generations that followed, the carriers of the next great movements, the Reformation and Counter-Reformation, transformed not just religious institutions and outlooks, but social and political attitudes. In these centuries, too, three political and economic movements helped turn Europeans into the dominant group of peoples on earth: the building of centralized states, the expansion into continents overseas, and the development of a commercial and industrial system known as capitalism. Finally, the early modern period witnessed the unfolding of the Scientific Revolution and of its unprecedented progeny, the antireligious and hypercritical era of the Enlightenment.

Fitting these movements together, and seeing them as the products of a single civilization, is the prime task of this segment of the course. But this period also happens to be the setting for much of the pioneering historiography of the past century. From Jacob Burckhardt and Max Weber to Fernand Braudel and the innovators of recent decades, the new ideas of historians have been animated by the search for the origins of the modern world, and the early modern period has therefore, quite naturally, been a favorite hunting ground. Consequently, it is in this segment of Western civilization that excellent opportunities arise for introducing students to current approaches, such as Ginzburg's study of Menocchio. Acquiring some familiarity with the principal movements of the age has to come first, but it is precisely against that background that the innovations can be given the excitement they deserve.

The modern world, despite its greater familiarity, is the hardest to teach because now the dangers of fragmentation increase. The age of the American, French, and Industrial revolutions can settle into straightforward patterns, but the nineteenth century offers almost an embarrassment of riches: titanic figures from Berlioz to Bismarck; bewildering shifts and advances in politics, empire-building, economic organization, science, and the arts; and overwhelming amounts of information about every level of society. To do justice to all aspects of this turmoil as well as its continuities, and at the same time indicate how the historian's horizons are expanding, is almost impossible. Here the teacher has to select more arbitrarily than before, but by this stage such choices can be turned to pedagogic advantage. The students should now have sufficient grounding in the themes and techniques of the subject to be able to set particularities into a broader perspective, and it can be a highly effective teaching device to discuss openly with them the bases for the choices. It could be, for example, that the course has emphasized the connections between politics and culture, has focused on the questions about coherence, conflict, and culture (numbers three, four, and six) in our list of ten. In that case the students themselves might be able to figure out that they will be paying special attention to topics like the Revolutions of 1848, Victorian values, or the political uses of opera, rather than to the second Industrial Revolution or the Crimean War.

The problem of choice does not subside in the twentieth century despite the obvious themes of world war, fascism, communism, and the modern movement in the arts. In the contemporary period the history of the West requires a global compass, a consideration of worldwide interactions vastly more complex than any that have come before. Again, the teacher has room to select where the emphases should lie, while encouraging the students to make the larger connections. At the same time, however, they should again be involved in the process of choice—to continue the example from the nineteenth century, this might favor such topics as the Russian Revolution or the influence of film rather than military strategy or the Spanish Civil War. Moreover, in this period the discipline of history may itself become a subject for study, because the new interests it has displayed are intimately linked to changes taking place throughout our society and culture.

What this outline suggests is that it is possible to sustain the traditional patterns of Western civilization, and do justice to the major issues that have exercised historians for centuries, without neglecting the new departures of recent years. It is true that the approach just outlined does reject—except for the twentieth century—the demand for an expansion of Western into world civilization. The techniques may indeed be applied on that larger canvas, but the danger (here considered decisive) is that the dilution of narrative coherence will then prove fatal. It is already hard enough, amidst the proliferation of topics and techniques, to retain pedagogic coherence even within the huge Western tradition—which, as our own ancestor, is the first element of the past with which American students should become familiar before they branch out. The problems become overwhelming when other, quite independent traditions, have to be integrated into the story. Rather than trying to encompass this vast agenda, therefore, the teacher would be well advised to concentrate on the task of finding a place in courses for the new departures of recent historical scholarship without fragmenting the discipline and its educational purposes. Indeed, the enterprise has to be limited, and not try to embrace geographic as well as topical enlargements, if these additions are to serve as expansions, and not confusions, of our traditional vision: as means of enlivening and broadening well-established structures.

The argument here is that only by keeping to one basic story, that of the West, can the teacher effectively use the technique of regular set-pieces—class sessions on popular culture, demography, gender roles, or the like—in order to blend both traditional narrative and new approaches. To take on other mandates is to blur this already difficult purpose beyond recognition. Only if limited to Western civilization can this means of presenting history become a comprehensive introduction that neither abandons the classic topics—and thus risks incoherence or too narrow a concentration—nor, on the other hand, ignores the latest specialties.

It may be that the magisterial assurance of the historian of fifty years ago will never return. We can no longer believe in a single, accepted subject matter, in unmistakable moral lessons, in exemplary models for action and behavior, or in the policies and beliefs of the elite as the essence of the historical enterprise. Instead, the traditional subjects, while still serving some of these purposes, have a new value for the teacher: their rhetorical effectiveness as a means of constructing a narrative framework for the subject. After this first stage, however, we can now call on a wealth of topics and methods to achieve a broad, nuanced understanding of the past. Rather than fearing this abundance as an invitation to chaos, the teacher should welcome it as a powerful set of tools that will enable students to perceive how societies function and how they have changed over the centuries. The means are at hand to make history once more the heart of the humanities and social science curriculum in the schools.

CHAPTER 12

Central Themes for World History

by Ross E. Dunn

One day not very long ago, I went into a fruit and vegetable market in my neighborhood. While looking over the avocados, I noticed that the clerks were speaking a foreign language among themselves. I thought it might be Arabic, but I was not sure. So I asked one of the clerks if the owners of the market had come from an Arabic-speaking country. The woman bristled slightly, then replied, "No, we are not Arabs. We are Kooor-dish!" Ever since then, my wife and I have called this store the "Kooor-dish market." In fact, the Kurds later sold it to people of Iranian descent. The Persians in turn sold it to the present owners, who are Arabs of Palestinian origin. Then there is the neighborhood meat and fish market that we frequent. Its proprietors are Arabic-speaking Chaldean Christians who emigrated from Iraq. Indeed, my Southern California city has become so cosmopolitan in the past decade that if I am to appreciate the cultural background and family origins of my immigrant neighbors, I can no longer think of classifying them crudely as "Middle Easterners" or "Orientals." I am obliged, rather, to know whether my neighbor is Kurd or Turk, Persian or Afghani, Palestinian or Syrian, Chaldean or Maronite.

The presence in America of newcomers from such diverse parts of the world is largely a manifestation of particular migratory movements that have developed only in recent years. As I drive down an avenue of my city and see commercial signs in Arabic, Persian, Chinese, Vietnamese, and several other scripts that are totally foreign to me, I wonder whether in their school classes my children will learn something about the places from which these settlers came and why they abandoned their natal homes for California. I wonder how their resettlement relates to the grand, world-scale patterns of migration in the late twentieth century as well as to the three centuries of earlier migration that contributed to the making of the American people.

HISTORY AND WORLD HISTORY

If the young people of my city are to make any sense at all of such issues as world migration, issues that impinge directly on their lives, their school curriculum ought to include world history, and as much of it as possible. Students must be offered the knowledge and conceptual skill with which they can at least begin to address intelligently the great global questions of our time. History must be the foundation of their world studies because only by examining the past will they locate themselves in humanity's drama and come to be aware that the world they experience is the way it is because of social processes that were activated decades, centuries, or millennia before they were born. To limit their global education to reviews of current events or to a purely contemporary study of other societies is to sow on much too shallow ground.

The idea that history education and international competence should be closely tied to one another in the school curriculum has been one of the themes in the national education debate of the past five years. Many teachers and scholars have been demanding that history as a discipline replace conceptually fragmented and excessively present-minded programs in social studies as the core of both the humanities and social science curricula. Many who share that view also specify a program of historical studies that replaces, or supplements, the traditional Western civilization course with one that embraces humanity as a whole.

Many educators, however, express uncertainty, if not alarm, about the practical problems of teaching world history. When teachers whose classroom experience has been limited to American history, Western civilization, or world geography agree (or are ordered) to plunge into world history, they may face multiple challenges of learning large new bodies of knowledge, abandoning topics that have been part of their canon for decades, radically reordering their periodization schemes, finding innovative classroom strategies, and even thinking about history in general as they never have before. Compared to Western civilization or the conventional geography course, world-scale history is still a comparatively unproven teaching field. Every teacher must be something of a pioneer in the search for an effective conceptual approach.

The most common blueprint for organizing a world history course has been simply to divide humankind into cultural or civilizational units, then to address each in turn, usually covering its history over a span of several centuries. Most textbooks take this approach, and indeed most educators and publishers seem to have assumed that world history must be primarily the serial study of a variety of foreign cultures plus the West. For example, Matthew Downey and Douglas Alder, both champions of world history, argue that "instead of discovering only their own Western heritage, students should learn to appreciate other cultures as well. . . . They need to know about cultures other than those of the West if the United States is to compete economically with . . . non-Western nations."[1] In *What Do Our 17-Year-Olds Know?*, Diane Ravitch and Chester Finn recommend that students "study the history of Western Europe for a full year, and the history of other major nations and cultures for another full year."[2]

GLOBAL HISTORY AS THE STUDY OF PROCESSES

The internationalist sentiment behind these recommendations should be taken seriously in all our schools. Defining world history, however, as fundamentally a study tour of civilizations in different parts of the earth has, I think, impeded the working out of a more integrated and dynamic conception of the global past. By assuming that civilizations are disparate chunks of humanity, bounded off from one another in space and time, and that therefore they must be the primal units of historical study, global educators have put themselves up a pedagogical tree where there may be nothing more to do except prune and shape the facts and concepts that are to be taught about each "culture."

The fact is that from the early Stone Age to the present, human beings have interacted in all sorts of aggregations that are not caged within one cultural tradition or another. Indeed, many of the most important events in history, even in ancient times, have been played out on a map bigger than any single country or civilization. If the aim of world history is, as it should be, to make sense of the larger, more extensive patterns of the past, then the patterns themselves, not separate cultures, ought to be the leading categories for sorting out and organizing the raw material that students will be asked to learn.

One of the recurrent complaints against the social studies in recent years has been that they are too abstractly analytical, too lacking in good narrative storytelling. Yet the very concept of "culture," and particularly "traditional culture," is often misleadingly presented to students as something static and immutable, having more to do with archaic institutions, immemorial customs, and ritual behavior than with dynamic and rationally explainable change. History as a series of separate, parallel culture stories is often not very exciting because in the end the narratives go nowhere. One week the students "do" African history, the next week India, and so on. None of the events occurring inside these "cultures" is related to a broader framework of world-historical meaning. So students miss out on some of the choicest dramas of world history, epic accounts played out across continents and oceans. These stories go unrecognized and unstudied because teachers and textbooks have found no way to bring them into the space-time limits of one conventionally defined culture or another.

Let us see how some of the recurrent questions about teaching world history might be answered if we imagine a course that takes the human community as a whole, rather than bounded cultures, as the primary field of study and that stresses in each era of the past the larger-scale patterns of change that have brought the world to its present state of complexity and interdependence. I will use the term "global history" as the most precise way to describe this kind of course, recognizing that the phrase has also and more generally been applied to any history studies that embrace the non-West as well as Europe.

Such a global history would be chronologically organized—that is, it would have a narrative structure, though a looser one than U.S. and European surveys often have. Students would follow a world time line that stirs awareness of the interrelations of societies from one century to the next and that invites continuous comparison of events occurring in different parts of the world. Each primary unit of the course would be organized around an important chain of events (and I use the term "event" broadly to include relatively long-term developments) whose impact was wide enough to involve peoples of differing cultures in a shared experience. These "big" events would provide the common reference point for investigating and comparing other events and trends that relate more narrowly to particular civilizations and cultural groups.

Moreover, such overarching events would also determine the periodization of the course—that is, the major divisions of time to be studied one after another. Making clear to students causal links between one "era" and another on the world-historical level is a challenge because we are so used to thinking about divisions of the past, excepting for the last century or two, only as they relate to particular countries or civilizations. World history cannot, as U.S. and Western surveys have done, trace a single narrative line of history, neatly sliced up, against the background of a relatively unified, coherent cultural development. Creative solutions to the problem of periodization in global history will in every case depend on teachers' willingness to stand back and scan the world scene for significant patterns of cause and effect from greater distances than they have usually done, and at the same time to break through civilizational categories that would predetermine the ordering of historical time.[3]

How might a major unit of study look in a course whose aim is to get students to think "globally"? Imagine an early unit whose primary focus is the invention and spread of iron technology, a historical event of great importance for large areas of Eurasia and Africa between about 1200 and 800 B.C. This development had a transforming effect on societies all across Eurasia and northern Africa. Moreover, set against the very long term of history, it affected much of the Eastern Hemisphere (though not the Western) in a relatively short span of time. The how, why, and where of the spread of iron would give rough geosocial and chronological shape to the unit of study and provide the leading comparative idea from which to launch discussion of other events in China, India, the Middle East, and the Mediterranean region during about a four-hundred-year period.

The objective here would not be to give the unit a narrowly technological focus but rather to provide students with a conceptual trunk line from which to undertake explorations of similarities, differences, and interconnections between one part of the world and another during *a particular period of time*. Students would be invited to think about an important, far-reaching change, such as the social effects of iron tool-making, as an integrated historical process, letting the process itself determine which cultural milieus are to be included in the study rather than fragmenting and obscuring the process by demoting it to merely a subsidiary aspect of the history of this civilization or that. Students could thereby observe events occurring in different parts of the world at the same time and consider how these events might be interrelated or at least compared.

In this course, then, students would at the broadest level of generalization be investigating historical processes rather than "cultures" on the map. By "process" I mean simply an identifiable pattern of change. Historical processes are like stories: They have beginnings, middles, and ends. As in a Western civilization course, students would study processes in different arenas of human action: Some would transcend the frontiers of a particular country or civilization (e.g., the Atlantic slave trade), others would not (e.g., the sixteenth-century Reformation). The aim of this approach is not to deny the importance of cultural forces in history. The ups and downs of particular civilizations are themselves important processes that need to be studied. The point is that the stories of civilizations should not be permitted to limit or confuse the teacher's efforts to help students see the "big picture" of world change in whatever age is being studied. History is distorted and ethnocentrism is only encouraged when we lead students to conclude that civilizations are self-contained and self-perpetuating and that their relationship to neighboring or distant societies is of no real importance. A major drawback of the traditional Western civilization course is its common presumption that the rise of Europe (and of the U.S.) to world economic and military dominance in the twentieth century can be adequately explained simply by looking back over the history of the West, neglecting the world context into which each age of Western history was born.

CONTENT OF A GLOBAL
HISTORY COURSE

Because the human community has moved over the long run of time from a sparse population and the isolated autonomy of small groups to global crowding and intricate interdependence, it is naturally easier to identify complex, large-scale patterns of change in the world in recent centuries than, say, in paleolithic times (except for fundamental but very long-term changes such as the progress of early tool-making or agriculture). Even so, the weeks of a course devoted to ancient history can still center on world-historical events that transcend the conventional civilizational modules. One of these would be the spread of iron already mentioned. Another might be the Indo-European expansion out of Central Asia between about 1700 and 1200 B.C., a phenomenon that deeply affected subsequent history all across Eurasia. A third might be the flowering of Greek commerce and culture from 800 to 200 B.C., a process that could be presented to students not merely as an early episode in the narrative of the "Western tradition," but more accurately and more dramatically as the rise of an Eastern Mediterranean–Black Sea civilization whose language, ideas, and aesthetics proved irresistible to peoples all around the rim of that dual sea and as far east as China.

In the millennium between A.D. 500 and 1500, patterns of human interaction involving very large numbers of people become increasingly evident. The remarkable growth of trans-hemispheric trade and travel, the long-distance migrations and predations of steppe peoples, and the rise of gigantic new empires that spanned two or more major civilizations all indicated the end of a world of divided regions. Indeed, it was during this period that all Eurasia, together with the northern and eastern rims of Africa, began to take on a kind of history of its own, a history that is almost completely obscured in the culture-based course. Some of the big events that might provide the main headings of study include:

- The rise of Islam as a movement not just of the Middle East but of the whole region of arid lands stretching from Iberia to India.
- The near industrial revolution in China under the Sung Dynasty and its effects on trade and economic development all across Eurasia.
- The military, economic, and cultural expansion of Latin Europe, a development that embraced an area stretching from Scotland to Palestine.
- The explosion of the Mongols and the hemispheric consequences of the conquests.
- The Black Death, not only as a chapter in the history of Western Europe but as a trans-Eurasian event that had long lasting effects on Central Asia, China, and the Middle East as well as on Europe.

In working up a syllabus for the modern age—that is, the centuries after 1500—international and truly global patterns are easily thrown into relief. Some of them are commonly taught in the traditional Western civilization course, but more as extensions of European history than as world processes. Some well-used topics recast in the global mold might include:

- Popular revolts and democratic revolutions between 1750 and 1850, not simply as aspects of European or American history, but as movements sweeping the "Atlantic basin"—that is, including Latin America and even West Africa.
- The early industrialization of Europe, not as a phenomenon entirely conceived and brought forth in England, but as a process involving economic interrelations worldwide.
- The New Imperialism, less as a study of intra-European conflicts abroad than as an encounter between Europeans and African or Asian peoples.

Some less obvious topics for the modern age might include:

- The demographic and cultural effects of the worldwide exchange of plants and animals that occurred in the century after Columbus.
- The surge of Islamic expansion in Eurasia and in Africa in the sixteenth century.
- The process in the twentieth century of environmental intervention and planetary pollution and their effects on world population and economy.

Insofar as students begin to think about world history, the remote and the recent past, in terms of such supranational topics as these, they should gain a more holistic view of their global heritage, as well as freedom from the perverse and narcissistic notion that "our" historical experience (America's and Europe's) has for all but the most recent decades been almost completely alien from "theirs" (Africa's, China's, and so on). Our profession has no greater responsibility than to offer students a broad base of world-historical knowledge and conceptual skill with which they may recognize and begin to confront the numerous problems of our planet, problems that no single nation or cultural group can hope to solve by itself.

THE SOCIAL SCIENCES OR THE HUMANITIES: WHERE DOES GLOBAL HISTORY FIT?

Implementing a more process-oriented world history will, of course, take more than merely adopting a new textbook and a revised set of outlines. Other commitments and choices must also be made that may or may not be compatible with the individual teacher's education, habits, and convictions. One question has to do with locating global history's disciplinary "home." Should it be in the care of humanists or social scientists, or of both?

The kind of world-scale history advocated here will inevitably engage the political, social, and economic behavior of people acting in groups (tribes, empires, trading corporations, religious communities, and so on). It will also emphasize many subsurface currents of change, like the effects on society of new technology, of which people were for the most part unconscious at the time the changes were happening. Therefore, teachers well grounded in the social sciences and the sorts of questions those disciplines ask might on the whole be more willing to innovate in global history than teachers inclined to humanistic subjects.

Since the humanities are eminently concerned with the values, achievements, and enduring styles of particular civilizations, some teachers might well be hesitant to offer a course that would constrain them from giving analytical primacy to the cultural and social continuities within each of the great traditions. But a clear choice must be made. A world history course can center on the serial study of several civilizations, stressing chronological strings of causation within each, as is commonly done in Western civilization courses. Or it can focus on the study of world-historical processes, emphasizing for each defined period of history those forces that embraced different peoples in shared experience. It may to some degree do both at the same time, but only at the risk of conceptual ambiguity and organizational confusion if one or the other approach is not clearly, explicitly dominant. Each approach is valid and teachable. But the global alternative, it should be made plain, does give precedence to the interrelations of peoples in each historic age over the cultural factors that divide them.

Since global history does carry something of a social scientific bias, teachers and textbook writers should be warned that the humane and dramatic dimensions of the past are no less important in this kind of course than in any other. If global historians fall so in love with economic systems-building, technological diffusion, or comparative demography that they forget to animate the past with personalities, deeds, and works of the mind and spirit, then their students will remain as indifferent to the discipline as they now generally appear to be. Global history may require new vocabularies and a certain amount of abstract formulation, but its classroom lessons must also be salted with vivid stories, artistic images, and the portrayal of great events and ideas.

GLOBAL HISTORY AND THE PROBLEM OF COVERAGE

When teachers consider world history for the first time, one hears a common refrain: "I could never get past World War Two in my Western civ class. How can I take on global history without running out of time at the Battle of Lepanto?" The simplest solution to the problem of coverage is, of course, to make the program of study longer. At present the world's past is surveyed in one year in most of the schools and universities where it is taught. A two-year sequence of global history is probably to be preferred. California addressed the issue in 1987 by designing a three-year program of courses: ancient history in the sixth grade, A.D. 500 to the late eighteenth century in the seventh, and modern history in the tenth.[4]

Yet even if world history is given generous scope in the curriculum, teachers must still carefully select what is to go into their syllabus and what is not. Skeptics about world history have often contended that such a course is impractical because no one can teach "everything" in a year's time. The charge itself is suspect since any ordering of the past involves a great deal of choosing between one potentially relevant fact and another. Indeed, the typical European history survey excludes mountains of historical information that is significant in some context. I know of no Western civ course that probes seriously into Charlemagne's conquest of Saxony, the commercial dynamics of medieval Amalfi, or the domestic politics of interwar Denmark. Western civ, rather, puts into relief the integrative, transnational patterns of European history (e.g., the Renaissance, the rise of fascism), anchoring them to empirical ground with concrete illustrations, examples, primary source readings, biography, and so on. A successful global history course will follow a similar scheme, except that the historical processes to be studied will often involve a larger scene of human interaction than one civilization or another.

The task of deciding which peoples to introduce to students and which to ignore is easier to accomplish if those choices are related to the world-historical processes to be studied. Australian aborigines might enter the scene only as they figure in a unit on the nineteenth-century overseas migrations of European settlers and their ensuing encounters with indigenous groups. Peoples of the Amazon basin or the Arctic Circle might reasonably be excluded from the course altogether. A textbook aiming to "democratize" world history by awarding a section or paragraph to every ethnic group in every corner of the planet would be chaotic and pointless. On the other hand, a course might go equally wrong if it focuses too narrowly on patterns of change among literate elites and urbanized societies. A genuinely global course could hardly neglect, for example, the tent-dwelling pastoralists of Central Asia, people who seem marginal indeed in modern times but who in earlier ages activated chains of events that reverberated all across Eurasia.

IS GLOBAL HISTORY INEVITABLY SUPERFICIAL?

Even if a global history course is assiduously selective, can time be found for more than superficial study of most topics? The new California *History–Social Science Framework* rightly commends the study of "major historical events and periods in depth as opposed to superficial skimming of enormous amounts of material," and it denounces syllabi and textbooks that make students "feel that they are on a forced march across many centuries and continents."[5] American history and Western civ surveys have long been notorious for skating over the surface of the past. When a world history course requires students to jog breathlessly across the chronologies of seven or eight different civilizations, they might indeed end up with less historical comprehension than they had at the start. We must reject any syllabus that substitutes memorization of countless free-floating facts for unhurried reflection on the meaning of the past.

Like an effective Western civilization course, a good global history avoids frantic exertions to "mention" as many facts and topics as possible. The difference lies in the questions asked. And the kinds of questions global historians should be formulating are far from superficial. Students can study momentous historical processes "in depth" as readily as they can study particular cultures. When they are allowed to rove over the whole world scene, they are likely to perceive important patterns of change that might not be identified at all in their Western civ class.

For example, what would a world-historical approach make of the fifteenth- to sixteenth-century Age of Exploration, a period usually treated in both Western civ and culture-oriented classes largely as a stage in the evolution of the Western tradition? Here are a few of the questions that might be asked: What relationship did European commercial enterprise in Africa and Asia have to the earlier expansion of a transhemispheric trading system run largely by Muslims? Why did Western Europeans succeed in discovering America and circumnavigating the globe when, as of the early fifteenth century, the Chinese were in several respects more likely candidates to undertake those adventures? How did the migration of old-world disease microorganisms across the Atlantic affect the success of Iberian conquest and settlement in America? What conditions all around the rim of the Atlantic led to the forced migration of millions of Africans to America?

Such questions are essential to explaining how the world's peoples and cultures got to be as thoroughly entangled as they are today. To grapple with these issues, students must learn how to think comparatively about the past and to recognize large-scale patterns. Answers to the queries posed in a global history class might be simple and straightforward or confoundingly intricate, but they will require more than superficial thinking and skimming. World history textbooks will probably continue to "mention" more facts than they should, simply because of the diverse requirements and tastes of the teaching market that uses them. But they can become more useful as they strive to integrate world history, to incorporate more discussion of the often hidden streams of change, and to accent comparative analysis.

GEOGRAPHY IN GLOBAL HISTORY

Geography is a vital partner in making world history intelligible. A global approach must inevitably emphasize the pervasive impact of climate, vegetation, and natural resources on the larger-scale events of history. It should also exhibit to students vivid mental pictures of the scenic travels of soldiers, sailors, merchants, and monks, as well as of the migration of religious truths, scientific ideas, and new technologies, spreading here and there over the surface of the earth.

Global history should require students to think about spatial geography, names and places, the locations of major mountains, rivers, islands, and straits, as well as empires, nations, and cities. But they should be discouraged from concluding that political and cultural boundaries are all they need to grasp geographical reality. Rather, they should develop an astronaut's view of the earth, a holistic grasp of the patterns that mountains, plateaus, ocean basins, and winds make in relation to one another. They should, for example, think of the whole Eurasian landmass as a single stage where important historical events have occurred. They should learn why so much history was carried on the oscillating monsoons of the Southern Seas. They should learn about the crucial role of pastoral peoples in world history by seeing that great band of arid land that runs all the way across the Eastern Hemisphere from the Sahara to the Gobi. To learn global history, in short, is to cultivate an integral vision of the world's geographical personality.

CONTEMPORARY PROBLEMS AND UNIVERSAL THEMES IN GLOBAL HISTORY

Whatever innovations teachers make to enliven global history, they would do well, I have argued, to lay the subject out along a chronological line. When it comes to organizing time, they should teach the old-fashioned way, starting somewhere back in the reaches of time and connecting the links of cause and effect as they move forward.

Some educators, however, hold a contrasting view: The study of the past should be wrapped up in a series of essentially sociological, humanistic, or contemporary topics—that is, on the persistent and ever-recurring problems of the race: war and peace, slavery and freedom, human rights, the condition of women, and so on. Such headings, they say, should determine the order of study, and students should be free to slide back and forth in time as they search for the "origins" of each "problem." This approach reflects the ideas of the "new social studies" movement of the past three decades in its advocacy of the study of contemporary issues "in historical perspective."

Many teachers have been skeptical of such a topical approach, and rightly so. In its more rigid forms, topic-centered social studies isolates selected aspects of history from the wider social context in which they are situated, and it treats historical facts as so many bits of "background information" to help explain conditions of the present. Students are denied the opportunity to learn the chronological relationship of events to one another or to contemplate the full range of possible causes and effects of processes being studied. History as data presumed useful to today's citizens erases history as story and drama.

On the other hand, meditations on the universal riddles of humankind should not be consigned brusquely to English and civics teachers. Indeed, a good global history course will not fail to wrestle with at least a few of the immemorial issues that inform our hopes, fears, and moral values. These questions can be embodied in selected themes that weave through the entire course in counterpoint to the narrative story being told. A teacher might select, for example, the impact of nationalism as a leading world-historical theme. When students mentally connect one era with another ("The demands of these African nationalists sound like the same things the leaders of the French Revolution were saying!"), the teacher knows they are following the thematic thread. One caution: play only a few topical songs. Attempting to work the students through too many of the ageless questions, however thought-provoking, can blur the conceptual structure of the course and detract from its central purpose, which is to reconstruct and interpret *history*.

Several prominent educators have argued vigorously in the past few years that since the political and cultural heritage of American society lies largely in the West, the history of the West should dominate the curriculum. Advocates of global education have answered that, yes, our children should learn about Western civilization, but they also must study other cultures in order to function intelligently in a shrinking world and to appreciate the diverse heritages of many new Americans. The argument of such internationalists is valid but inadequate on its own. It assumes that a variety of "world cultures" can reasonably be investigated *ad seriatim* and largely in isolation from one another, and that then the result can rightly be called world history. But their approach obscures the fact that the social context of all history is ultimately the globe itself. And it fails to refute the argument that since the crowded curriculum allows no time for detailed study of several cultures, schools should devote their time to "our own."

The remarkable role of the West in world history must obviously figure large in a global history course. The fact remains, however, that even if the Western tradition shaped must of *us*, the rise of that tradition occurred within a world context that shaped much of *it*. However valuable it is to work the study of Western civilization and several other selected heritages into the school day, the fundamental question is whether we can afford to permit young Americans to graduate without having at least tried to erect in their minds a framework for thinking about the long run of change in the world in something grander than narrow cultural or nationalistic terms. Are the supracultural processes that, in all their complexity, shaped our own world worth understanding? If so, then the search for a teachable world history becomes more imperative every day.

NOTES

1. Douglas D. Alder and Matthew T. Downey, "Problem Areas in the History Curriculum," in *A History in the Schools*, ed., Matthew T. Downey (Washington, D.C.: National Council for the Social Studies, 1985), p. 17.

2. Diane Ravitch and Chester E. Finn, Jr., *What Do Our 17-Year-Olds Know?* (New York: Harper & Row, 1987), p. 208.

3. On the problems of periodization in world history see Peter N. Stearns, "Periodization in World History Teaching: Identifying the Big Changes," *The History Teacher* 20 (August 1987):561–80; and my article "Periodization and Chronological Coverage in a World History Survey," in *What Americans Should Know: Western Civilization or World History, Proceedings of a Conference at Michigan State University, April 21–23, 1985*, ed. Josef W. Konvitz (East Lansing: Michigan State University, 1985), pp. 129–40.

4. *History–Social Science Framework for California Public Schools, Kindergarten through Grade Twelve* (Sacramento: California State Department of Education, 1988).

5. Ibid., p. 5.

CHAPTER 13

History for a Democratic Society: The Work of All the People

by GARY B. NASH

When Bostonians awoke on August 14, 1765, they found a rag-clad effigy of stamp distributor Andrew Oliver hanging from the great elm tree on the Orange Street thoroughfare that connected their maritime center to the mainland by a narrow neck of land. All day townspeople and country farmers participated in the ritual humiliation of this wealthy Boston merchant who had chosen to accept a Crown appointment that proved to be obnoxious to most American colonists. Then, at dusk, a crowd of working people gathered for a mock funeral of Oliver. Artisans cut down the effigy as dark came on, carried it through the streets to the Town House, then marched to Oliver's new brick office near the South End wharves whence the stamps were to be distributed. They leveled the building in less than half an hour. Before the evening was over, the crowd had stomped off to Oliver's luxurious mansion at the foot of Fort Hill and wreaked their vengeance on his stable house, his chaise and coach, and the mansion itself. In the thoroughness with which they pillaged the mansion were signs of the long-standing hostility they bore to a man who for years had disparaged those who worked with their hands.

Twelve days later, the crowd gutted the mansion of Thomas Hutchinson, lieutenant governor of the Bay colony and a man long hated by laboring Bostonians for his haughty disregard for the plight of the economically distressed and his many attempts to dismantle the town meeting system of local government. The fury of the crowd on these two evenings—undoubtedly the strongest denunciation of constituted authority since the overthrow of Governor Edmund Andros in 1688—initiated a chain of events that led to the American Revolution.

At the head of the crowd on both August 14 and August 26 was a twenty-eight-year-old shoemaker named Ebenezer MacIntosh. The son of a Scots-Irish immigrant who himself never escaped poverty in the New World, MacIntosh was a veteran of the Ticonderoga campaign against the French in 1758 and a fervent Protestant. In the early 1760s he became a leader of the South End Pope's Day company, the organization of laboring men that displayed its antipapist beliefs on November 5 (Guy Fawkes Day) each year with pageants and processions that warned of the danger of popish Stuart pretenders to the English throne who would revoke hard-won English liberties.

MacIntosh acted entirely out of character for a poor shoemaker in eighteenth-century Boston. Such uneducated and undistinguished persons were supposed to follow not lead, deferring to the superior wisdom and political experience of the elite. Yet his leadership in the violent protests against the Stamp Act in Boston played a critical role in the politicizing of laboring people—a process that continued in the years after 1765. Patrician revolutionaries soon hustled him off center stage, apprehensive of their own positions if the streets of Boston fell under the control of a poor shoemaker. But briefly, MacIntosh was the man of the day; indeed, he might have been man of the year.

One hundred and ninety years after the Stamp Act crisis and over a thousand miles south of Boston, a forty-two-year-old

Black seamstress boarded a bus in Montgomery, Alabama, sat down near the middle of the vehicle just behind the section marked "Whites Only." Several stops later, after the bus filled up, two white men boarded, and the driver called out "Niggers move back." Three black passengers complied, yielding their seats and standing in the aisle to the rear. Rosa Parks wouldn't budge. Swearing under his breath, the driver pulled the bus to the curb and came back to her seat. "I said move back. You hear?" Mrs. Parks stared out the window, her face expressionless. And in that moment a revolution began that would challenge and ultimately change patterns of behavior in the South and in the rest of the nation, patterns that had never squared with the principles of equality, natural rights, and the idea that all Americans should play their full part in our system of government.

Rosa Parks was arrested on that day in 1955 for not "knowing her place." But her defiance of established authority, like MacIntosh's, touched off a movement that led to a revolution, though this time of a different kind. The boycott of Montgomery's bus system by the city's Black population, inspired by the gritty refusal of Rosa Parks to endure any longer what Afro-Americans had reluctantly accepted for generations, showcased the power of nonviolent protest and, after similar events in other cities by politically awakened Black Americans and white supporters, led to the emergence of Martin Luther King, Jr., as a national leader.

MacIntosh and Parks: two obscure individuals—one white, one Black; one male, one female. Both were virtually unknown beyond their own neighborhoods. Both initiated action that had profound effects on history and then faded into the shadows. Blacks in their celebration of past victories have remembered Parks, whose courageous act is also recorded in the history books, usually in a single sentence, because the civil rights movement was a part of the lives of those who are now writing history books for classroom use. MacIntosh, for the most part, still escapes notice because class-conscious acts have hardly ever been accepted as touchstones of remembrance in American society.

The larger significance of these two individuals is that they demonstrate that social movements, leading to historical transformations, are often touched off or deeply influenced by ordinary people who step outside the roles assigned to them by their superiors. Even if social and political movements are not led by ordinary people, they cannot succeed without the participation of common folk, who, once involved, often alter the course and character of their movements.

The view that history is with the people is not only more fitting for a democratic society, in which it is assumed that an active citizenry is essential to the maintenance of liberty, but it is more accurate. The need for such historical revisionism was seen long ago. In 1856, Frederick Law Olmsted remarked that

> men of literary taste . . . are always apt to overlook the working classes, and to confine the records they make of their own times, in great degree, to the habits and fortunes of their own associates or to those of people of superior rank to themselves. . . . The dumb masses have often been so lost in this shadow of egotism, that, in later days, it has been impossible to discern the very real influence their character and condition has had on the fortune and fate of the nation.

Tolstoy, in writing *War and Peace*, echoed that thought. "To study the laws of history," he wrote, "we must completely change the subject of our observation, must leave aside kings, ministers, and generals, and study the common infinitesimally small elements by which the masses are moved."

The peculiar disjunction of fabricating an elitist history for a democratic society has been challenged for at least a century by a long but thin line of historians connecting the contemporary scene with past generations. The closest the historical profession earlier came to adopting an inclusive approach to American history was during the Progressive period when a number of early twentieth-century historians argued much for the role of ordinary people in history. However, they were almost always inattentive to gender and rarely overcame the virulently racist thinking of the period. Thus, the history of racial minorities found little or no place in their work. A few early advocates of women, labor, and racial minorities took up the cudgels for these groups, but in the main their work never found its way into textbook treatments of American history.

Such early advocacy of a more democratically conceptualized history slumped badly as the so-called Consensus school rose to prominence in the period following World War II. But the revival of a national history sensitive to gender, race, and class has proceeded powerfully since the early 1960s—in ways that would probably have pleased Olmsted and Tolstoy but do not at all please some elder statesmen and stateswomen of the profession today. The presentation of our history has undergone fundamental changes in part because historians of the last generation have been much influenced by the many-sided struggle for social and racial justice in the 1960s and because the social, gender, and ethnic composition of the profession has changed considerably since the 1960s. Black history, though it has attracted some attention for more than a century, became a major topic only when the civil rights movement of the post–World War II period made the country reverberate with rhetoric, demonstrations, violence, and armed government intervention at the local level, and when Blacks and their white allies increasingly became involved in the writing of history.

Attention to the history of other ethnic groups, such as Native Americans, has been prompted by their own increasing social awareness and political determination. Still others, motivated by the civil rights movement of the beginning in the mid-1950s, and by Black power movements and the radical anti–Vietnam War protests of the 1960s, became increasingly sensitive to class consciousness and class conflict as significant themes in the American past, often conjoining such factors with those of gender and ethnicity. When women began to enter Clio's ranks in substantial numbers, and did so because the powerful feminist movement that unfolded in the 1960s began to open up careers in a variety of previously male enclaves, the field of women's history blossomed.

The principle of inclusiveness is central to the attempts of historians who try to write a democratically conceived history today, and this is what sets them apart from the Progressive historians of the early twentieth century who concentrated on the struggles between "the haves and the have-nots" but largely ignored women and racial minority groups. The guiding assumption today is that students can truly learn about the historical processes that have produced present-day societies only when they understand the roles played by all constituent parts of the society under study. Therefore, these historians, often labeled "social historians," strive to include the history of women; racial, ethnic, and religious minorities; and people of all classes and conditions. Moreover, the attempt is to avoid the "powdered-sugar approach"—that is, tacking on mention of women, Blacks, and laboring people—which was the common practice as textbooks began to change in the 1970s. Rather, the effort is to integrate fully the history of these groups in the presentation of the particular period.

History written in this way implicitly seeks to overcome the great man theory of history. Thomas Carlyle wrote in the middle of the nineteenth century that "the history of the world is but the biography of great men," and more than we care to admit, that theory has continued to pervade history textbooks. Of course, it would be absurd to say that great individuals have not played important roles in history, and that some of these notables, acting heroically or despicably, have changed the course of local, national, and international events. The vital task in teaching history in a democratic society is to show the interaction of the great political and religious leaders, scientific geniuses, captains of industry, and military officers with the mass of ordinary people and to show how each group influenced the other.

We cannot understand the Great Awakening of the 1730s and 1740s, the first mass movement in American history, without delving into the role of Jonathan Edwards, George White-field, and other highly educated clergymen. But neither can we understand it without noticing that it was transformed and extended far beyond what its first leaders imagined or desired by women and youth, servants and slaves, farmers, and artisans who often offended the purported leaders by taking the Awakening in new directions. The American Revolution would have looked very different, or might not have been successful at all, without its steadfast Washington, its charismatic Franklin, its sagacious Jefferson; but neither could it have succeeded without the participation of ordinary people, who, once involved, altered its course to the dismay of many from whom they had initially taken their marching orders. The antislavery movement of the antebellum period had its Garrisons, Welds, and Grimkés; but without the willingness of thousands of anonymous individuals, Black and white, to take unpopular and often dangerous stands, it would have failed miserably. Thus it is the interaction of elite and nonelite, the complex and fascinating stories of how social, political, and religious movements changed as elites tried to persuade and enlist ordinary people and ordinary people pushed forward their own agendas in ways that changed and sometimes displaced leaders, that we need to place at the heart of our national history.

In stressing the participation of ordinary people in history, we must also remain mindful that fundamental restructurings of society and economic systems, such as the rise of capitalism, Europe's colonization of overseas societies, industrialization, and urbanization have wrought alterations that ordinary individuals have been relatively powerless to change. But rather than completely dictating human life, these overriding, long-range processes have worked to set general boundaries within which most people carry on their existence, while still retaining the ability to shape their individual destinies to a considerable extent.

Several dangers lurk in the attempts to write history that takes into account all of the constituent parts of which a society is composed. The first is that when we try to include the forgotten people of history, we are often writing about Blacks, women, and laboring people who were exploited and disdained. Covering their past has had a way of turning into victims' history; and, as victims, these groups too often have been seen as passive figures, always acted upon but never themselves the agents of history. Africans were not merely enslaved. Indians were not merely driven from the land. As Ralph Ellison, the Black American writer, has reasoned: "Can a people live and develop for over three hundred years by simply *reacting*? Are American Negroes simply the creation of white men, or have they at least helped to create themselves out of what they found around them?"

To include African slaves, Native Americans, women, immigrant laborers, or any other group in our history books in this way, simply as victims of the more powerful members of society, is ultimately to deny their full humanity. It is to render voiceless and powerless people who deeply affected the course of our historical development, and the same can be said of the excluded, exploited, and enslaved in other societies around the world.

A second danger in trying to correct the white, male-oriented, hero-worshiping history that still persists is the tendency to restock the pantheon of national heroes with new figures of a different sex and less pale skin and think the job is done. This is simply a revised form of heroic, and essentially elitist, history. A revised history that merely trades in a male monochromatic set of heroes for a mixed-gender polychromatic set of heroes is not revisionist enough, because, while dealing with some of the fallacies of male-dominated and white-dominated history, it does not correct the severe class bias that has characterized most of our history. Native American leader Vine Deloria, Jr., pointed out some years ago that much of the supposedly revisionist "new" history still "takes a basic 'manifest destiny' white interpretation of history and lovingly plugs a few feathers, woolly heads, and sombreros into the famous events of American history." That could not be done if we agree that the history of any society cannot be properly understood without taking account of the activities of *all* its constituent parts, which means people of all classes, regions, and conditions.

Let us return to our initial examples as a way of showing how history can be taught so as not simply to replace the "old" political history with the "new" social history, but how the history of elites and of ordinary people intertwined. We will take first the case of Rosa Parks and the civil rights movement of the 1950s and 1960s and then, in greater detail, examine the case of Ebenezer MacIntosh and the American Revolution.

Rosa Parks was more than a lone individual struggling against racial injustice in her society, and she certainly did not start the civil rights movement after World War II. But her spontaneous act of defiance on December 1, 1955, did have a catalytic effect, setting in motion events that mobilized large numbers of previously uncommitted people. Several years before she stepped on the bus in Montgomery, she had attended a workshop for civil rights workers at the Highland Folk School in the hills of Tennessee. She had also been a member of the National Association for the Advancement of Colored People (NAACP), as well as a member of the International Ladies Garment Workers Union. In the South, in these years, it took courage to join such organizations. But it was the specific training imparted by such organizations and their group solidarity that fortified courage and deepened conviction. Parks, in other words, was a humble individual who had decided to fight against the daily injustices suffered by Black Americans, and she found organizations through which to act on this determination. It was through local chapters of such organizations that individuals began to make a national impact in the 1950s on America's most persistent problem—the problem of race.

For almost a year a local leader of the Black community, E. D. Dixon, had been trying to organize a boycott of the city's buses to end the hated Jim Crow rules. But Montgomery's fifty thousand Black citizens were far from unified and many relied on the buses to get to work. Even if alternative transportation had been available, many feared losing their jobs by participating in a movement that challenged white segregationist authority. But in a kind of chain reaction, Parks's fateful bus ride roused the courage of many hundreds to participate in a one-day boycott organized by Dixon. When that action succeeded beyond expectations, Dixon convinced a twenty-seven-year-old Black minister who had recently accepted a pastorship at the Dexter Avenue Black church, but had no record as an activist, to accept leadership of a boycott to the bitter end. Martin Luther King, Jr.'s leadership produced a massive boycott involving people who for the most part had never engaged in such a confrontational action before. And from King's involvement came the founding of the Southern Christian Leadership Conference (SCLC) in 1957, and three years later a more radical offshoot, the Student Non-Violent Coordinating Committee (SNCC).

Rosa Parks was by no means the first Black American in Montgomery to protest against discrimination—the local NAACP had been carrying on that fight for years. But it was her spontaneous refusal to obey a command to move to the back of the bus that galvanized other Black leaders to organize a boycott of the city's transportation system. Moreover, the action of this dignified middle-aged woman, with her coiled, braided hair and rimless spectacles, inspired thousands of anonymous Blacks to refuse to ride Jim Crow buses in a boycott that the leaders themselves had grave doubts would succeed. "There was no plot or plan at all," Parks said later about her defiant act. "I was just tired from shopping . . . and my feet hurt."

By the late 1950s local action in different parts of the South, inspired in part by the successful boycott of Montgomery's segregated buses, had produced many rivulets of action that were beginning to conjoin into a mighty stream. At each step, as the Black struggle became more militant, grass-roots groups sprang up to enlist more and more previously quiescent Blacks and whites. In many cases, new recruits pushed their leaders further than they had intended to go. By the time John F. Kennedy reached office in 1961, the evening news was filled with sounds and pictures of racial confrontation in the South that created widespread sympathy for the civil rights struggles of Black Americans and forced the new president to take a much more advanced position than he had intended, fearing as he did the alienation of white Southern Democrats. The Civil Rights acts of 1964, 1965, and 1967 were, in effect, the culmination not of moral and political leadership exercised by a white elite, though it was a white legislative elite that passed these bills, but of an insistent movement of thousands of virtually anonymous Americans who put their reputations, their jobs, and their bodies on the line in order to end generations of degrading discrimination that made a mockery of the principles on which the nation claimed to exist.

It is fitting to conclude with the American Revolution and the role of ordinary individuals like Ebenezer MacIntosh. The Revolution is, of course, a staple topic in every textbook and course in American history, for it ushered in independence and laid the foundations for the political system under which we live. But to judge by its treatment in textbooks currently used in the nation's schools, the great man theory of history is still very much in vogue and the historical amnesia about large constituent parts of the American society has not yet lifted.

In treating the Revolution, almost all textbooks that I have examined ignore the principle of inclusiveness, passing over the experiences of huge groups in colonial society or simply homogenizing all colonists into one undifferentiated mass, except for the Loyalists who are pictured simply as those who could not summon the courage to fight against the Crown. Almost completely ignored are the tensions that divided the American rebels—tensions that originated in the agendas for change held by such men as Ebenezer MacIntosh, agendas that conflicted with those of upper-class politicoes.

Almost all textbooks employ the great man theory of history to explain the advent, process, and outcome of the Revolution. They focus the student's attention on Washington, Franklin, Adams, Jefferson, and a few other political and military leaders; and they work teleologically to the ultimate outcome, thus smothering the contingency and complexity of the Revolution and robbing it of much of its democratic force. Students learn of ordinary people only as doughty farmers, artisans, and shopkeepers who were energized and led by brilliant statesmen and dauntless military leaders, never as self-activating men like MacIntosh who assumed leadership himself when his social superiors were dragging their feet.

In this way the Revolution is primarily rendered as a war of independence—and even that story is told primarily in terms of military and political history with scant attention to what was happening on the homefront during the war. Textbooks rarely present the competing ideologies and jarring revolutionary agendas constructed by different groups of people who brought varied experiences into the years of imperial crisis and therefore had different expectations and sought different results in the revolutionary fray. They ignore the differential rewards and losses of the war years among farmers, mechanics, merchants, the clergy, and other groups in different regions of the country. In recent years, many textbook writers have added paragraphs on women. But they stress only the occasional female contributions to male wartime activities—such as Deborah Garnett, who dressed like a man in order to fight, and Molly Pitcher, who carried water to slake the thirst of soldiers on the battlefield—rather than the rising consciousness among women about expanded female roles under a new government. They add a few sentences on early abolitionist stirrings, but these concern what whites thought and did (or did not do) about slavery. Still ignored is how thousands of Afro-Americans created the greatest slave resistance movement in American history by fleeing to and fighting with the British.

It is also telling that almost all textbooks entirely ignore the complicated process of drafting state constitutions—a process that revealed the different political ideologies, economic interests, and social agendas present in every state. The Revolution takes place in the Continental Congress and on the battlefields, and that is all. Missing is the struggle to define a new system of government and to forge a regenerated society that takes place at the local and state levels—precisely the loci where the homogeneous and consensual view of the Revolution must give way to a more complex and contingent, a more human and dramatic process. Given the patriotic and smoothed-over version of the Revolution served up in most textbooks, students are often stunned in college to find how laboring people in the cities pushed their social superiors along the road to revolution rather than being led into the revolution. They are surprised to discover how differently Pennsylvania and Massachusetts, or North Carolina and Virginia, worked out their constitutional-political arrangements and how people from many strata of society figured in the outcome. They are amazed to find that large numbers of Blacks fled to the British in order to gain their freedom. They are surprised (and sometimes dismayed) to find that the men of 1776 muzzled the opposition press, abridged civil liberties we take for granted today, and exiled pacifists. They are taken aback to learn that fierce contests of will and competing ideologies regarding the economic order wracked the American cause and even led to bloodshed as patriot fought patriot.

Why has the American Revolution been sanitized in the textbooks, emptied of all drama except that which flows from the battle of David against Goliath, the guerrilla against the gorilla? Perhaps the answer resides in the ancient feeling that the responsibility of history teachers is to inculcate *amor patrie*, and that this is best accomplished by showing a nation's past in untarnished, heroic terms. However, does this not lead only to passive patriotism of the flag waving kind that is most appropriate in authoritarian regimes? Such stainless steel versions of our Revolution are not likely to lead to active citizenship, to the moral, political, and social inquiry that is the highest form of patriotism in a democracy. Frederick Douglass's words are worth remembering in this regard: "Those who profess to favor freedom and yet deprecate agitation are men who want crops without plowing up the ground, they want rain without thunder and lightning. They want the ocean without the awful roar of its many waters."[1]

A more realistic view of the American Revolution is *more* likely to inculcate a commitment to democratic principles than the view offered in most textbooks used in the schools today. The Revolution is an epic example of the role played by people at many levels of society, in many regions, from different backgrounds, and with different points of view; all were involved in the revolutionary moment to some degree; all had to make difficult choices and decide what freedom was worth; and a great many were eager to participate in the making of their own history and the shaping of the society under which they would live. Some saw more of their agenda for America accomplished than did others. Some suffered keen disappointment but drew upon revolutionary principles, as they understood them, to continue their struggles after the Revolution. But nearly all were drawn into the civic process in one way or another and became part of an often disorderly and often exhilarating campaign not only to win a war but to define the future of the American Republic. In the course of their participation they created streams of change that those in high places did not always like but learned were more powerful than themselves. "Swimming with a Stream which it is impossible to stem," "yield[ing] to the torrent if they hoped to direct its course" were the metaphors used by one of New York's leaders, Robert R. Livingston, Jr., who recognized how the Ebenezer MacIntoshes of America had abandoned follower roles and become instead the makers of history.

The ruminations of John Adams on the Revolution, conveyed to a friend who was writing a history of the event, are worth remembering. Reflecting on one of the revolutionary figures who is studiously ignored in most textbooks, except for his authorship of one galvanizing pamphlet, Adams wrote of Thomas Paine: He was "a mongrel between pig and puppy, begotten by a wild boar on a bitch wolf," and added that "never before in any age of the world" was such a "poltroon" allowed "to run through such a career of mischief." Yet Adams was an astute observer as well as maker of history. Thus he added (writing in 1805): "I know not whether any man in the world has had more influence on its inhabitants or affairs for the last thirty years than Tom Paine. . . . I am willing you should call this the Age of Frivolity, and would not object if you had named it the Age of Folly, Vice, Frenzy, Brutality, Daemons, Buonaparte, Tom Paine, or the Age of the Burning Brand from the Bottomless Pit, or anything but the Age of Reason. . . . Call it then the Age of Paine."

We need more pain in the textbook accounts of the Revolution; in fact, we need it in the accounts of all periods of American history. That is to say, we need more of the diversity, struggle, contingency, competing points of view, and compromise that occurred. Almost automatically this will provide an antidote to the great man theory of history, not denying the role of great men but putting it into perspective and tempering it with an understanding of the many situations when the first became last and the last became first. This is not only a more accurate and three-dimensional history, it is also the kind of history that will nourish in our students an understanding of the relevance of the past to the present, the complexity of social and political problems, the necessity of active citizenship. Students come to understand from the kind of history that includes the experiences and involvement of people of all classes and conditions that little is inevitable in history—that is, beyond human control. They learn that almost all events and movements are explicable in terms of the particular choices and decisions made by men and women in places high and low. Surely this kind of history provides a more usable past for a democratic society.

NOTES

1. Quoted in Leon F. Litwack, "Trouble in Mind: The Bicentennial and the Afro-American Experience," *Journal of American History* 74 (1987):336.

PART V

Toward Better History in Schools

CHAPTER 14

Obstacles Teachers Confront: What Needs to Change

by John Arévalo, Marjorie Bingham, Louise Cox Byron, Claudia J. Hoone, and Charles Shotland

Nobody is more anxious for teaching to be effective, lively, and memorable than teachers themselves. It is the substance of every morning's hope, of every day's striving, of every evening's reflection on what went right or wrong. As members of the Bradley Commission with many years of experience in elementary and secondary school classrooms, we know the ups and downs of hundreds of thousands of our colleagues across the country. If we dwell here on the downs—the obstacles to good teaching—it is not because we forget the joys that are also part of teachers' lives, but because we believe that no campaign to improve American education will get very far until all those concerned clearly recognize the obstacles teachers confront, and build into their campaigns the changes that need to be made to remove or reduce those obstacles.

Over the years, too much of the public and too many officials, administrators, experts, and academicians have assumed they already knew enough about the realities of the classroom to decide what to change and what to leave alone. Have they not all spent at least twelve years of their own lives

251

in classrooms, sitting in front of the teacher's desk? How much else would they have to know? A great deal more, our experience tells us. The full range of problems teachers face cannot be understood even by the most attentive parents who drop their children off at school each morning and listen to supper-table accounts of what went on that day. It is not a matter of parents or would-be reformers lacking sympathy or good intentions. Teachers recognize and appreciate the support and encouragement they get from many quarters. But anyone not sitting behind the teacher's desk necessarily must fail to one degree or other in comprehending the teacher's life, just as anyone not gripping the deck of a trawler can never quite know the fisherman's life, or anyone aboveground sense what it's like to be a coal miner a mile below. Not that sensible, sensitive observers cannot come close. In regard to teaching, we think of Theodore Sizer's insights into the life of Horace the English teacher in *Horace's Compromise*, perhaps the single most valuable book of the many that have appeared out of the reform movement of the last decade.[1]

Our particular subject here is the history teacher who, beyond the bundle of problems common to all classroom practitioners, faces an added bundle arising from the special nature of history teaching. Of the two bundles, the first is easier to describe. Parents, principals, superintendents, school board members, teacher educators, and university professors are likely to know more about problems of teachers in general. These crop up in PTA and school board meetings, faculty gatherings and educators' conventions, newspapers and magazines, sometimes on television when other programming is in short supply. And for any reader desiring a quick refresher course on the daily obstacles teachers confront, reading *Horace's Compromise* will do wonderfully well as a beginning.

History teachers, to be sure, share fully in the good, the bad, and the merely dull or vexing in the typical teacher's life. On the secondary level, they must deal with all the problems of adolescence, peer pressure, and popular culture with their many powerful pulls away from formal learning. They must manage not only the classroom, but five or six classfuls a day, each of which may differ sharply from all the others. Second period: "How do I break up that bright, gossipy gang in the left corner?" After lunch: "Will Joe and Johnny be out of it on drugs or drink again?" Last period: "What will half the boys, at a soccer game away, be missing?" History teachers, like all others, face the classroom tensions arising from sex, social class, and race; from contrasts in ability and learning styles; and from differing home backgrounds and prior schooling. And particular, unpredictable problems abound. The morning may demand a wrenching concentration on the needs of a deeply depressed student, the afternoon merely a demeaning little struggle to make oneself heard over the cackling of the p.a. system, which asks no permission to interrupt at any time, without regard to what may be a crucial moment in the lesson.

There may be a shortage of texts for the students and a surplus of paperwork for the administrators. More surely, there are too many students and too little time for coaching, for thoughtful marking of papers. Horace, says Sizer, is lucky. His suburban school assigns him five classes with a total of 120 students. His inner-city counterparts may have 175 or more. Good teachers want their students to write, but there is so little time to read their papers. It takes Horace ten hours to give each student's homework and compositions a five-minute look. Doing this only twice a week adds twenty hours to a "lucky" teacher's twenty-plus hours of class time—over forty hours are used up so far and we have not yet counted the hours needed for reading and selecting materials, for preparing for each of five classes five times a week, for administrative chores, department and school meetings, special academic or disciplinary problems after school, extracurricular duties, meeting parents, counseling students, writing letters of recommendation. Nor have we yet touched upon keeping up with good books and articles in one's field or working with colleagues on curriculum, course design, and teaching methods, or mentoring practice teachers.

Very little leisure can be wrung out of teachers' evenings and weekends during the school year. Contrary to popular notions, their much-envied vacations do not make up the disparity. Teachers' work-hour years are commonly longer than those of most people who work for fifty weeks and are very often substantially better paid. And the summer is not so long or so free as it may seem to outsiders. There is added income to be earned at one job or other, and university courses to be taken, whether for financial or professional reasons. There are new books to be read, new courses to be prepared for September. The great common needs of teachers devoted to their work are time and the energy to use it well, from year's beginning to year's end.

Horace, Sizer concludes, should not have to compromise so much; he should be responsible for 80 students, not the 120 or 150 or more that are common in schools today. But reducing overall teacher load is "a low agenda item" for unions and school boards. Instead, Sizer observes,

> the administration will arrange for in-service days on "teacher burnout" (more time away from grading paragraphs) run by moonlighting education professors who will get more pay for giving a few "professional workshops" than Horace gets for a year's worth of set construction in the theater.[2]

Relax, the consultants say, and work at improving your attitude.

Although Sizer does not dwell on the matter, top-down prescriptions for coping and for change from outside experts have been far from the least of the obstacles American classroom teachers have had to face over the years. So few reformers have ever thought to ask teachers what they think is broken or not broken, and what most needs fixing. To the extent that campaigns for educational improvement have been conducted by people who are not classroom teachers and never have been, many of the perennial problems teachers face have been left unaddressed, made worse, or added to, despite the talents and good intentions of those involved. Instead of looking closely at classrooms, and facing up to the long, often costly, and unspectacular work of gradual improvement, outside experts and commissions have promoted those recurrent fads that sweep over the schools every few years (Life Adjustment, Career Education, Futures Learning, Back-to-Basics, Doing-a-Value, Global Consciousness), each one promising salvation in a hurry. As school boards and administrators flail about to keep up to the minute, the curriculum is skewed this way and that; the broader, abiding educational needs of students and society are left aside, and teachers stand awash in the debris left by successive tides of fashion.

Happily, the Bradley Commission on History in Schools was one of the exceptions to the customary rule of teacherless panels. In all, we five represented a century of experience in elementary, middle, and high schools, and two of the Commission's three staff members—Elaine Reed and Joseph Ribar—were also veteran teachers. From the start, the Commission operated as a conversation among equals, a common effort of university historians and classroom teachers. It was important to the Commission's work that this be so, for our purpose was not simply to deplore what was happening to history in the schools and to preach on the need for greater time in the curriculum. More than either, it was to examine what was already being done well in history classes, and to reduce every barrier we could to its being done more widely, in more schools of many kinds, for more students of all kinds. For such a purpose, the presence of working teachers on the Commission was vital.

Collaboration between distinguished scholars and seasoned teachers was also important to the Commission's determination to promote better kinds of history—thoughtful, analytical, rich in lively narrative and varied methods, organized around questions significant for students and for the wider society. We sought the kind of historical study that would sweep away the familiar complaints of tedium and irrelevance, that would truly engage and educate students at all grade levels. Here again, teachers could help their colleagues on the Commission to consider how such new-style history might be taught—and what particular, added obstacles might arise to its being taught effectively.

What follows is an elaboration of our conversations on some of these issues in the several meetings of the Commission. Our summary report, "Building a History Curriculum," minced no words: "Decisive changes will be necessary not only in curricular and course design as addressed in these pages, but in every other condition that affects the teaching of history in the classroom."[3]

To combat the frustrations common to all teachers of academic subjects, the Commission argued for lower student/teacher ratios, fewer extracurricular duties, less administrative paperwork, more flexible schoolday schedules—to allow for seminars, debates, and extended discussions—and greater teacher authority across the board, from curriculum making to textbook choice, to the design of both preservice and in-service teacher preparation programs. Here the Bradley Commission joined other voices calling for fundamental change in the role of teachers throughout the entire educational enterprise. As in other true professions, the practitioners themselves should determine the aims and methods, the standards and preparation, for their own professional work.

The true professionalization of teaching careers is critical to excellence in history, as it is in the other academic subjects. But the many reform movements spurred by "A Nation at Risk" in 1983 are ominously divided between those pressing for greater teacher authority and autonomy, and those insisting upon greater bureaucratic centralization and top-down imposition of detailed curricular content and standardized teacher "evaluation" and student testing. The latter trend is professionalism's polar opposite, casting teachers as machine operators in sausage factories. But it seems to have the upper hand for now, as school authorities and public officials succumb to the temptation of quick, "efficient" responses to what they hear as public outcries for school improvement and "accountability." We are not encouraged to see methods that have in recent times been discredited in industry now thoughtlessly applied to education, where they make even less sense.

As historians, we are not surprised at impatient searches for shortcuts. We also know the high failure, not to say disaster, rate of shortcuts, no matter how convincing their show of action. There are simply no quick, or cheap, or universally applicable, all-purpose fixes for the obstacles we know to be out there. And historical experience also suggests that a good number of those obstacles will never be neatly removed, will always be there as part of daily reality, requiring our daily effort to counter or reduce their effects upon us. One of these, which has affected the role of history in the curriculum since the early 1900s, is the powerful utilitarian twist in American notions of schooling in general. As David K. Cohen has noted, we manage to revere education in the abstract and discount, or even belittle, book-learning in practice. This love-hate impulse goes back a long way and appears, as Cohen reminds us, in the most popular literature Americans grow up on, such as Mark Twain's *Tom Sawyer* and *Huckleberry Finn*.[4] And we all know its vogue in our modern sitcoms and movies.

"What good is it?" is a fair question, but it takes a long answer in history's case, as it does in literature, philosophy, and the arts, and many are the professional educators in twentieth-century America who have not stayed around to listen. So we cannot be surprised by a certain public apathy, which is passed on to the young. We can hope that the Bradley Commission report, this book and others like it, and the many projects being conducted by historians and teachers across the country (some of which are listed on page 10 and in Appendix A) will help to make history's case to public officials, school board members, parents, and school administrators, and win their support from above. But motivating students will always be a natural part of our work, an obstacle only insofar as it sometimes takes over-much time from the material we are anxious to present.

Fortunately less common than apathy, but more of an obstacle when it appears, is outright hostility to historical studies in the schools. In their chapters, Hazel Hertzberg and Diane Ravitch have touched upon some of the struggles between history and other subjects for space in the social studies curriculum since the early part of the century, and upon the arguments made ever since against the uses and importance of history. Unless the Bradley Commission and its allies succeed in reshaping the social studies curriculum around a history-geography core, the scarcity of curricular time will remain the single greatest obstacle history teachers face. The campaign for more time may be long; we cannot yet predict its outcome. But this broader struggle against skeptics or opponents among professional educators is not the only issue here.

Unhappily, history teachers in certain localities must deal with the active hostility of certain single-issue or special interest groups. Their complaints range from general annoyance with a subject that fails to offer comforting answers of black and white, right or wrong, to questions they want to believe are simple—all the way to hotly partisan rejection of the slightest criticism of their favorite groups and causes. By its nature, historical study always challenges myths and wishes with inconvenient fact, so even the blandest textbook may draw the wrath of true believers. And so will teachers who deal with important questions. Wherever school authorities fail to shield teachers from bullies or fanatics, the history taught will be watered-down indeed, for almost no historical question of significance to society and its young is without potential controversy. Screening it out of our courses undermines everything our commission hopes for.

Turning to other obstacles directly hurtful to the better history we want to teach, we may cite the common absence of clear state or local policy on the place of history in the curriculum. Whether out of apathy, or various sorts of hostility, or simply out of inability to hold a steady course amid the ever-shifting currents of educational fashions—so many of which are dumped into the social studies—school authorities fail to articulate why history should be taught, what kinds are most worth teaching, and how much of each is needed. We hope, again, that our "Building a History Curriculum" will bring decisive improvement here, because without it many state and local guidelines for the social studies will continue to raise obstacles to sensible curriculum and course planning.

Ill-conceived guidelines issued from above can hurt in two ways. They can be so brief or abstract that they allow every fad or local interest a clear field to dominate, or disrupt by constant change, the curricula of local schools. At the other extreme—and this is likely to be the greater problem in the near future—they run on to great length and detail through pages listing endless facts, "concepts," and "social studies skills" utterly beyond the capacities of teachers in real classrooms to cover effectively. Even to try would exhaust and frustrate teachers and students alike. Such overambitious guidelines leave no time for developing history's "habits of the mind" or for exploring central questions of significance in depth, or for using methods that actively involve students in their own education.

Depending upon local circumstances, teachers have sometimes been able to ignore such overbusy guidelines. But the vogue of assessment is upon us, and wherever states and localities move to force the coverage of skills and subject matter by "objective" standardized testing, we have an added obstacle all but impossible to overcome. That sort of testing, the Bradley Commission clearly warned, "limits school autonomy, forbids curricular and methodological flexibility, and discourages the thoughtful, conceptual history we believe to be necessary."[5]

Teachers are under heavy pressure (in some places, test scores are published not only school by school, but class by class!) to drill for right answers to testlike questions, rather than to teach for reasoned understanding. The problem is critical.

We are aware of no standardized test suitable for mass administration that is equal to the task of evaluating what is most important in historical studies. Bad tests will almost compel teachers to teach bad history. The Bradley Commission's concern is expressed in its plea for a continuing alliance of classroom teachers, university historians, and faculties of education to work at devising tests that will help and not hurt the quality of learning.

As teachers, we are convinced that this kind of collaboration between school and university people is absolutely indispensable to reaching any of the Commission's goals. We want and need professional autonomy from bureaucratic centralization that swallows up resources and limits our flexibility, but we do not want isolation. In its campaign to bring and to keep school and university historians together, our commission argues again and again that each party has much to tell the other. Only together can we remove or reduce the obstacles to our work.

Are textbooks dull, overstuffed, and badly organized, thereby presenting impediments rather than aids to learning? Of course. But only teams of seasoned, imaginative scholars and teachers can make them better. The same is true for every kind of auxiliary material, from collections of primary sources to audiovisual and computer-assisted learning programs. Collaboration can make them better, as well as provide those regular critical reviews of texts, materials, and programs that the Bradley Commission calls for.

Is inadequate teacher preparation in our colleges and universities an obstacle to improved historical studies? Of course. Again, only that triple alliance of experienced teachers and university departments of history and education can bring together the several pieces of the puzzle. For far too long the subject matter programs of prospective teachers have been divorced from their programs in education, and both programs have suffered from failure to keep in touch with the school classroom itself. Another major obstacle is in state standards for teacher certification. Some are so loose and permissive as to require not a single history course for certification in social studies. Others are overburdened with specifics and credit requirements, often in out-of-date education courses with no relation either to subject matter or to the practical problems of the classroom. The right kind of reform can be expected only from the concerted action envisioned by the Bradley Commission, whose resolution on the matter is categorical: "That the completion of a substantial program in history (preferably a major, minimally a minor) at the college or university level be required for the certification of teachers of social studies in the middle and high schools."[6] Even then it will not be easy, for state requirements are often set by vested interests in the colleges and departments of education, concerned to maintain their flow of credit-seeking students.

In-service programs are also likely to be next to useless unless working teachers with high standards are involved in their design. Not only do colleges and departments of education need to examine themselves and reorder their priorities, but so do many university departments of history, for the structure and content of history major programs are frequently ill-adapted to the needs of prospective teachers. Having paid little attention to the latter as undergraduates, history departments are not well equipped to follow up with helpful contributions to in-service programs for the teacher's ongoing career. Yet in many districts, the teacher's only path to advancement and higher pay is to pile up credits in postgraduate courses. Without effective action to transform them, such courses, whether in history or education, will amount only to dreary added barriers, wastes of precious time and energy.

Teachers suffer isolation not only from the university historians and the teacher educators who do so much to shape, or misshape, their preparation, their work, and the tools of their work, but they suffer isolation from each other. Here the main culprits are the bureaucratic organization of schools and that perennial obstacle, shortage of time. The rhetoric of the education world exalts teamwork, open discussion, and participatory decision making as the ways to wisdom and high morale. Reality is very different. Decisions that properly belong with teachers—choices of texts and materials; design of curriculum, courses, and tests; methods and standards; the uses of time in the school schedule; even turning on and off the loudspeaker—are handed down from above. Insofar as they lack the power to influence so many factors that affect them, teachers have rather little reason to interact with colleagues on matters of academic substance or other professional issues. Nor do they usually have the time.

We have sketched above the multiple demands of the teacher's routine that so quickly add up to a sixty-hour week. There is no time, in most schools as presently organized, for the collaboration or collegial decision making that marks a true profession. When decisions are arbitrary, hasty, and ill-considered, when morale is low, the reasons are quite evident. But our final concerns here are the obstacles that time presents to the history teacher in particular, even when other factors may be favorable. The central plea of the Bradley Commission is that historical study be given more time in the curriculum, at both the elementary and secondary levels. All else follows upon this. The rush to cover American history, or Western and world civilizations, in a single year of secondary school makes for hurried, rigid, superficial surveys, without the chance to immerse students in the nuances, the personalities, the complexity of forces that make history come alive. At the elementary level, the absence of rich historical literature, of story, myth, and legend produces impoverished minds and imaginations; it deprives children of the background and perspectives upon which to build their later studies, forcing upper-grade courses into banal and superficial forms. These issues are forcibly argued in "Building a History Curriculum" and elsewhere in this volume, so we need not repeat them here.

What we can add are a few specific observations on the barriers to our spending enough "time on task"—that is, time spent on each student's intellectual experience of our subject.

Obviously, class size is vitally important at all grade levels, and especially so if the teacher must deal with several levels of ability, whether in reading, writing, "listening," or in prior knowledge of history and geography. At the secondary level, class size is perhaps less important than is the number of classes—and the number of different (and new, sometimes last-minute) preparations—the teacher is assigned in any given term. Teachers know that small classes are best for some things and larger ones for others, but that in all cases the total number of students for whose learning the teacher is responsible determines the quality of education that is possible—not certain, of course, but *possible*. Teachers (and parents) also know that those experts who can never seem to find "objective" evidence that the student/teacher ratio is important for effective learning invariably send their own children to schools where the ratio is low.

Two other eaters of time and morale are inflexible class-hour schedules and overrigid prescription of teaching methods. There is no objective reason, as far as we can determine, but only encrusted habit, that enforces a five- or six-time fifty-minute lockstep march through the middle and secondary school day. How many adults would stand for such a regimen, or profit from it, even in the pursuit of subjects they know and love? The system precludes the imaginative mix of approaches to learning that common sense and all of our own experience tell us is essential. There should be time for genuine seminars, for extended discussion once students are engaged, for films and debate, for field trips (without ruining the teaching plans of colleagues in other departments), for shorter lectures, and varied slots of time for tutoring and group projects.

Not only rigid schedules but top-down prescriptions of teaching methods present obstacles to the teacher's ability to do effective work. Fashions come and go very quickly in American educational methodology, including fashions of history teaching. For a while, it may be "postholing," then group projects, then the "inquiry method," followed by simulations and role-playing, or history-as-current-events, or history-ashandy-example of social science concepts. Each may be thoughtlessly pressed upon teachers, whose evaluations may suffer if they fail to follow suit. Ironically, the lecture is never in pedagogical fashion, but school schedules and mandated coverage compel teachers to resort to it repeatedly, no matter what else they might prefer. The point here, and explicated in "Building a History Curriculum," is that all such methods are useful from time to time, but that each loses its effect when it is overused. In most cases, the choice of method—and schedule—should rest with teachers, who know their own strengths best, who know what is right for their classes, at particular moments, to deal with the lesson at hand.

Pushers of single pedagogical fashions ignore the obvious: Different subjects, and topics within subjects, are learned best in different ways, ranging from memorizing and drill to brainstorming and independent study. Schools, and courses, must be free to be both disciplined and easygoing, fixed and flexible, hierarchical and egalitarian, at different times for different subjects at different levels. The Bradley Commission argues that good history teaching must apply the rule that variety is the spice of learning, just as it is of life: "There is no right answer, no one best way, but only a sensible mixture put together by each teacher according to circumstances, to the subject and students being taught, and to that teacher's particular strengths."[7]

In conclusion, we do not pretend to have covered here all of the obstacles that the present conditions of American society and American schools put in the way of good teaching. Inequalities of school financing and irresponsible budgetary priorities produce schools without maps, globes, or even up-to-date textbooks. And many American schools have no better prospects of setting up libraries, buying new books and materials, or modern equipment, than do the schools of impoverished societies in the Third World. Conditions are generally worst of all in those urban school districts plagued by poverty, absenteeism, drugs, and violence. The American public is told on the one hand that its expenditures on schooling are extravagant, but then is told on the other hand that schools should be expected to solve all of society's problems from reckless driving to the trade deficit. Since so many of the supposed cures and crash programs wind up in the social studies curriculum, the time spent on substantial academic subjects is further reduced. Paradoxically, we might get much more and better education from our schools if we expected less of them, especially in regard to those problems that the larger society needs to handle for itself.

Two reasonable questions may remain in the reader's mind. First, is there not a conflict between the Bradley Commission's urging state and local policymakers to adopt and enforce its guidelines for the history curriculum, and our repeated insistence on teacher autonomy and decision making? We believe not. A careful reading of "Building a History Curriculum" will reveal the very broad range of options in curricular patterns, in course design, and in teaching methods that we and our commission colleagues offer. Coupled with the proper role teachers ought to play in state and local decision making, the Bradley report sets up what we see as a healthy tension between outer guidelines and inner implementation. We recognize that autonomy is not license to do anything we please. Nothing of what we have said should be taken to imply that all teachers, left entirely to themselves, would automatically become ideal practitioners. Just as doctors, lawyers, and engineers must work within the imperatives of their professions, so must we. And we believe that some of the central imperatives of the history teaching profession, from kindergarten through graduate school, are embodied in the nine major resolutions of the Commission.[8]

The other question we need to answer may arise from our litany of obstacles to the history teacher's work. If things are so bad, why do we not seek other employment? Here we must return to our opening remarks. We are and remain teachers because we also find great joy and satisfaction in our work. If readers forgive mountain climbers for devoting most of their narrative to cold, snow, ice, and wind, to crevices and cliff walls, before getting to the glories of their view, we ask the same for ourselves. There are glories in our work with the young. We do not pretend to be more burdened with problems and constraints than are most people. But we have laid our problems out as fully as we could because there must be no misunderstanding of the effort and time it will take to achieve genuine improvement in American schooling. So many attempts at reform have failed in the past because obstacles were minimized and quick change was guaranteed, because it was pretended that schools alone could perform miracles against larger forces in society that devalue and undermine everything that schools stand for. The public has gone through repeated cycles of unreal expectation followed by disillusion. As historians, we must emphasize the need for patience and long-term planning. No worthwhile change will be quick or easy. Many of the barriers we cite will require no less than a decade of steady, purposeful transition—curricular reform is one of these. Some, such as better preparation of teachers, will probably take longer. Let us also add that a good number of the obstacles we describe are obstacles we have chosen to set for ourselves because we are aiming high, because we want teachers in all kinds of schools to have the chance to teach more and better history. If we were content with things as they are, certain of our "obstacles" would disappear. But so, too, would the purposes and rewards of our work in the classroom and on this Commission.

NOTES

1. Theodore R. Sizer, *Horace's Compromise: The Dilemma of the American High School* (Boston: Houghton Mifflin, 1984).

2. Ibid., p. 21.

3. The Bradley Commission, "Building a History Curriculum" (Westlake, Ohio: Bradley Commission on History in Schools, 1988), p. 26.

4. David K. Cohen, "Teaching Practice: Plus Ça Change . . ." (East Lansing, Mich.: National Center for Research on Teacher Education, 1988), p. 2.

5. "Building a History Curriculum," p. 28.

6. Ibid., p. 8.

7. Ibid., p. 24.

8. Ibid., pp. 7–8.

CHAPTER 15

Toward Better Teacher Preparation and Certification

by Suzanne M. Wilson and Gary Sykes

History teaching as envisioned here by our fellow authors is exciting. Instead of the familiar trudge through endless dates, names, and facts, school history would be alive and breathing and meaningful. We envy future generations the experience of such classrooms and teaching, wishing that we could revisit school to hear the stories, work at the activities, witness the events described in this volume.

Reforms of current practice, however, will require extensive changes in teaching, teachers, and schools. The lack of attention to such comprehensive changes, essential to reform, offers a partial explanation for why past reforms, sounding much the same call, have fallen short. In this chapter we explore one of those necessary changes: the preparation and certification of the teachers who must both lead and carry out this movement. We address four questions: (1) What is good history teaching?; (2) What do teachers need to know about history and about teaching in order to teach this way?; (3) How are teachers to acquire these understandings, skills, and dispositions?; and (4) When and where should we expect that teachers acquire such knowledge? We conclude with particular recommendations for the improvement of history teaching that go beyond what our colleagues have recommended thus far.

WHAT IS GOOD HISTORY TEACHING?

Our fellow authors ground teaching in subject matter, broadly construed. History teaching as pictured here does not require students to memorize lists of facts—the rivers of central Africa, the kings and queens of England, for example. Rather, a disciplinary-based conception of history teaching sets as its major goal the communication of knowledge about both the most significant substance of the discipline *and* the nature of the methods employed by historians—for example, their modes of interpretation, of the use of evidence, and of the integration of new realms of scholarship. Teachers need to teach students about both aspects of the discipline of history for a number of reasons.

First, teaching that focuses solely on the content of a discipline runs the danger of misrepresenting that discipline to students. If students learn only to recite verbatim the stories they read in textbooks, they never discover that historical knowledge comes from hard thinking on the part of scholars about diverse bodies of evidence. Nor do they learn that historical knowledge is often qualified and contingent. They come away from such schooling believing that knowledge is static, that there are bodies of truth buried out there in the social world, waiting only to be exhumed by graybeards living in libraries.

But it is not simply a matter of misrepresenting the discipline to students. Teachers must also teach about the "stuff" of the subject matter as well as about the methods of the discipline to keep students from drawing wrong conclusions about their own learning and knowing. If students are not exposed to the dynamic aspects of the subject matter—the ways in which new knowledge is created, the interpretive aspects of knowing that are assumed and accepted by historians—they see themselves as sponges, responsible only for absorbing the information presented, not for thinking about it. They learn to be passive recipients, unaware of the ways in which they could actively participate in learning. Moreover, they may see nothing inherently interesting or exciting about the subject matter. Nor should they be expected to. Kammen and Craig, Ravitch and McNeill would be no more excited by much of the dry material that finds its way into history textbooks than are schoolchildren. Rather, what excites and motivates historians is historical inquiry, knowing that factual information provides us with ways to interpret the thought and action of past generations, drawing multiple, and sometimes conflicting, meanings out of the events that appear so fixed and stagnant in textbook accounts. We cripple ourselves if we do not allow students to see the creative forces behind history writing, for it is in those forces that we can find ways to motivate and interest students in the continued study of history. Hence, history teachers need to emphasize the interpretive aspects of history in order to engage students in critical thinking. They need to use the diverse methods that historians use for thinking about social, political, economic, and cultural problems so that students may develop similar, albeit less sophisticated, skills.

The image of the teacher emerging from these chapters is one who deeply understands the subject matter to be taught, who wants to communicate that understanding to students, and who also understands that this is possible only through a variety of pedagogical strategies that are appropriate for the particular content and students at hand. Such teaching requires, in turn, elaborate understanding of schools and schooling, students and subject matter.

WHAT DO TEACHERS NEED TO KNOW?

The conception of history teaching that we advance is daunting and requires much of teachers. Rather than attempt a complete accounting here, we will focus on the two most fundamental requirements: subject matter knowledge and subject-specific pedagogical knowledge.

Subject Matter Knowledge

We start with a simple, and rather obvious, assertion: Teachers whose responsibility is to teach American history should have studied American history in depth. But usable knowledge of American history is not easily measured. It is not simply a matter of quantity—the ability to recite more dates, recognize more names, recall more events. Rather, it requires elaborated, coherent understanding of historical phenomena. Usable—and teachable—historical knowledge has four main characteristics.

First, deep and usable knowledge is *differentiated*—that is, teachers understand the various components and subcomponents of a concept or event. For example, an American history teacher can know that multiple conditions and ideas were at work to produce the American Revolution, many causes both long-range and immediate. Differentiated knowledge of the subject matter means that a teacher perceives and understands the several dimensions of a particular topic in history.

A second characteristic of deep knowledge of the subject matter is *elaboration*. Here teachers possess detailed knowledge of an event, person, concept, or idea that goes beyond the skeletal pieces associated with differentiated knowledge of subject matter. Relevant details allow the teacher to build a lively, engaging story. Furthermore, details often provide new insights into old questions and allow historians to generate more refined or novel explanations for phenomena. In other words, knowledge of detail often reveals the complexity of problems historians wrestle with, those subtle distinctions that make the obvious not so obvious.

A third aspect of deep historical understanding is its *qualification*, the awareness that historical knowledge is often qualified and tentative. Historians explicitly acknowledge that the conclusions they draw are both defined and limited by the spatial, temporal, and ideological contexts within which events took place and by the fragmentary nature of their evidence.

Teachers themselves must have grasped the qualified nature of knowledge in order to convey it to students. If they can effectively teach that knowing something involves searching for clues, sifting through evidence, and arguing about perspectives, students may be more interested in what is being taught, for often the processes through which new knowledge is generated are more intriguing and enlightening than the results of those processes. Yet all too often students see only end products of scholarship, not the drama of discovery.

A final dimension of deep understanding of subject matter is *integration* or relatedness. Events, for example, can be integrated by looking at the causal relationships between them. On the other hand, events or figures can be interpreted in light of a common theme, providing another way of integrating historical knowledge. Teachers need to know how one event is tied to another, both causally and thematically, in order to make ideas and events meaningful. Students who fail to arrange facts into broad patterns are unlikely to develop historical understanding or to recall much of what they have learned. Communicating the connectedness of historical knowledge is essential to learning that lasts, essential to making the past usable in future thought.

All four aspects of deep knowledge of subject matter—differentiation, elaboration, qualification, and integration—are central to fostering analytic thinking. Proficient teachers understand these several ways of knowing in history. Thus, they are able to expose their students to various models of critical thinking and to teach students to apply them to the information they encounter in history classrooms and textbooks.

Subject-Specific Pedagogical Knowledge

But lest we assume that knowledge of history as a discipline is sufficient for teaching, we need to recall certain brilliant historians each of us has encountered who had little capacity to teach. Knowledge of history is certainly necessary, but history teachers also need to know *how* to teach the history they know. Such a complex capacity involves many kinds of knowledge, skill, and disposition, but here we concentrate on one kind of understanding that Lee Shulman and his colleagues have labeled "subject-specific pedagogical knowledge." Such understanding is the joint product of reflection on teaching, learners, and subject matter, all at once.

Subject-specific pedagogical knowledge is understanding how to teach particular subject matter to learners to meet defined goals. Teaching history requires more than knowing history because a third party, the learner, is always present. Good teachers know that their students already have beliefs, knowledge, preconceptions, and experiences that affect what they learn. They are not empty vessels or blank slates to be filled up with information, but active elements in the process of learning. The story one student hears and takes away from history class will be much different from the story another student hears. Teachers who are unaware that students filter, twist, construct, and reconstruct the information they hear are naive about the processes of learning. Just as the final listener in the party game "Telephone" receives a different message than the first, students come away from stories well told in history class with a dismaying range of understandings.

Teachers with subject-specific pedagogical knowledge know how students typically construct their understandings about the history they are taught. Such teachers know the most common misconceptions students have about revolution, about leadership, about chronology, about government. They also know what kinds of prior experience students have had that can be used as springboards into discussions of new material. It is not accidental, for example, that so many teachers use the metaphor of the mother-child relationship when discussing the bonds between England and her colonies. However, teachers also know that students have qualitatively different conceptions of such relationships, and they acknowledge that when using such metaphors in their teaching.

We call the process of thinking about the subject matter, about the learner, and about how best to teach a *transformation*. In transforming the subject matter into effective educational experiences for students, teachers create *representations* of history. Talking about the relationship between England and the colonies in terms of a mother and child is but one representation of that relationship. Other illustrations, metaphors, examples, and analogies might cast the relationship in a different light, providing yet other representations.

Teachers encounter many students with backgrounds, experiences, and values that differ substantially, often quite sharply, from those of the teacher. To make connections, teachers must find multiple ways to engage students in the subject matter. They must have a repertoire of representations. In response to students' misunderstandings or lack of engagement, teachers must be ready to reconsider their explanations and invent new illustrations and metaphors. While a single representation may have led to the teacher's personal and private understanding, teaching is a public activity, requiring that ideas and insights historians leave buried in the recesses of their minds be made public by teachers so that students can explore and understand them. To do so, teachers need multiple representations.

We have only scratched the surface of the kinds of knowledge and skill required in teaching. Subject-specific pedagogical knowledge includes other kinds of understandings as well—

the goals of history teaching, for example, and the ability to judge and augment curricular materials such as textbooks. Teachers also need to know, more generally, how to manage classrooms and alternative learning environments. They need to know the contexts in which they teach, theories of learning, reasoned educational aims and objectives. A full, careful cataloging and analysis of such knowledge and skills could take up an entire new volume. The simple point is that it is not sufficient to proclaim what should be taught in history classes and how. It is also crucial to consider the many sorts of understanding and skill that teachers need in order to be engaging and effective. Future work by commissions such as this one should go on to explore these issues.

HOW WILL TEACHERS ACQUIRE THESE UNDERSTANDINGS?

We cannot expect teachers to teach a kind of history they have never learned. In today's elementary, secondary, and university classrooms, students may encounter history in all its richness and glory, but we suspect that this is not the norm. History classes in the schools are despised by too many students who see them as endless parades of facts requiring rote memorization. Undergraduates frequently fare no better. They may listen to or read the stories of different historians, but never learn that historians do not agree with one another about the kinds of questions to ask, the ways to answer those questions, or what a reasonable historical explanation may be. They frequently manage to escape doing original work of their own. Intent on marching through as much material as possible, their instructors do not stop to reflect on the debates still raging about whose story counts and whose may not. Too often students assume that only one story is possible.

If we want teachers to convey the pleasures and excitements of history, then we must share that kind of history with them when they are elementary and secondary school students, when they are undergraduates, and when they are practicing teachers. We cannot continue to count on the fact that occasionally a child or adult will trip over a good piece of historical writing, be swept away in the drama and conflict of our past, and become inspired to spend his or her life sharing that excitement with others. Hence, the call for reform in the teaching of history in elementary and secondary schools requires that we change liberal arts teaching in the colleges as well. If we are to expect future teachers to learn the history we want them to present in schools, professors in liberal arts departments must learn to reflect about what and how they are teaching, and not teaching.

Consider an example. Some instructors, intent on covering Middle Eastern history from 1700 through 1948, have little time to cover a multiplicity of interpretations if they are to get to the twentieth century. If they presume too quickly that students understand that the material they present is based on varying interpretations, they may never take time to say so or to discuss it in their classes. But students do not necessarily acquire such understanding on their own. They may well leave college without any usable grasp of the material they have temporarily absorbed. Instructors must examine the assumptions they make about the deeper understandings they want students to take with them. They must then make those assumptions explicit to their students. Preparing for such teaching is not a simple task; it requires time and effort in an environment that does not often reward either. However, the reform of history teaching called for in this volume requires just such introspection and change.

Parallel changes are required in teacher education; teacher educators must explicitly address the issue of subject-specific pedagogy. For example, it is not enough for novice teachers to guess about students' prior knowledge of slavery. Rather, prospective teachers must develop the skills and knowledge necessary to discover what students already know or believe about slavery and about the Civil War. An adolescent who has just seen *Gone With the Wind* or read *The Color Purple* is likely to have powerful but incomplete and distorted images of slavery. Teachers need to learn how their students' preconceptions influence how and what they learn, and how those preconceptions can foster or impede learning.

Most current teacher education is not adequate in this area. New courses that marry history and pedagogy are necessary, courses in which teachers think about the subject matter, consider what students know and believe about it, and develop skills for assessing that knowledge and belief. Imagine, for example, a course entitled "Learners and Learning in History" in which prospective teachers use learning theories to think specifically about the teaching of history. They could interview a number of students before and after exposure to a given topic in a history class, and then analyze how the students' prior knowledge and beliefs influenced their subsequent learning. Prospective teachers could examine what kinds of preconceptions students bring to particular topics, and could develop the disposition and skills to use students' knowledge and beliefs to enhance classroom learning.

We also need to develop new courses in which teachers learn to transform knowledge of content and students into usable pedagogy. Teaching involves more than laying an instructional template on a particular piece of content. It requires critical examination of the ways in which methods realize the purposes of instruction. Teachers don't simply need to learn *how* to create a role play of Congress or a simulation of the Battle of Lexington. They need to understand the connections between methods and students' learning—for example, that students who write newspaper accounts based on original sources learn differently from students who read textbook accounts and engage in heated discussion. While no one form of pedagogy is necessarily superior to another, teaching strategies convey their own varied lessons—around the "same" topic. Teacher education needs to promote in prospective teachers the critical analysis of pedagogy, learning, and subject matter, for the choices and the consequences are complex and multifaceted.

If, for example, generating representations of the subject matter is central to good teaching, a course might be developed to help teachers think about this aspect of their work. Since there is a burgeoning literature on representations of knowledge in the fields of cognitive psychology, cognitive science, artificial intelligence, and computer-assisted instruction, such a course might require students to look at how various scholars think about the role that representation plays in knowing and learning. Entitled "Knowledge, Its Representations, Its Transformations," such a course might require that teachers reflect, first, on their own mental representations of the subject matter, second, on representations generated by scholars, and finally, on instructional representations of knowledge they want to present to their students. Using their developing understanding of learners and learning, teachers could practice generating multiple representations, testing them against the standards of knowledge set forth by the discipline *and* the students they are teaching.

All this suggests that there is much room for innovation both in teacher education and in the liberal arts curricula. Liberal arts educators and teacher educators alike share the responsibility for seeking out the changes that must take place in institutions of higher learning and professional education if we are to prepare the teachers we wish to have in our classrooms.

WHEN WILL TEACHERS ACQUIRE THESE UNDERSTANDINGS?

History teachers should be lifelong students of history and of teaching. History is a living discipline and the cultivation of the historical imagination requires steady nourishment. If teachers are to represent the inquiring and interpretive aspects of history, they must engage the subject in this manner, and so exemplify such habits of mind. The history teacher's vision, however, must be bifocal, concentrating at once on the subject and on the teaching of the subject. Teaching is a complex craft that requires continuous learning. The practicing historian must stay abreast of trends in historiography: the disparate challenges of cliometrics, psychohistory, and the Annales school, for example, and the more general blurring of modes that proceeds apace in the social sciences. So, too, the teacher of history should engage continuously in exploration and re-finement of the teaching craft—the subject, the students, and the methods.

Learning to teach, then, should unfold over a career. But when we turn our gaze from the ideals of history teaching to daily reality, the prospect is discouraging. It exaggerates little to note a systematic bias against deep engagement with history and its teaching at every stage of life and work. Learning to teach begins with going to school. When young adults take their first teaching assignment, they already have had twenty years of experience in observing their own teachers' efforts. Attempts to change patterns of history teaching in the schools, to depart from overemphasis on lectures, textbooks, and standardized tests, and from the chronological quickstep through people, places, and events, encounter the weight of traditional practice reinforced through thousands of hours of instruction at school and university. No other profession faces quite this challenge of professional *re*socialization: The work of medicine, the law, accounting, or architecture is largely invisible to the layman, and the professional school is the student's first introduction to the mysteries of professional knowledge and practice. In edu-cation, however, students already have well-formed notions of what teaching involves and powerful models—both positive and negative—of what teaching is like. A handful of courses and ten weeks of practice teaching is hardly sufficient to alter the deeply rooted conceptions of teaching, learning, and subject matter that have accumulated over the years, and that often receive further reinforcement in liberal arts courses at the uni-versity.

Present credentialing requirements do little to disrupt traditional patterns or to promote intellectual engagement with the teaching and learning of history. In recent years states have returned to testing teachers, a licensing practice initiated in the mid-nineteenth century then gradually abandoned by the early twentieth. By the mid-1980s, over forty states had mandated tests for licensure, while half also had mandated tests for admission to teacher education programs. The three types of tests in use cover basic skills (reading, writing, mathematics), professional knowledge, and subject matter knowledge. Most common is the National Teacher Examination, divided into a core battery including general knowledge, professional knowledge, communication skills, and a series of subject area examinations. Professional knowledge, as defined by these tests, does not include the subject-specific pedagogical knowledge that we discuss in this chapter, nor do the tests of subject matter knowledge measure the depth of knowledge that we find indispensable.

In recent years, many states have extended assessment into the first year of teaching, typically relying on a standardized instrument to evaluate performance in the classroom. Some states also have created beginning teacher programs that provide assistance as well as assessment, but the emphasis is on evaluation, not on support. Those new performance-based assessments concentrate on generic teaching skills such as classroom management, lesson structure, or the efficient use of time. Such assessments neither focus on teaching subject matter nor recognize the possibility that teaching may differ across subject matters.

These trends in state standard-setting concentrate on generic competencies derived from research on basic skills teaching at the elementary level, deemphasize disciplinary knowledge, and separate what is taught from how it is taught. "We will assess your basic skills, maybe your knowledge of historical fact, and some knowledge of teaching," the states seem to say, "but we will not assess your knowledge of teaching history." This implicit formula is nicely calculated to support the status quo, underscoring that there is apparently nothing special to know about teaching the subject matter of history as opposed to anything else.

If contemporary approaches to credentialing fail to emphasize history teaching, traditional arrangements also make entry to teaching a "sink or swim" experience in which the novice works in isolation, receiving little support or assistance from peers or supervisors. The brief, vivid, sometimes traumatic, experience of practice teaching is quickly followed by the assumption of full professional responsibilities, with little attention to induction or formal socialization. Worse, in many districts, seniority-based teacher transfers impose the most difficult teaching assignments on the novices, as veterans seek easier duty. Predictably, many new teachers leave in the first few years, while those who stay learn survival skills, not teaching strategies, adjusting their ideals to fit their immediate circumstances.

As teachers advance in their careers, opportunities to continue the study of history and of history teaching are relatively infrequent and informal. Spurred by salary inducements and state requirements, many teachers take courses at nearby universities according to convenience, related neither to their discipline nor to their teaching. Unusually dedicated teachers may seek out opportunities for study during the summer, or form teacher study groups to meet on weekends and in the evenings. And they may participate periodically in the development of curriculum, sometimes alone, sometimes with colleagues. What is notable, however, is the weakness of institutional support for ongoing professional development. School policy and norms, school resources, peer culture, and work incentives all fail to support continuing engagement with history teaching.

Finally, history teaching must be viewed against the backdrop of schoolteaching in general. The discipline of history (in both senses) competes with many other demands for history teachers' attention. Elementary teachers are expected continuously to deepen their knowledge of many subjects—mathematics, science, art, literature, music—and skill areas such as reading and writing. Secondary teachers must attend to an equally broad range of subjects within the field of social studies, either through individual courses or through interdisciplinary programs. In many high schools, particularly those serving rural areas, teachers are generalists, not specialists, and must become adept at myriad tasks. Whereas the disciplines—more particularly specialization within disciplines—provide the primary source of identity for university professors, the schoolteacher's identity is, to say the least, more diffuse. The American history teacher may also coach volleyball, sponsor the student council, teach two sections of geography, advise the Latin club, and supplement her income with a summer job.

As both Larry Cuban and David Cohen have noted, these patterns in teaching are deeply rooted in the historical evolution of schooling and of the teaching profession. Clearly, they challenge any teacher's ability to learn to teach in productive ways. They apply to all teaching, but the teaching of history carries its special burdens. There is first the long-standing ambiguity about the boundaries of the field. At the university, disciplinary boundaries are strong and clear, but this is not true for elementary and secondary teaching. History teaching coexists uneasily with the "social studies," complicating efforts to forge consensus on the aims and organization of curriculum and on the knowledge required of teachers. This ambiguity is reflected in most states' credential categories. To accommodate various patterns of practice in schools, teachers are not typically licensed in areas such as history, geography, or economics, but in "social studies" or "social science," or in multigrade and content configurations such as kindergarten to grade eight. Consequently, the match between qualifications and teaching assignments is often very weak, a problem that equally plagues science teaching. Moves to introduce specialist credentials provoke strong opposition from local educators who seek flexibility in their school staffing. Such tensions have played out over many decades.

TOWARD REFORM IN HISTORY TEACHING

The reform of teaching, then, means entering a circle. The current practice of teaching history at school and university exerts a powerful influence on future generations of history teachers. Professional education alone is not likely to be a sufficient counterforce, even if it were substantially reformed. Tomorrow's teachers are today's students, sitting in school and university classrooms where much pedestrian teaching takes place. The schooling system feeds itself, maintains itself. What is required is not learning from experience, but breaks with experience—the experience of mediocre teaching that too often greets the student. An agenda to improve the quality of history teaching and learning for teachers and students alike must have three strands.

First, the teaching of history in our schools and universities must be honored and improved. At the elementary and secondary level this means strengthening teachers' connections to and identification with history. At the university level, this means strengthening historians' connections to and identification with teaching. If such symmetry is not pursued, then we believe little progress will be made. At issue is whether historians and history teachers form one or two professions. Here, too, the tendency is to pull apart that which is better joined—the school to the university, our teaching to our scholarship. The best history teachers in our schools know a great deal about teaching. They can profit from connection to imaginative historical scholarship. Historians may stay abreast of and contribute to research, but they typically fail to learn much about teaching. The first strand of reform, then, must encourage status-equalizing opportunities for historians and history teachers to learn from one another, so that research and teaching may be mutually educative, so that a common professional identity may begin to form.

The second strand looks to the formal preparation of history teachers, encompassing standards, university coursework, and the structure of opportunity for practice and induction in the schools. Teacher educators also belong within the profession of history teachers. They will be responsible for much of the research on teaching and learning history, and should work closely with colleagues in history departments on the preparation of teachers and the improvement of teaching. This means establishing closer collaborations across departments within the university and between the universities and the schools. Rather than regarding the university curriculum as a zero-sum contest for control of credit hours, historians and history teacher educators should acknowledge their complementary expertise and work together to strengthen the intellectual content and the integration of coursework for prospective teachers.

State standards should likewise begin to focus on pedagogical and curricular knowledge of history. A promising lead in this regard is the emerging work of the National Board for Professional Teaching Standards. This body was established in 1987 to develop procedures for the voluntary certification of teachers. Research and development work under way on innovative assessments has begun to suggest promising approaches that states might draw upon, and the Educational Testing Service has already announced a multiyear effort to reform the National Teacher Examination to take advantage of these emerging developments. So it appears that promising changes are under way, changes that will at last emphasize deep knowledge of subject matter and subject-specific pedagogical knowledge.

States also should press forward with plans to create induction experiences for beginning teachers. A sensible approach might provide the first-year history teacher with a reduced load, assistance from a mentor teacher, and a continuing seminar at a nearby university. Such structural arrangements may be set in the context of extended teacher education and/or licensure requirements, for the supervision of initial practice provides a performance base for evaluation. Here, too, however, standards and criteria must emphasize subject matter teaching in addition to generic teaching skills. Beginning teachers understandably are concerned with the management problems of the classroom, but this preoccupation can drive out attention to the teaching of subjects. States can begin to support teachers in ways that will allow them to avoid this imbalance.

The final strand must look to the school as a place for a veritable *career* in history teaching. Sociologists have long noted differences between bureaucratic and professional forms of control within organizations. Professionals tend to establish lateral connections through associations with peers who form their reference group. This model applies most obviously to research-oriented university faculty members whose institutional bonds are often as weak as their disciplinary affiliations are strong. Bureaucratic organizations foster greater organizational allegiance, for careers are vertically structured. School-teaching is a mixed form, featuring an undifferentiated and imperfectly professionalized work force operating within a public bureaucracy.

These observations underscore the complexities in fostering commitment and competence in history teaching on a widespread, systematic basis. To be sure, individual projects around the country engage teachers in the continued study of history, and these are exciting and valuable endeavors. But the mainstream occupational and organizational processes remain untouched and continue to exert powerful control. The schools must change, to provide greater support for history teachers to deepen and extend their expertise, to form professional affiliations around history teaching through regular connection with historians and with their own teaching colleagues, to work on curriculum, to undertake their own local inquiries into the conditions of learning and teaching, to experiment with new forms of instruction, to encounter greater variety in work and responsibility over their careers.

The ideas and ideals set forth by the distinguished contributors to this volume cannot flourish without a supporting social and educational structure that implicates the organization of the university and the schools, the preparation of teachers, and the shape of the teaching career. As efforts go forward to promote the study of history in our schools, we ask for much closer attention to the pragmatic conditions that must support such noble work.

CHAPTER 16

For Better Secondary Teaching: Stories Old and New

by JOSEPH P. RIBAR

NO ONE CAN DO EVERYTHING

The scholars and teachers of the Bradley Commission on History in Schools were acutely aware that no student can gain an adequate background in history in only one or two courses. It requires a cumulative and sequential program, beginning in the elementary grades and continuing through twelfth grade. For that reason, the Commission forcefully recommended that school curricula include more time for history, and in particular, it called for four full years of history sometime between seventh and twelfth grades.

These are, however, goals that have yet to be reached. In actuality, as a present-day high school teacher you are likely to find that students have little or no preparation in history when they enter your class. And yours may be the only course they will take in their entire secondary school careers. You must be able to make the best of the fact that although you may offer a superb course, your students may well graduate without an adequate background in history because of the structure of the curriculum.

You alone cannot make up for a curriculum that is deficient in time devoted to history by trying to cram everything that has been left out of K-12 into *your* course. If you truly love history and understand its value, you may be greatly tempted to try. But you must resist the impulse, for you will succeed only in destroying your own course. Far from saving the students, you are very likely to dispel whatever interest they might have had in history, or even make them hostile to it.

No matter how good a teacher you are or how much you know about history, no matter how much your department, district, or state tells you to cover, the fact remains that you cannot teach your students everything they ought to know about history, all of its drama, its nuances, and its techniques, in your single course. The strongest, unanimous conviction of the Bradley commissioners was that learning history takes time. That became their central plea to policymakers at all levels: devote more time in the curriculum to the study of history.

The first step in teaching well, then, is to limit what you try to do to match the time in which you have to do it. Good and great teachers use a wide range of methods to succeed at this. One technique was especially recommended by the prize-winning historians and master teachers on the Bradley Commission: "Tell them a story." History offers the greatest stories ever told, full of adventure, comedy, melodrama, tragedy, and mystery. The great teacher is able to take the best, most engaging stories from each era of history and set them as stepping stones through his or her course.

Case studies and narrative history breathe life into a course and keep the students' eyes from glazing over at the recital of names and dates. History teachers can, after all, compete with the best that movies and television have to offer. In planning their courses, they have access to all the same stories and biographies used by the entertainment industry. Through such stories history teachers can turn passive entertainment into active learning.

History teachers need not and should not stop at the entertainment value of a good story, as do some Hollywood producers. By using the analytical techniques of the historian, teachers can draw out of that same story the "Vital Themes" and "Habits of Mind" suggested in Chapter 2, "Building a History Curriculum." But the balance must be kept between analysis and storytelling. Analysis must not submerge the human drama. *Teachers must not forget to tell the story*, for it is the power inherent in the stories of history that will take students to the intellectual goals that teachers set.

Motivation is the engine that drives all the rest. With it, the study of history is a pleasure and students look forward to class. If the story is well told students will be eager to find out what happens next; they will be concerned with the people in the story, they will want to find out what happened to them, what they did, and why they did it. By first presenting history as a story, teachers can be well on the way to overcoming the apathy many students show toward history when they ask, "Why do we have to study this old stuff anyway?" The first answer is not because it is good for them, or even that it is good for our society; the first answer is "Because you'll like it!"

A STORY TO WORK WITH

Once upon a time, the most powerful country in the world sent an army of its finest soldiers halfway around the globe to fight an indigenous force of a different race in a tropical climate. They expected a swift and crushing victory. In fact they met defeat due to the geography, the climate, and the diseases of the country in which they fought and the resistance of the guerrilla forces they sought to subdue. The defeat marked the beginning of the end of the powerful country's influence in that other half of the world.

Of course, this is a synopsis of the story of Napoleon's elite troops who were sent to Santo Domingo in 1802 to put down Toussaint L'Ouverture's rebellion of Blacks in the French colony. It obviously, perhaps transparently, invites students to think of the United States's experience in Vietnam and could be used to explore at least two of the Bradley Commission's vital themes: comparative history of major developments, and conflict and cooperation. In an American History class, it could be used in relation to such topics as the changing role of the U.S. in the outside world, and the major successes and failures of the United States. The same story might serve in a World History class in studying such topics as historical success and failure, the interplay of outside forces and local culture, and the impact of the American and French revolutions outside their borders. This, however, is only one way to tell and but a few ways to use this particular episode of history. As we proceed, we shall try to envision its use in a variety of ways.

CONTEXT FOR FACTS

Using narrative history helps students learn, and remember, more factual information because the *story gives a context for data*. Names, dates, legislation, places, struggles, and choices have meaning as the building blocks of the story. When students remember the human adventure of the story, they will also remember its most important factual detail.

One of the time-honored techniques in developing memory is the use of association. Typically, memory specialists show off by repeating endless strings of discrete bits of unrelated information. They do it by building in their minds a fantasy story line around the bits of information. They remember the story they've created, and the bits of information are readily associated with pieces of the story. Our task is ever so much easier and enjoyable. We don't have to create fantasy stories and our information is anything but unrelated; it is the very stuff of narrative history.

The sample story of the French defeat in Santo Domingo can be the peg upon which innumerable pieces of factual information are hung: the time and the main actors; the location of the island and its geography, climate, resources, and diseases; the then current methods of communication, transportation, and warfare; the ambitions and ideas at work. It may also serve as a place marker for data that explains the episode and its significance. For example, Napoleon was in power in France, Jefferson was president of the U.S., and the Louisiana Purchase followed a year after. The riveting story of the underdogs' victory over the powerful French can evoke all of these pieces of information in students' minds.

A BASIS FOR ANALYSIS

Narrative history is also best at teaching the thinking skills and analytical techniques of the historian in a natural way. By starting with the stories of history the teacher is assured that there will always be some*thing* to think about, some*thing* to analyze. The story is the raw material upon which the historian practices his or her craft, and students can learn to do it too, all the while keeping the story in its proper context and related to what went before and what was to follow.

A history class is not merely story hour at the library, nor is it an exercise in memorization of encyclopedic facts. It can call into play an entire range of skills and modes of judgment or "habits of the mind": distinguishing evidence from assertion and fact from conjecture, the assessment of motive, the development of historical empathy as opposed to presentmindedness, the search for cause and effect, the understanding of the relationship between geography and history, the recognition of the importance of individuals who have made a difference in history, the comprehension of interplay between continuity and change, and distinguishing the important from the inconsequential. None of these skills can be developed, tested, or refined in a vacuum. They must be applied and reapplied to real cases time after time.

Again our story of the French in Santo Domingo in 1802 is helpful. To cite only one instance, the story can develop the historian's habit of mind that looks for the complexity of historical causation. Although this episode, at first glance, seemed to have no effect on the United States, it turns out to have had a significant impact on the Louisiana Purchase and our entire future. Jefferson, at the time, was engaged in a campaign of both intrigue and diplomacy in an attempt to purchase New Orleans from France. Napoleon was preparing to resume his European wars. The defeat on Santo Domingo made him realize the great obstacles to holding a North American empire in the face of American and British opposition. He decided to sell not only New Orleans but the whole of Louisiana and to concentrate his resources in Europe. Ironically, Jefferson, an anti-federalist Republican who opposed a strong central government, accepted Napoleon's offer only to be opposed by the Federalists who supported a strong central government but, in this case, argued that Jefferson's administration did not have the authority to make such a momentous agreement! In addition to revealing complex relationships, the story also lends itself to an examination of Jefferson's own impact on the development of the young American republic, both physically and politically.

WHAT IS A STORY?

The stories of history, like stories in literature, are made up of basic elements: characters, setting, and plot or action. All three elements are needed to tell a successful story. For this reason, if you "stick with the story," you must necessarily become a better historian than if you merely relied on a single textbook to provide the story. You may need to search through several sources to find clear and lively information on all three elements. Moreover, by sticking with the stories of history, you most likely will have to cut back the scope of what you try to cover if you are to make enough time for complete stories. Since it may take several classes to tell a worthwhile story effectively, you will need to make difficult choices of what to leave out— and to work at explaining such choices to your students.

In developing characters, setting, and plot or action of a historical episode, your first tasks as a historian are those of a good newspaper reporter. You will want to present the who, what, where, when, how, why, and so what of the episode. One of your principal tasks is bringing the characters to life. You will find out what kind of people they were, how they got that way, and how they interacted with each other. You will know what they looked like, how they conducted themselves, what their ideas were, how their ideas developed, what their motives were, who their friends were, what they liked and disliked. Thus you will have found answers to the reporter/historian's questions of who and some of how and why. Our France/Santo Domingo story should bring to life the French commanders, their soldiers, Toussaint L'Ouverture and the island people, and the French and American leaders and diplomats including Napoleon, Talleyrand, Jefferson, Monroe, and Livingston.

You need to establish the setting of the story, its location and time, to give your students a feel for the terrain, the distances, the climate, the technologies of transportation and communication available. You will sketch a background of the times, the daily lives and notions of the people. Who and what else were in their world and in their minds? What were the prevailing political, religious, and economic orthodoxies? How could the time and place have influenced the characters and the action of the story? You are dealing here with the reporter/historian's questions when and where, and more of how and why.

The plot/action is usually the most compelling part of the story. Teachers who tell the stories of history have command of the action. They realize that the most interesting plots turn on conflict—historical conflict between individuals, groups, countries, or ideas. There can also be conflict between people and the environment, or even a blind battle with the as-yet unknown. Conflicts arise over love, honor, duty, revenge, power, wealth, property, land, water, religious or political convictions, or simply misunderstandings. Struggle can be mental, physical, or emotional; military, economic, or scientific.

One basic method for structuring the plot/action of historical episodes is to lay out three stages: problem, action and reaction, and results. First, identify what is the conflict and who are the antagonists. Second, relate what actions were taken and by whom and what the reactions to them were. Third, present the result of the action and reaction in the same terms used in the initial problem statement.

Historical storytellers have no requirement (as many fiction storytellers have) to make sure the result of the story is either a solution or a resolution of the problem. Indeed, one historical habit of mind is to be prepared to live with uncertainties and exasperating, even perilous, unfinished business, realizing that not all problems have solutions. While all history stories do have results, it may well be that those results do not resolve the problem, do not punish the wicked or reward the virtuous or heal the sick. In fact the results of the action and reaction in a conflict may not change the situation at all, or the outcome may even be new and larger conflicts.

Because teachers are often pressured to "cover" a certain amount of material, they may try to substitute a synopsis of the plot for a complete telling of the tale. It is as if, in a study of classic films, the curriculum declared it sufficient to read only plot summaries from a TV magazine, because there was not enough time to watch all the classics during the course. Thus *Casablanca*, for instance, would be reduced to an absurdly simple line: "American expatriate in North Africa helps an old love escape from the Nazis during WWII." Without the action and subplots, without the richness of character, without the conflicts and surprises and turning points, what is left of *Casablanca*? Only a meaningless, wholly unmemorable string of words.

The same is true for a story of history. If a teacher were to use our story of the French troops in Santo Domingo in 1802 only as it has been related here, or in most textbooks, without filling in the lively details of setting, characters, and plot, it would receive—and deserve—a lukewarm reception (at best) from students. The synopsis alone utterly fails to answer the reporter/historian's questions of what, how, or why and does not even consider the so what, the what of it. We must have the whole story, with all of its human appeal and excitement, and its larger significance.

HOW TO USE A STORY

A story ought not to be started before the teacher has decided where to go with it. Which of the vital themes of history are particularly appropriate to draw out of the story? Which of history's habits of the mind will be helpful in telling and analyzing the story, and which will the story itself nourish or reinforce?

Good stories of history may be interesting to tell and to listen to. But for veritable teaching the story is not complete until it is analyzed. Not only should students have a grasp of the who, what, where, when, how, and why of the story, they should be able to use the techniques in "History's Habits of the Mind" (page 25) to take the story apart and to think about it. Students should be able to evaluate evidence, to tell fact from conjecture, to assess human motives, to understand the way people saw and experienced the events and issues at the time rather than judging them by present-day standards. They should be challenged to search for cause and effect, to comprehend the interplay of continuity and change, and to distinguish the important from the trivial.

The saga of the French in Santo Domingo in 1802 can be told in many ways and with many different emphases, depending on where the teacher wants to go with it. If it is to be used to work on the theme of comparative history of major developments, the story might be told deliberately in general terms, as in our first sketching of it, to invite an initial confusion that would then lead to discussion of comparative history. On the other hand, if the story were to be used for the theme of human interaction with the environment, it would be told with an emphasis on geography, technology, resources, disease, and the choices made by people in reaction to their surroundings. In each instance, the purpose for which the story is used substantially affects the way it is told.

Knowing what you want to do with the story *before* you start to tell it will help you focus the tale. It will also help you decide what style of storytelling would work best, the methods you might use to present the characters, setting, and plot most effectively. And it is important to keep in mind that varying your style of storytelling will provide variety and changes of pace for your classes. There are many ways of presenting given characters, setting, and plot or action. From the movies you have seen and the books you have read, you already know many styles of telling a story. Among them are linear storytelling, flashback, and "discovering" the story.

In a straightforward, linear rendition, the plot/action is the organizing principle of the story and reveals characterization, setting, plot twists, and subplots in the order in which they come up in the story. Your personal dramatic flair may itself be enough to make the story compelling to the students. Another technique is to start at a highly dramatic point in the story, a conflict or skirmish or debate. Bring your students into the action, get them involved with the characters, then cut the story at the point where "all the blood is pumping"—as writers say, "let it bleed," while you flash back to fill in the background of the characters and setting. When you return to the main story line you will have the students anxious to find out what happened.

The French disaster in Santo Domingo could be useful, for example, in a World History course as a way to flash back to a study of Napoleon Bonaparte, the man who sent the elite troops across the sea in the first place. Once we get the French to the island and take them to the eve of the decisive encounter, we can turn back to the emperor. We can discuss why he sent them, how he came to power, his early years, his philosophies, his faults, and (perhaps) what happened to him later and at the end. The Santo Domingo incident will serve as a way into the study of the importance of individuals in history and the significance of personal character, for both good and ill.

A third way to go about telling the story is to challenge students with an intriguing question or problem from the story. Ask them what they would need to know to resolve the problem, to "discover" the essence of the story. How could they find out? Have them use the reporter/historian's questions. Challenge them to find and bring in pieces of information and apply them to the story. To do this well, you must have researched the episode yourself and you will know in advance when your students are starting down a blind alley. Know beforehand how you may redirect them and get to the destination, to the kind of historical understanding you wish them to have.

An example of this technique with reference to our story of Santo Domingo might be to begin the study of U.S. History topic number 3 (page 28) suggested in Chapter 2, "Building a History Curriculum." That topic focuses on the gathering of people, cultures, and traditions that have contributed to American heritage and society. Instead of merely relating the story, the teacher might begin by challenging the class to discover the meaning and veracity of the statement: "An early Haitian victory is the main reason why citizens of Billings, Montana, do not usually speak French today." To discover the story behind such a statement, students must frame useful questions, gather data, evaluate the data for accuracy and for relevance, and then use it to formulate new questions. The object would be to have students tell the story of the France/Santo Domingo episode and explain the proposition that it was significant, through the Louisiana Purchase, to our present national culture. They would thereby have reached the reporter/historian's ultimate question: So what?

MEMORIZATION AND HIGHER-LEVEL THINKING

Although we have been discussing the imaginative use of narrative as a primary tool and technique for the teaching of history, it is important that history teachers come to grips with the question of memorization. Other disciplines have made their peace with memory, mathematics for instance. Math teachers see no contradiction in asking students to carry multiplication tables around in their heads. They do not see this as antiintellectual, or that theirs is therefore not a sophisticated mental discipline. They simply recognize and accept the fact that higher-level thinking about math requires people to have at their immediate disposal a certain amount of basic information.

In the same way, history teachers must acknowledge that higher-level thinking in history requires that students must have a certain amount of basic historical information on immediate recall. History teachers may well feel discomfort at being criticized (or praised) for the job they are doing on the single criterion of students' ability to recall basic historical facts about this country and the world. Some beginning teachers feel it is somehow demeaning to acknowledge that one of their objectives is to have students learn and retain a body of factual information. There is no reason to feel this way. There is no conflict between the retention of factual information and the higher-level analytic techniques and understandings we also strive to teach. Our students *should* be able to retain the basic who, what, when and where of the episodes we study. We should expect it of them, and they should be told why we expect it: Facts are indispensable to deeper understanding, which in turn explains the meaning of facts.

The other side of the coin, however, is that we must also *teach* for that dual result. The math teacher drills the multiplication tables before expecting the students to remember them, but then uses them again and again in higher-level math work. In the same way the history teacher should use techniques that help students learn and retain the basic factual material, and then use that material in various ways to achieve higher skills and understanding.

TEACHING AND EVALUATION

History teachers are dedicated to helping their students learn history. They spend most of their time, talents, and tools to do that. Yet two of their more powerful tools, tests and grades, often seem to be used *against* the student, rather than *for* the student. Tests and grades are too frequently aimed at finding out what the student does *not* know, has *not* learned. But why should teachers, when testing and grading, have to think of themselves more as judges or evaluators than as instructors? Teachers should feel free, and be left free, to use their tools of testing and grading to help students learn and only secondarily to evaluate them.

Everyone hates getting bad grades and taking tests that may result in bad grades. But think of the converse. Students love getting good grades and taking tests on which they know they can do well. For example, a "final" history exam can be given on the first day of class. Students can be told that it is the same exam they will take at the end, and that since this is the "final" exam they are not expected to know much of it. They can even get a "0" now and it will be quite all right. But they should say or write everything that comes to their minds. One result could be that the teacher would discover how much students already know about what he or she is planning to teach, or what notions and preconceptions students arrive with. That kind of information will help focus teaching goals, methods, and materials.

On their part, students would have a good picture—preview—of what is important, what they should know, and be better able to recognize it when it comes up during the course.

Since even a "0" is no handicap, they will feel no pressure to pretend and instead they are likely to feel proud about whatever it is they *do* know and can say. As the teacher gave the same "final" exam at the end of each week, or each unit, students would recognize the material as it appeared in class. They would get progressively better grades and might well come to enjoy taking tests.

The point is that teachers already have the tools of testing and grades. Why use them to prove only what students do not know instead of using them to make students want to learn? A novel testing process need not take any longer than the conventional quizzes and tests. Neither need it replace time devoted to telling the stories of history, to the analysis of them, or to the teacher's evaluation of class participation and discussion. Testing and grades can be employed to repeat and reinforce the who, what, where, when, how, and why of the narratives studied during the year. Significant changes could emerge in the teacher's own attitude toward testing, and in students' rising confidence in their own abilities.

CONCLUSION

History teachers, take heart. You can be better teachers and take more pleasure in your work. Insofar as your situation allows you, shrug the world off your shoulders. Do not let others expect you to teach your students everything that can be known about your subject and the skills that go with it, all in your one brief course. Identify an appropriate number of interesting and important episodes, research the stories, and decide on the most engaging ways to present them. Use tests and grades to help your students show off how much they are learning and have remembered. You may not turn them all into Ph.D. candidates in history—and you probably wouldn't want to—but at the very least, you will not have turned them away from history, and you may possibly have turned many of them on to a study that, in the words of the Bradley Commission, "provides the only avenue we have to reach an understanding of ourselves and of our society, in relation to the human condition over time, and of how some things change and others continue." To the extent that you succeed in this, students will remember you as important in their lives. Years from now, among their "school stories" will be ones about you and your history course. The stories they tell about you will be rooted in the power and importance of the history stories you are telling them now.

CHAPTER 17

For Better Elementary Teaching: Methods Old and New

by ELAINE WRISLEY REED

Preceding sections of this book have made the case for *why* history should be taught in schools, and have also suggested *what* kinds of history and historical ways of thinking ought to be learned at each level—including those all-important foundation school years of kindergarten through grade six. It is the intent of this section to offer answers to the *how* questions for elementary grades, to suggest methods and strategies teachers can use to proceed with the teaching of history and history's habits of mind.

To begin with, the members of the Bradley Commission were careful to emphasize the equal importance of worthy subject matter on the one hand and effective teaching methods on the other. As every seasoned teacher knows, neither is of much help to students without the other, no matter how excellent each alone might be. Nor did the Commission see any dichotomy between teaching the facts of history and developing the skills of thinking critically about them. Quite the contrary. The historical perspective, from which citizens can derive thoughtful judgment, arises only from solid knowledge of past events. And it is equally certain that what happened in the past is best remembered insofar as it bears upon significant issues that students are impelled to think about. The Commission members' emphasis was as much, if not more, on thinking about history as on describing what happened in it. To nurture such thinking—what the Bradley Commission called "History's Habits of the Mind"—let us take each of the habits in turn (see page 25) and apply them to history instruction in the elementary school years.

At every grade level, kindergarten through grade six, teachers may start by talking with youngsters about what habits are. What are some health habits? What habits have you developed at home to be helpful to other members of your family? What are some of your safety habits in getting to school? What are some work habits we have already talked about in school that help us learn? (Students may respond with such things as doing one's homework, finishing one's work on time, doing one's best work, etc.) Tell students that as we go about studying history, there are some other habits of thinking that we are going to try to use regularly.

TO UNDERSTAND THE SIGNIFICANCE OF THE PAST

The first objective for history teaching in the elementary school should be to help students, through their own active learning, to understand the significance of the past to their own lives—both private and public—and to their society. If history is the study of the past, let us begin with children by developing the concept of the "past" and why it is important to us. Professor William H. McNeill writes about history as memory, both private and public, and that the lack of knowledge of history is somewhat analogous to amnesia. Tell the children a story about waking up one morning and not having any memory at all. Go through your actions during a typical day and ask children to indicate which ones would be impossible without your memory. Would you be able to get dressed? Would you know how to eat breakfast? Would you remember to brush your teeth? Would you know how to treat the members of your family? Would you know who your friends are? Would you know what communities you are a member of? And so on; then extrapolate to our public, collective memory of the past.

Or try historian Michael Kammen's analogy of driving a car without a rearview mirror. Even though elementary students have not actually driven, their experience as riders can be profitably brought to this discussion. Ask: How does a rearview mirror help us? How is history like a rearview mirror? How is it *not* like one?

After connecting the words "history" and "the past," ask children to give you examples of what we as people can remember that animals cannot. (They will suggest all sorts of things, from words and tunes to Abraham Lincoln's birthday.) Ask how humans are different from animals in this respect (people can remember what happened "long ago"; memory of our recorded past is what makes us human). Have children put together a sentence using the words "past," "memory," and "history." To further develop a sense of the past, have students ask an older person in their family about his or her past: What toys or sports did they play in the third grade? What kind of clothes did they wear at the age of eight? What time did they have to go to bed? What did they like about school? Did they ask *their* parents questions like this?

HISTORICAL EMPATHY

To develop historical empathy as opposed to present-mindedness, students should be encouraged to perceive past events and issues as they were experienced by people at the time. Teachers who use weekly current events or newsmagazines with their classes can encourage children to view current events as though they were tips of icebergs. Talk about looking to see what's underneath, or what's gone before in the case of a news story. Have students identify as many items in their weekly news as they can that would be difficult, if not impossible, to understand unless they had some background knowledge of what went on before. In following weeks, encourage children to ask habitually "What's the background for that event?," or "What went on before?," or "What's the history of that group of people?," or "How do you suppose these people feel about what is happening?," or "What do they hope and fear?"

Developing historical empathy in children may mean asking them to "get behind the eyeballs" of someone in history, to "feel their way into the culture of the age." Teachers who encourage creative writing in their language arts classes may want to use an assignment where students are asked to imagine that they are children of the 1600s, 1700s, or 1800s. Ask students to place themselves in a seat in school beside a child of that time period: How would they do? What could they talk about? What words or terms might each use that the other wouldn't know? Alternatively, historical documents such as diaries and letters can be used to help children perceive the context of events. A letter from a girl in a covered wagon train heading west through Donner Pass can show students how "the westward movement" was viewed by a person at the time—who may or may not have known that she was a part of that movement identified later by others, even though it was a "current event" when she was experiencing it.

To aid fifth and sixth graders in perceiving past events and issues as they were experienced by people at the time, help them analyze epic decisions in history through the eyes of the decision-maker. Examples are such decisions as Queen Isabella's to bankroll Columbus, or President Truman's to drop the atomic bomb. Use questions that help students identify alternatives and consequences: What did President Truman want? What other options were open to him at that time? What were some of the probable consequences of those various options?

THE MANY AND THE ONE

Students of history should acquire at one and the same time a comprehension of diverse cultures and of shared humanity. It is here that elementary school teachers could proclaim a "search and destroy" mission: to get rid of all the stereotypical assumptions that our children have had handed down to them from generation to generation about people of other cultures. Through studying world history (religious beliefs, customs in other places and other times, diverse family patterns, social structures and institutions), children can learn how differently various human groups have tried to cope with the world around them, how so many basic human needs—food, clothing, shelter, security, companionship, hope—have always been the same. They can begin to recognize sameness and difference throughout the recorded past. They will learn as much about themselves, and how they resemble and are different from others, as they will learn about colonial Americans or the Greeks and Romans.

Children's literature about times past is particularly useful for discovering fears and hopes like our own. Children love to read the epic poem about an ancient Mesopotamian king, Gilgamesh, his friendship with Enkidu, and his heroic yet futile quest for immortality.[1] Students cannot help but feel a sense of shared humanity that cuts across time and culture. An example from a medieval Japanese noble woman, Lady Murasaki, is a story that has been called the world's first novel, *The Tale of Genji*.[2] It tells of the adventures of another child in his elementary years, Prince Genji, a son of the emperor.

Another example of literature-based instruction is *Pioneering Spirit* for grade three, or *American Dreams* for grade five.[3] Each thematic series contains ten different paperback titles of fine children's literature that teams up with history to bring the past to life, such as *On the Banks of Plum Creek* by Laura Ingalls Wilder. There is also a read-aloud book for grade three, *From Path to Highway: The Story of the Boston Post Road* by Gail Gibbons, and an audio cassette for listening—which provides a model for oral reading—or reading along with the story of an early American family, *Sarah, Plain and Tall* by Patricia MacLachlan. The integration of literature makes historical learning more productive; moreover, reading about what people did in times past enlarges students' sense of the potential that resides inside human beings for both good and evil.

CHANGE AND CONSEQUENCES

Students should be helped to understand how things happen and how things change, how human intentions matter, but also how their consequences are shaped by the means of carrying them out, in a tangle of purpose and process, in the words of William H. McNeill. The easiest way to introduce the concept of change is to use time lines. Like maps and globes in geography, time lines are a concrete expression that is unique to history. Reading, that symbol system most children try to learn, is in many ways more abstract than what youngsters have to deal with when they first begin working with time lines. Time itself is a developing concept in the elementary school years—not a developed one. Students first learn the idea of sequence as preparation for later introduction to chronology and dates as a very, very specific way of placing things and events in sequence.

Personal time lines show changes children have experienced themselves. Fourth-grade teacher Claudia Hoone, a Bradley commissioner from Public School #58 in Indianapolis, gives students a vertical number line for ten years. This focuses on a short span of time, and notes events close to the experience of her children. Their assignment is to write about one or more things that happened to them in each year of their lives. As you might expect, her youngsters include such items as their birthdays, when they got their baby sisters, when they started school, when they moved, but also such things as "I got my first ribbon in track" and "I made the A-Team at School #58" and "I met Mrs. Hoone in fourth grade!" A class that shares its time lines can discuss which things have changed, and which have stayed the same. Take children one more step and ask whether or not they expect any differences, changes, or similarities in the future.

In the context of American history or world history in fifth and sixth grades, students can be asked to make a pictorial time line on a roll of shelf paper to show changes in a field such as the technology of transportation or communication across the years or centuries. Another pictorial time line could show the story of food-getting, from the development of irrigation, domestication of animals, invention of agriculture, use of machines, etc., all the way up to the delivery of pizzas from a regional, computerized service center. Class discussion of the final product time line is important; the habit of thinking about change is too important merely to hang the time line on the wall and forget about it.

WHAT'S IMPORTANT AND WHAT'S NOT

Students should be able to distinguish between the important and the inconsequential, to develop the "discriminating memory" needed for a discerning judgment in public and personal life. Professor Michael Kammen writes that "worse than no memory at all is the undiscriminating memory that cannot differentiate between important and inconsequential experiences" (Chapter 5). Here again, time lines can be a useful device for thinking about history.

A computer software program that helps students make choices for time lines is available.[4] When using it, students themselves input the data about events and personalities, and the software develops the scale and prints out the time line sideways in a large, easy-to-read banner format. Students can choose to construct time lines for one day, one week, one year, or many years. In discussions of their time lines, students begin to understand what is appropriate to include and what is not; they evaluate the comparative significance of events and then go back and revise their time lines on the computer keyboard. For instance, one student at first included going to a particular concert on his time line. If he had been doing a time line for one year about fourth grade, this would have been appropriate. However, he was doing a time line of his whole life, and it contained many different activities he had done. When he looked at his first draft, he realized that one concert in one year was not significant. As a visual aid, this computer program helps students better understand what a "discriminating memory" is, and they go on to apply what they've learned from personal time lines to those they create in American, Western, and world history.

CHANGE AND CONTINUITY

Students should comprehend the interplay of change and continuity, and avoid assuming that either is somehow more natural, or more to be expected, than the other. Collect from an attic or borrow a boxful of "old" things: antiques, old pictures, old dolls, old coins, or whatever concrete objects you can find that fit the category "old." Bring this "mystery box" to class and have one child at a time come up and pull out an object; see if the children can figure out what it is or was used for a long time ago. Then discuss what life was like "long ago." Talk about which things in the mystery box have changed, and which have stayed the same. Children may want to follow this discussion by bringing in old things their families have saved.

In the context of community studies, young children can

focus on how their community has changed over time. Here again old photographs will help; students can look at the older buildings to see how they differ from the newer ones. They can write sentences about some change in the neighborhood they noticed either going to or from school yesterday. Invite a senior citizen to come to class and tell the children what life was like in your community in the past. Old newspapers, oral history, diaries of early citizens, historical museum trips, and trips to historic buildings will also help students to think about continuity and change.

Historians caution us that events from the past can never be replicated exactly, that we should learn to expect change as well as continuity, and that the so-called lessons of history cannot be transferred unreflectively from one historical period to another. To study history is to learn about some of the possibilities, but historians are not in the business of making absolute predictions. Children enjoy knowing that history shows us some surprises, too: The German blitzkrieg tactics in World War II were quite a surprise to the French defenders dug into the Maginot line of fortifications. The French believed that the "lessons of history" from World War I taught them how to defend against any attack, but they were conquered when the Germans went around the Maginot line to the north, at a speed they hadn't imagined possible.

HISTORY IS UNFINISHED BUSINESS

Students should prepare to live with uncertainties and exasperating, even perilous, unfinished business, realizing that not all problems have solutions. The story of mankind's continuous search for solutions to problems can be fascinating, but fourth, fifth, and sixth graders should know what historian Gordon Craig meant when he wrote that "what may appear to be solutions today are merely tomorrow's headaches."

Use examples from whatever history the class is studying;

if American history, an instance could be the discussions of slavery that arose during the framing of the Constitution. Was slavery a good solution to the problem of shortage of labor? Ask students if the three-fifths compromise was the final solution to the problem, when did it come up again, and in what setting? Was the problem over with the Emancipation Proclamation? Was it solved with the Civil Rights Act of 1964?

In world history, an example is the problem of watering the crops in ancient Sumer. A solution that turned out to be a headache (as well as one of the reasons Sumer became the first civilization of which we know very much) was the invention of irrigation. Through the years, evaporation of the water used for irrigation accumulated salt in the soil, eventually becoming a serious problem for the Sumerians, and for later generations of Americans as well.

Again in the category of "unfinished business" are the struggles for freedom of a variety of peoples in the past, along with their need for order and control. Elementary school students can find this tussle in their study of the Greeks, the Romans, feudalism in Europe or Japan, the English, American and French revolutions, and certainly in their inquiry about the entire history of democracy in the United States.

THE CAMPAIGN AGAINST MONOCAUSALITY

Students should begin to grasp the complexity of historical causation, respect particularity, and avoid excessively abstract generalizations. By the later elementary school years, when children are trying to construct simple systems for interpreting events, teachers can help by explaining that events have causes—with an emphasis on the plural. This usually means helping students see and make connections, and identifying effects as well as causes. Case studies from the past are often less threatening and easier to understand for the very reason that we are not as close to them as we are to what happened on the playground yesterday.

Time lines with events illustrated by children on a separate sheet of art paper, and then strung on a piece of rope or clothesline, are a good springboard for a discussion of causation. You can remove one of the pictures and ask, What else will we have to take out?, or, Which events on our time line would not be here if I removed this picture? Follow with a discussion of the idea that events usually have several related causes. The year 1914 and the events leading up to World War I carry lessons about the complexity of historical causation.

For another example, when you are studying the American Revolution, draw a "word wheel" on the chalkboard, with "American Revolution" written in a circle in the center. Then draw lines radiating out from the center like spokes of a wheel. On each of these lines, note the variety of reasons students can give from their reading and other learning about the war. Your "spokes" may have such phrases as taxation without representation, ideas from writers about independence and freedom, population growth in the colonies, actions of the British Parliament and king, ideas from France, the Proclamation Line of 1763, the Boston Massacre, the Boston Tea Party, the shots at Lexington and Concord, and so on. Then draw a large circle around all the spokes, so children see that they are all related to the event we call the American Revolution. Ask students if they would have seen the whole picture if they had stopped with just one cause or reason for the war. You may want to deepen the discussion by asking if students see any groups or kinds of causes: Are there economic spokes? Geographic spokes? Are some causes more important than others?

Use the word wheel technique again when complex events come up in the study of history; it will not be long before students will start using it independently, and by the end of the elementary grades students will reject a single cause as being an insufficient explanation. History teachers can smile when they hear students say, "I suppose the fall of the Roman Empire is going to have more than one cause, too, just like everything else we've studied."

HISTORY'S TENTATIVE NATURE

Students should be helped to appreciate the often tentative nature of judgments about the past, and thereby avoid the temptation to seize upon particular "lessons" of history as cures for present ills. If you asked elementary-grade children "Who discovered America?," many might immediately answer "Christopher Columbus." You could then introduce evidence that the Vikings had been here earlier, and that the American Indians were here even earlier than that. Tell your students that some scientists theorize that the American Indians were actually from Asia, and that they came to our continent during the Ice Age by way of a land bridge where the Bering Strait is today, thereby discovering America long before Columbus. Ask students how their answers to your first question changed as new evidence was introduced. Were they open to new information? (They may be interested in reading about two boats named the *Kon-Tiki* and the *Ra-2*.) Tell them that historians are continually looking for new information to help understand the world, and that at some point in the future there may be new historical information about the earliest peoples in America.

PEOPLE WHO MADE A DIFFERENCE

Students in the elementary grades should recognize the importance of individuals who have made a difference in history, and the significance of personal character for both good and ill. If sociologists study groups and classes, and economists study "Economic Man," then historians study individuals, and look at them in *all* of their various activities. Many elementary teachers are already using biographies, both of famous and not-so-famous-but-interesting persons of the past. One set of biographies for your class or elementary school library is the *People of Distinction* series.[5] It includes such individuals as Marco Polo, Mark Twain, Jim Thorpe, Mary McLeod Bethune, Daniel Boone, Thomas Edison, Frederick Douglass, and Mozart.

An example of an autobiography that is well suited to reading aloud to children age eight and up is that of Helen Keller.[6] This use of biography works well because young children find other people fascinating; they are very curious about others. It also works because it takes advantage of the motivation intrinsic to history: the "people" motive or the desire to find out why people behave the way they do, the identification motive or the desire to be like others who have been famous, and the related success motive or need for achievement that children feel and identify with when they study achievers of the past. These intrinsic motivations make the content of history exciting to children—and teachers' jobs easier.

THE UNINTENDED AND UNEXPECTED IN HISTORY

Although much in the human adventure is the result of intentional, or at least volitional, action, students should also begin to appreciate the force of the nonrational, the irrational, the accidental, in history and human affairs. While a classic case of the accidental in history is the discovery of the Americas by Christopher Columbus, another instance is from the context of the Civil War, or War Between the States. General "Stonewall" Jackson was mistakenly shot and wounded in the arm by his own men in the Battle of Chancellorsville. Upon the amputation of Jackson's arm, General Robert E. Lee said, "He has lost his left arm, but I have lost my right arm." A few days later, Jackson died. Fifth graders can speculate on how the result of the Battle of Gettysburg might have been different, how Lee's hesitation on the first day enabled the North to obtain high ground positions on Culp's Hill and Little Round Top and what the advantages of these positions were, and whether, if "Stonewall" had been there, he would have taken and held the high ground for the South.

Examples of the irrational in history come up when elementary grade youngsters find out about the assassinations of Abraham Lincoln, John F. Kennedy, and Archduke Francis Ferdinand. Younger children could be asked to write sentences and paragraphs to finish the sentence, "If President Lincoln had not been shot . . ." Archduke Ferdinand and his assassin in Sarajevo could be the beginning point for an essay by older children on the consequences of human actions in history.

TIME AND PLACE ARE INSEPARABLE (OR THE ROLE OF GEOGRAPHY)

Students should understand the relationship between geography and history as a matrix of time and place, and as context for events. One of the first questions to ask when learning about any event in times past is, Where did it happen? And then, What influence did that place and its distinguishing characteristics have on the event? Examples for discussion are the breakup of the Spanish Armada in the winds and currents of the English Channel, or the death of Napoleon's and Hitler's armies on the Russian winter plains, or the rise of civilizations in such areas as the Tigris, Euphrates, Nile, and Indus River valleys.

The role of geography in history may seem clear, but we know of classes where map and globe skills are saved for Friday afternoon. Just as an indicator map helps adults when they are watching television news to tell where an event is "happening," so does information about place give children a frame of reference for historical events. Any data collection chart students use for classifying information about early civilizations of the world (or early North American settlements, etc.) should have *place* as one of the categories.

Fourth graders who are studying state history could prepare a list of historical landmarks in their state, identifying their locations, and then analyzing the reasons for these locations. Fifth graders could determine the specific reasons for the location and later growth of selected cities (or colonial settlements) in North America. Examples of reasons may include nearness to water, transportation routes, natural resources such as coal or oil, sources of power, some special physical feature, or historical accident. How do geographical factors explain why some cities grew faster than others? Sixth graders studying world history could identify through the use of historical maps how a place, such as the continent of Africa or Europe, has changed over time.

EVALUATING EVIDENCE

Students should read widely and critically in order to recognize the difference between fact and conjecture, between evidence and assertion, and thereby to frame useful questions. To begin developing this habit of the mind, construct an "event" with the cooperation of the teacher and class next door. It need not be anything dramatic or elaborate; it could take only the first five minutes of a class or lesson. If possible, arrange to have the "event" videotaped. The following day, tell your class that you have heard about something that happened yesterday in Mrs. X's class. Ask them for suggestions on how to find out what happened. Your students will probably mention asking someone from the other class, or asking their teacher. Ask for five volunteers to go to the other classroom and interview five persons there about what happened. They should find out what time the event happened, where the persons involved were standing or sitting, who said what and in what sequence, what the teacher said and did, and so forth. Have your interviewers question each person individually, so that they do not hear the others' descriptions, and jot down the five responses to report to your class.

After each of the five descriptions is read aloud, talk about the similarities and differences in the accounts of the event. Point out the need to consider more than one source of information, in order to ensure accuracy. (Recall this discussion when you are attempting to get students to use more than the encyclopedia in their next written reports.) Play the videotape of the event for your class and compare it with the eyewitness reports. What may account for the discrepancies? Which elements are facts rather than opinions, evidence rather than assertions?

Also discuss the difference between statements by witnesses and others who heard about the event and then retold it, but were not physically in the classroom when it happened (these might include the principal, other teachers, other children, family members at home). Upper-grade children can use the terms "primary" and "secondary sources." Have students classify descriptions of an event as fact or opinion, recalling the example of yesterday's classroom event, and then moving on to historical primary source documents and other accounts of events.

Teachers may want to share "rules of evidence" from the legal profession—that is, statements by witnesses, written documents, or objects. One must know the source for it to be considered evidence. There are several questions students can use to evaluate evidence in their history texts and in their library research. Is it a primary or secondary source? Did the source have any reason to distort the evidence? Is there any other confirming evidence? Is the evidence public or private? Your class members may want to make posters of these key questions as guidelines. As students master the questions and use them regularly, take the posters down.

VARIETY IS THE SPICE

Looking back over history's habits of the mind and the teaching methods suggested for developing them, we can only conclude that there is no one best method or exclusive strategy for teaching historical thinking and perspective-taking. Everything from entering the exciting and glamorous National History Day contest to everyday class discussion works; we have suggested here such diverse strategies as oral history interviews, current events, creative writing, historical documents, children's literature, time lines, computer software, mystery boxes full of old things, local community studies, storytelling, word wheels, biographies, and, naturally, maps. They are designed to take into account various learning styles of students, as well as the multitude of strengths in teaching styles.

Awareness of learning styles seems particularly important in teaching history. Too often, educators have inherited the idea that schooling means students working quietly, sitting quietly in their own seats most of the time. That idea fits some students well, but does not serve students who learn best when they can test ideas in talk and action, and for whom action is a forerunner of the next important step, reflection. Abstract symbols such as words on the printed pages of history textbooks are effective with some; they value vicarious experience in books because it nourishes their imagination. However, those students who find the concrete world, as perceived by the senses, far more real than symbols on a textbook page, need to be engaged in new experiences and their own active learning, so that abstract symbols will make more sense to them as representations of experience.

While the suggested strategies in this chapter are many and various, they are directed toward one specific objective: to help students *habitually* ask questions. Where did that event happen? What was the background of it? What were the causes? Are there any stereotypes involved? What is the evidence for that? What does this mean for my life? What did it mean to the people living at the time it happened? Was it a change? Is it important or not? Who were the individuals who made that difference? By framing these useful questions, children can benefit from prudent judgment applied to all areas of their lives, and they can enjoy thinking sensibly about history and about their own lives as part of history.

NOTES

1. Bernarda Bryson, *Gilgamesh* (New York: Holt, 1967). Read-aloud, grades two to six; independent reading, grades four to six.
2. Lady Murasaki, *The Tale of Genji* (New York: Random House, 1985). Paperback, read-aloud.
3. *Pioneering Spirit* and *American Dreams* series (Cleveland, Ohio: Modern Curriculum Press, 1989).
4. TimeLiner (Cambridge, Mass.: Tom Snyder Productions, Inc.). For grades kindergarten to twelve.
5. *People of Distinction* series. (Chicago: Children's Press, 1987). 22 volumes, for grades four and up.
6. Helen Keller, "The Story of My Life," in *More Classics to Read Aloud to Your Children* by William F. Russell (New York: Crown Publishers, Inc., 1986).

APPENDIX A

Sources of Information about History

The Bradley Commission on History in Schools encourages persons interested in history to contact the following organizations for information and materials:

American Historical Association
400 A Street, S.E.
Washington, D.C. 20003
(202) 544-2422

Council for Basic Education
725 Fifteenth Street, N.W.
Washington, D.C. 20005
(202) 347-4171

Education for Democracy Project
American Federation of
   Teachers
555 New Jersey Avenue, N.W.
Washington, D.C. 20001
(202) 879-4575

Geography Education Program
National Geographic Society
Washington, D.C. 20036
(202) 828-6640

History Teaching Alliance
Department of History
University of Florida at Gaines-
   ville
Gainesville, FL 32611
(904) 392-0271

National Center for History in
   the Schools: A Cooperative
   UCLA/NEH Research Pro-
   gram
Dr. Charlotte Crabtree, Director
University of California at Los
   Angeles
405 Hilgard Avenue
Los Angeles, CA 90024-1521
(213) 825-4702

National Council for the Social
   Studies
3501 Newark Street, N.W.
Washington, D.C. 20016
(202) 966-7840

National Endowment for the
   Humanities
1100 Pennsylvania Avenue, N.W.
Washington, D.C. 20506
(202) 786-0428

National History Day
11201 Euclid Avenue
Cleveland, OH 44106
(216) 421-8803

Organization of American
Historians
112 North Bryan Street
Bloomington, IN 47401
(812) 335-7311

Organization of History
Teachers
Earl Bell, President
History Department
University of Chicago
Laboratory School
1362 East 59th Street
Chicago, IL 60637
(312) 702-0588

Society for History Education
California State University,
Long Beach
1250 Bellflower Boulevard
Long Beach, CA 90840
(213) 985-4503

World History Association
Raymond Lorantas, Editor
Department of History and
Politics
Drexel University
Philadelphia, PA 19104
(215) 895-2471

For other information regarding the Bradley Commission on History in Schools, contact Elaine Wrisley Reed, Administrative Director, 26915 Westwood Road, Suite A-2, Westlake, Ohio 44145, (216) 835-1776.

APPENDIX B

The Bradley Commission on History in Schools: Commission and Contributor Profiles

JOHN M. ARÉVALO teaches world history and American history, regular and advanced placement sections, to sophomores, juniors, and seniors at Harlandale High School in San Antonio, Texas. He directs the Junior Historians and the Academic Decathlon and chairs a Principal's Advisory Committee. During his fifteen years as a teacher, Mr. Arévalo developed advanced placement curricula for American and European history, and wrote *Mexico's Archbishop Mora y del Rio: Symbol of Resistance in the Church and State Struggle, An Exile in Texas* for the Texas State Historical Association. He also teaches history at Palo Alto Junior College in San Antonio.

THOMAS BENDER is a professor of history and university professor of the humanities at New York University. A cultural historian with a particular interest in cities, his books include *Toward an Urban Vision, Community and Social Change in America*, and *New York Intellect*. Most recently, he edited *The University and the City: From Medieval Origins to the Present*. He has served as Visiting Professor at Columbia University and the New School for Social Research. The recipient of the Frederick Jackson Turner Prize of the Organization of American Historians, he is the author of the forthcoming book *History and Public Culture*.

MARJORIE WALL BINGHAM teaches Western civilization and advanced placement European and American history at St.

Louis Park Senior High School, St. Louis Park, Minnesota. Dr. Bingham is director of the Women in World Area Studies Project. She has been elected to leadership positions in both the American Historical Association's Teaching Division and the Organization of American Historians and is a founder of the new Organization of History Teachers. Dr. Bingham also serves on the executive boards of the Minnesota Women's History Center and the Minnesota Humanities Commission.

LOUISE COX BYRON'S teaching career spans a period of twenty-eight years in the Atlanta Public School System. During that period she has taught at the elementary, middle, and high school levels. For the past twelve years she has served as a core instructor of world history and international relations in the Humanities Magnet at Booker T. Washington High School, the first public high school for Blacks in Atlanta and one of the largest public high schools in the Southeast from its infancy in 1924 to present. She has participated in curriculum revision and social science projects for the Atlanta Public School System. She is also a member of the core team to introduce strategies for implementation of the Socratic method and the Paideia Proposal.

CHARLOTTE CRABTREE is a professor in the Graduate School of Education at the University of California, Los Angeles. Her specialty is curriculum theory, to which she brings the perspective of developmental psychology; her special interests are in the learning of history in childhood and adolescence. Professor Crabtree was an adviser to the National Endowment for the Humanities in its 1987 study of the state of humanities in the schools and she was principal co-writer of the new California *History–Social Science Framework, 1987.* She is the director of the UCLA/NEH National Center for History in the Schools.

GORDON A. CRAIG is J. E. Wallace Sterling Professor of Humanities Emeritus at Stanford University. Dr. Craig is an authority on German affairs and military and diplomatic history. His numerous books include *The Politics of the Prussian*

Army, 1640–1945; Germany, 1866–1945; The Germans; The End of Prussia; and *The Triumph of Liberalism: Zürich in the Golden Age, 1830–1869.* A former U.S. Marine Corps officer, Dr. Craig is a past president of the American Historical Association and the recipient of the Goethe Medal in 1987.

Ross E. Dunn is a professor of history at San Diego State University. His specialty is African and Islamic history. He is the author of *The Adventures of Ibn Battuta, A Muslim Traveler of the 14th Century* and *Resistance in the Desert: Moroccan Responses to French Imperialism, 1881–1912.* Professor Dunn has a particular interest in the reconceptualization of world history. He was elected first president of the World History Association and is senior author of the innovative school textbook, *A World History: Links across Time and Place.*

Robert H. Ferrell is Distinguished Professor of History at Indiana University, Bloomington. Professor Ferrell's most recent book is *Woodrow Wilson and World War I.* Long interested in the quality of history teaching in U.S. schools, he co-authored *Teaching of American History in High Schools* in 1964. In addition, he has written *Peace in Their Time,* five books on Truman, and *American Diplomacy,* now in its fourth edition.

Hazel Whitman Hertzberg was Professor of History and Education at Teachers College, Columbia University. An authority on social studies reform in American schools, she wrote widely used curricula in local history and Iroquoian studies. Twice a Fellow at the Woodrow Wilson International Center at the Smithsonian for work on Native Americans, she was also a Guggenheim laureate for social studies research. Among her books are *The Search for an American Indian Identity: The Modern Pan-Indian Movements, The Great Tree and the Longhouse: The Culture of the Iroquois,* and *Social Studies reform, 1880–1980.*

Claudia J. Hoone teaches history to fourth graders at Public School #58, an inner-city elementary school in Indianapolis, Indiana. She served on the Indiana Department of Education Committee that developed social studies proficiency standards for students statewide. Ms. Hoone is a member of the steering committee of the Indiana Historical Bureau's Broadsides program, which introduces primary source historical documents into elementary and middle school classes.

NATHAN I. HUGGINS is the W.E.B. DuBois Professor of History and Afro-American Studies at Harvard University. He is the author of *Protestants Against Poverty, Harlem Renaissance*, and *Slave and Citizen: The Life of Frederick Douglass*, and has served on the executive council of the Organization of American Historians. Professor Huggins is also on the board of advisers of the Children's Television Workshop.

BARBARA B. JACKSON chairs the Department of English at Blind Brook High School in Rye Brook, New York, and is English coordinator for the Blind Brook–Rye School District, which received the nation's Excellence in Education Award in both 1985 and 1986. In a twenty-year career, Mrs. Jackson has taught at all secondary school levels and at the university level. As an educational consultant, she conducts workshops in classroom strategies and teacher leadership, and acts as a peer-coach for several school districts. She has been cited as one of the Outstanding Leaders in Elementary and Secondary Education.

KENNETH T. JACKSON (Chair) is the Mellon Professor of History and of the Social Sciences at Columbia University. Dr. Jackson is the general editor of the thirty-volume *Columbia History of Urban Life* and author of several books including *The Ku Klux Klan in the City, Cities in American History*, and *Crabgrass Frontier: The Suburbanization of the United States*, which won both the Francis Parkman and the Bancroft prizes. He is co-author of the forthcoming *Silent Cities: The Evolution and Meaning of American Urban Cemeteries*, and is editor in chief of *The Encyclopedia of New York City*.

MICHAEL KAMMEN is Newton C. Farr Professor of American History and Culture at Cornell University. He won the 1987 Francis Parkman Prize, given for the best book published in American history, for *"A Machine That Would Go of Itself": The Constitution in American Culture*. Professor Kammen won the

Pulitzer Prize for History for an earlier book, *People of Paradox: An Inquiry Concerning the Origins of American Civilization*. He also wrote *A Rope of Sand: The Colonial Agents, British Politics and the American Revolution*.

WILLIAM E. LEUCHTENBURG is the William Rand Kenan Professor of History at the University of North Carolina at Chapel Hill. Professor Leuchtenburg has served as president of the Organization of American Historians and the Society of American Historians. He is recognized for his work about the Great Depression–New Deal era. His book, *Franklin D. Roosevelt and the New Deal*, won the Francis Parkman and the Bancroft prizes. Professor Leuchtenburg's book, *The Perils of Prosperity*, is widely used in college courses in American history.

LEON F. LITWACK is Alexander F. and May T. Morrison Professor of American History at the University of California at Berkeley, where he won the Distinguished Teaching Award. Professor Litwack's book, *Been in the Storm So Long: The Aftermath of Slavery*, won the Francis Parkman Prize, the American Book Award, and the Pulitzer Prize. He has served as the president of the Organization of American Historians and as a visiting professor at Moscow State University and Beijing University.

WILLIAM H. MCNEILL is Robert A. Millikan Distinguished Service Professor of History Emeritus at the University of Chicago. Among his many works are *Plagues and Peoples* and *Mythistory and Other Essays;* his *The Rise of the West: A History of the Human Community* won the National Book Award and is a recognized classic in the field. Professor McNeill has served as president of the American Historical Association. He is on the board of editors of the Encyclopaedia Britannica and is vice-chairman of the Christopher Columbus Quincentenary Jubilee Commission.

GARY B. NASH is a professor of history at the University of California at Los Angeles and associate director of the UCLA/NEH National Center for History in the Schools.

Among his many books are *Quakers in Politics: Pennsylvania, 1681–1726; Class and Society in Early America; Red, White and Black: The Peoples of Early America; The Urban Crucible* (runner-up Pulitzer Prize in History); and most recently, *Forging Freedom: The Formation of Philadelphia's Black Community, 1720–1840.* Professor Nash serves on the executive board of the Organization of American Historians, and on the national advisory council of the John Carter Brown Library.

THEODORE K. RABB is a professor of history at Princeton University and is founder and co-editor of *The Journal of Interdisciplinary History.* He has published extensively in his field of early modern Europe. Professor Rabb's work for the effective teaching of history includes consultancies to dozens of colleges and schools for the National Endowment for the Humanities, the directorship of the Community College Internship Program, chief historian of the Renaissance television series, and authorship of widely adopted textbooks, problems books, and audiovisual aids for high school and college courses. His forthcoming book is *Sir Edwin Sandys (1561–1629): A Life and Times.*

DIANE RAVITCH is a professor of history and education at Teachers College, Columbia University. Her books include *The Great School Wars, New York City, 1805–1973; The Schools We Deserve: Reflections on the Educational Crisis of Our Times;* and *The Troubled Crusade: American Education, 1945–1980.* She is co-author of the 1987 study, *What Do Our 17-Year-Olds Know?,* and is director of the Educational Excellence Network. Professor Ravitch was the first person chosen from the field of education studies to serve as Phi Beta Kappa Visiting Scholar in 1984–85, and she was principal co-writer of the "California History–Social Science Framework, 1987" (for which she was made an honorary citizen of the state of California).

CHARLES SHOTLAND teaches American history to seventh- and eighth-grade students at Blind Brook High School, Rye Brook, New York. During his twenty-nine-year career, Mr. Shotland has taught history at all middle school grades, fifth through eighth. Chairman of the Social Studies

Curriculum Committee and coordinator of the Middle School Humanities Program, he also finds time to be president of his teacher association. Both schools in which Mr. Shotland has taught have received a President's Award for Educational Excellence.

GARY SYKES is on the faculty of the College of Education, Michigan State University, and is staff director to the Holmes Group. An authority on teacher education, Professor Sykes is the co-author of *Value Conflicts and Curriculum Issues* (with J. Schaffarzick) and *Handbook of Teaching and Policy* (with L. Shulman). He has taught at both the elementary and secondary levels, and has special interest in the professionalization of teaching. Dr. Sykes served on the California Commission on the Teaching Profession and is currently consultant to the National Board for Professional Teaching Standards.

SUZANNE M. WILSON is on the faculty of the Department of Teacher Education, and is senior researcher of the National Center for Research on Teacher Education, at Michigan State University. Her special interest is the integration of subject matter knowledge and pedagogy in the field of history. An experienced teacher of mathematics and social studies at the secondary level, Dr. Wilson has authored and co-authored many articles, book chapters, and professional papers on research and policy in teacher preparation and certification, and is consultant to the National Board for Professional Teaching Standards.

C. VANN WOODWARD is Sterling Professor of History Emeritus at Yale University. A recognized authority on the history of the South, Professor Woodward's books include *Mary Chesnut's Civil War*, a Pulitzer Prize winner, *The Burden of Southern History*, *The Strange Career of Jim Crow*, and *Origins of the New South (1877–1913)*, which won the Bancroft Prize. Professor Woodward is a past president of the American Historical Association, the Southern Historical Association, and the Organization of American Historians. He also won, in 1986, the prestigious Bruce Catton Prize for Lifetime Achievement in the Writing of History.

STAFF

PAUL A. GAGNON, a professor of history at the University of Massachusetts at Boston, is principal investigator for the Commission. Professor Gagnon is the author of *France Since 1789*, the American Federation of Teachers (AFT) report, *Democracy's Untold Story: What World History Textbooks Neglect*, and of a recent report on high school textbooks for American history. He is also a member of the national board of the Fund for the Improvement of Postsecondary Education (FIPSE), and of the Paideia Group.

ELAINE WRISLEY REED is administrative director for the Commission. She is executive director of the Ohio Council for the Social Studies and serves on the board of National History Day. Her prior experience includes work on the Educational Research Council's Social Science Program, "Concepts and Inquiry." A former fourth grade classroom teacher, she has particular expertise in history and social sciences in the elementary school curriculum.

JOSEPH P. RIBAR is consultant to the Commission on research and communications projects. An independent consultant for eight years, Mr. Ribar works with small businesses and nonprofit organizations on marketing and publications projects. Mr. Ribar's prior experience includes eight years of high school teaching (American history and political philosophy) and seven years as a writer of school textbooks (elementary and secondary social studies, and elementary health education).

INDEX

Adams, Charles Kendall, 4, 17, 73–74, 77
Adams, Herbert Baxter, 72, 77
Adams, John, 245, 247–248
Adelson, Joseph, 175
Administrators, school, 18, 252, 253, 255, 256, 257
African history, 24, 30, 39, 44, 65, 221, 223, 224, 225, 229, 241
Agricultural history, 27, 28, 31, 61, 151, 167, 184, 308
Alabama, 236, 242–243
Alder, Douglas, 218
American culture, 28–29; heritage phenomenon, 138–154; public, in contemporary historical writing, 189–202
American Federation of Teachers, 16, 21
American Heritage, 148
American Historical Association (AHA), 3, 10, 18, 20, 46, 67, 72, 111, 135; Commission on the Social Studies, 91–93; Committee of Five (1911), 79, 87; Committee of Seven (1899), 61, 76–79, 82, 83, 85, 88–89, 90, 94
American history, 19–20, 24, 26, 28–29, 59, 60, 61, 74, 78, 106–107, 108, 218, 224, 229, 234–248; democratic issues in, 28, 234–248; in elementary school curricula, 34, 35, 36, 63–65, 148, 184–187, 308, 311–316; and foreign policy, 166–169; ignorance of, 52–58, 138–139; in secondary school curricula, 37, 38, 39, 40, 59, 63–65, 148, 289–292; synthesis, in contemporary historical writing, 189–202; teachers' subject matter knowledge of, 271; topics for study of, 28–29. *See also specific periods*
American Philological Association, 178
American Revolution, 28, 30, 31, 65, 182, 213, 235, 240, 242, 244–248, 271, 312
American Women's Heritage Society, 143

Analysis, narrative history as basis for, 291–297
Ancient history, 29, 60, 61, 70–71, 78, 80, 87, 219; in elementary school curricula, 184, 185, 187, 306, 311, 313, 315–316; in Western civilization curricula, 209–211; in world history curricula, 223, 227. *See also specific countries; cultures; periods*
Annales school, 204, 279
Annalistic history, 88
Anthropology, 22, 43, 59, 125
Architectural preservation, American, 141–143, 147
Area studies, 19, 95
Arts, 22, 26, 28, 31, 43, 60, 125, 257; in elementary school curricula, 34, 184, 185; in Western civilization curricula, 210–214
Asian history, 24, 30, 39, 65, 223, 224, 228, 229. *See also specific countries; cultures; periods*
Asian school systems, 9
Association, and memory, 290–291
Association of History Teachers of the Middle States and Maryland, 79
Assyrian history, 210
Audiovisual programs, 45–46, 260
Auxiliary materials, 45–46, 75–76, 260

Bailyn, Bernard, 127–128
Beard, Charles A., 79, 93, 136, 195; *The Rise of American Civilization* (with Mary Beard), 188, 197, 199
Bemis, Samuel Flagg, 148
Bettelheim, Bruno, 176
Bill of Rights, U.S., 54, 185
Biography, 44, 60, 74, 288; in elementary school curricula, 33, 34, 36, 62, 177, 178, 313–314; in secondary school curricula, 37
Black history, 27, 28, 106, 139, 143, 194, 236, 238, 239, 240, 241, 242–244, 245, 246, 311. *See also* Civil rights movement; Slavery
Bobbitt, Franklin, 81, 92
Bode, Boyd, 93